113

113

Indians, Settlers, and Pioneers

IN NEW YORK STATE

CATHERINE URELL, PH.D.,
Research Associate,
Bureau of Educational Research, Board of Education
of the City of New York

JENNIFER CHATFIELD, M.A.,
Instructor, Department of Public Instruction,
American Museum of Natural History

FOLLETT PUBLISHING COMPANY
CHICAGO   *New York*

Table of Contents

This boy is telling his class a story about an Indian pipe and its history.

Exploring New York State

Do you like to read stories? Most boys and girls do. Maybe you like to make up stories, too. Maybe you like to tell true stories about yourself or your friends. Which do you like better, true or make-believe stories?

Did you ever think that everybody has a true story? Your life is a story, and you live some more of it every day.

Most of the stories you know are about people, but places have stories too. If you live on a farm, your farm has a story. If you live in a town or a city, there is a story about your town or your city. The true story of a place is called its *history*.

You know some of the important things that are happening in your town or city or farm right now. These things are part of its history. Do you know any important things that happened before you were born, maybe long, long ago? These, too, are part of history.

Most of the boys and girls who are reading this book live in New York State. Your state has a history and a very interesting one, too. Every farm and town and city in your state has a history. In some ways, their histories are alike, because they belong to the same state. In some ways, their histories are different, because the places are different. Different things happened in them. Different people came to live in them. Some places were settled long ago, and some were settled later. Some have mountains

and some are flat. Some have lakes and some are on the seashore.

Indians Lived Here Long Ago

The long-ago history of every part of the state is the same. Long ago, Indians lived everywhere. There were different tribes living in different parts of the state. Perhaps you know the name of the tribe that used to live where you now do. Some of the tribes belonged to a great group called the Iroquois. Other tribes belonged to another great group which spoke the Algonquin language. The large groups and even the tribes had some different ways of living, but they were all alike in many ways.

Early Settlers Come to Our State

When white men came here later, they brought their ways of living. The Indians and the white men began to share the same land. Sometimes they shared it peacefully. Sometimes there were fights. Many Indians did not want to share their land with the white men. Some of the white men were not fair with the Indians.

The first white people to make real homes here were the Dutch. Before that some white men had come to buy furs from the Indians. Others had come to teach the Indians the Christian religion. But these Dutch settlers were different. They brought their wives and children. They planned to settle here and make farms and towns where their children could live when they grew up.

6

Living in New York from Indian times to our own.

The first Dutch settlers came to the place that is now our state capital, Albany. After a while, they had trouble with the Indians, and went to live in a safer place, which is now New York City. Later many of them went back to their earlier homes. The Dutch settled many towns in the eastern part of our state.

Later, many English people came to our state. People from other lands came too. Some of the newcomers settled in the eastern part of the state. Many, however, wanted to move farther west. But the Indians in the western part of the state wanted to keep their land. They drove many of the white men away. So western New York State was not settled until many years later than the eastern part.

Explore Your Own Community

In what part of the state do you live? Was your community first settled by the Dutch? Or do you live in the central or western part of the state, where the Indians kept their homes longer? Was your home community settled by people moving from the eastern part of the state? Maybe it was settled by people who came from New England or other eastern parts of our country.

How can you find out about your own community? You might visit a museum that shows models or pictures of the first settlers. There you could see the things these people used, the way they dressed, the kinds of homes they lived in.

7

New York
Our State

0 10 20 30 40
Scale of Miles

Watertown

LAKE ONTARIO

Oswego

Oneida

CANADA

Lockport

Niagara Falls

Rochester

N. Y. State Barge Canal
(Erie Canal)

Syracuse

BUFFALO

Auburn

Niagara R.

Genesee River

FINGER LAKES

LAKE ERIE

Ithaca

Hornell

Jamestown

Olean

Elmira

Binghamton

OHIO

WALK ON WATER

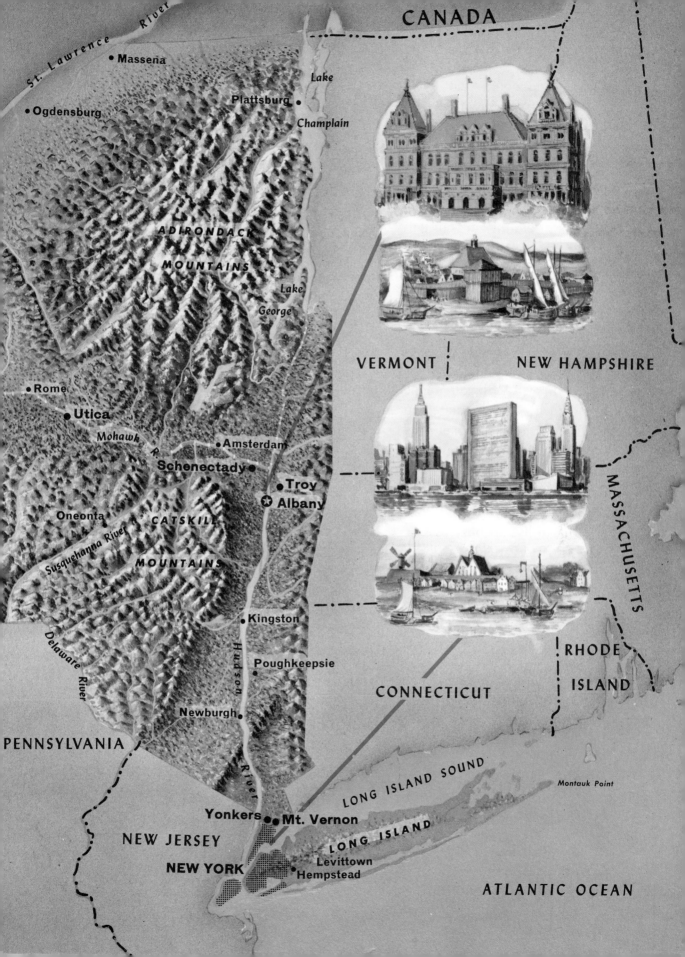

CANADA

St. Lawrence River

Massena

Ogdensburg

Plattsburg

Lake
Champlain

ADIRONDACK

MOUNTAINS

Lake
George

Rome

Utica

Mohawk R.

Amsterdam

Schenectady

Troy

Albany

Oneonta

CATSKILL

Susquehanna River

MOUNTAINS

Kingston

Delaware River

Poughkeepsie

Hudson River

Newburgh

PENNSYLVANIA

VERMONT   NEW HAMPSHIRE

MASSACHUSETTS

CONNECTICUT

RHODE

ISLAND

LONG ISLAND SOUND

Montauk Point

Yonkers   Mt. Vernon

NEW JERSEY

NEW YORK

LONG ISLAND

Levittown

Hempstead

ATLANTIC OCEAN

If there is no museum nearby, you may be able to find books that tell of the early days in your community. Better yet, you may know some grandmother or grandfather who can tell you stories of the old days. The older people in a community can remember true stories that their grandparents told them long ago.

There may be things in your neighborhood that were left by the early settlers. Maybe there is an old, old house. Maybe there is a fort. Maybe there is a battlefield where early settlers fought for their homes and their freedom.

Children of Early New York State

This book will tell you about three families that lived in this state long, long ago. The first story, "Cokoe the Owl," tells about an Indian boy and his life with his family and his friends.

The second story is about a Dutch boy and a Dutch girl who came across the stormy sea to live in our state.

The third story tells of a family who made the long trip from eastern to western New York State in pioneer days. They settled beside a lake. How many of you have a lake near your home?

These stories tell you some of the history of our state. They tell you about boys' and girls' games, and about the kinds of work that children had to do long ago. They tell of early homes, of the food people enjoyed, of the clothing they wore. They tell how people traveled and how they sent messages from place to place. They tell you how the boys and girls of olden days talked and how they felt about all sorts of things.

You will be surprised to find that these long-ago children were a great deal like you. Their parents were like your parents. Families worked together and played together as they now do. Children did most of the things their parents wanted them to, but sometimes they got into mischief. They all learned in some way, whether or not they went to school.

In museums we can see objects used by people in the early days. Here the children see a warming pan.

Older people can remember things about your community that you can't find in history books.

Of course, you will find that these children's lives were different from yours in many ways. They had to eat the food that came from nearby, or go without. Food was not then brought in ships, trains, and trucks from all over the world. They had to wear the clothing their mothers could make for them. When they were still quite young, they learned to work like men and women, because there was so much work to do in newly settled homes. There was no electricity to make work easier at home or on the farm. There were few factories to make the kinds of things you buy at the store today. There were no movies or radios or TV shows.

How Did People Live Long Ago?

But these are all things outside of people. Inside, these children and their mothers and fathers were very much like your friends and neighbors. Even the Indians weren't very different. All the groups who have lived in our state have helped one another. They have had some sort of government. They have worked and taken care of their children. People have laughed. Babies have cried. Children have played. Everybody has been scared sometimes and angry other times. Men and women and children have done brave things. People have been kind to one another.

As you read these stories, ask yourselves, "Did people like these live in my community in the old days? How were our Indians like Cokoe and his family? How were they different?

"Did Dutch people like Lisbet's family ever live where I do? Did our first settlers come from across the sea or from other parts of our own country?

11

"Did our pioneers have the same troubles as the family at Polly's Falls? Were their lives harder or easier? Why did pioneers come to our part of the state? Was there rich soil? Was there water power for mills? Was there a river or a lake to make transportation easier? Were the Indians friendly, like old Beaver Tail? Did they fight like the Mohawks near Beavertown?"

You will like the boys and girls in the stories, and the grownups, too. Some of the people are real, and their stories are true. Some of the people are make-believe, but their stories tell what people really did in the olden days.

There is no use in telling you anything more. You will enjoy the stories more if you find out for yourself about the children and how they lived.

Today it is easy for us to prepare meals or choose our clothes. We have machines, too, to help us build our houses. But the people who lived in New York long ago, perhaps in your own community, had to grow and make these things for themselves.

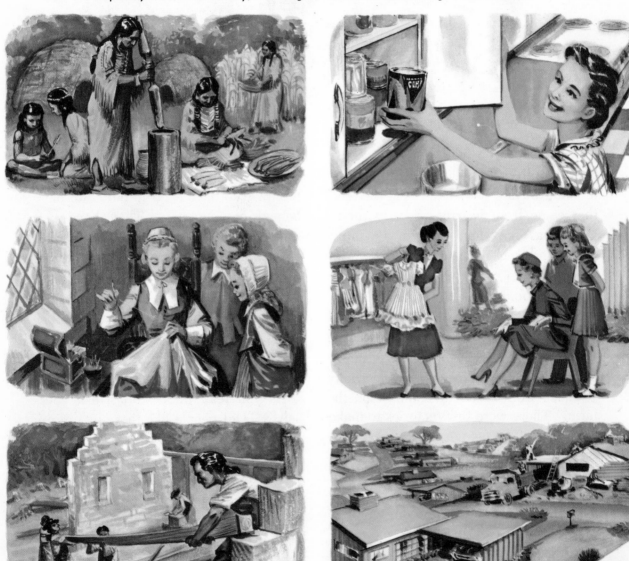

ONE: Cokoe the Owl

Cokoe the Owl

This is the story of Cokoe, a *Woodland Indian* boy. In the year 1600 he was just ten years old. He lived in a village on the west bank of the Hudson River.

Cokoe's people called themselves the *Lenni-Lenape*. In the *Algonquin* language, which Cokoe spoke, this means "real people." There were many other Indian villages up and down the river and off in the woods. The people on the east bank of the Hudson were *Mohicans*. They, too, spoke Algonquin, but not quite the same way as the Lenapes did. Cokoe had to listen very carefully to understand the Mohicans. At least they were friendly with Cokoe's people.

But up the river to the north, and beyond the Lenape to the northwest, there were other Woodland Indians who spoke a different language. They were the *Iroquois*. Cokoe had heard the grownups in his family speak of these Indians as "the enemy." He trembled when he heard their names.

Cokoe lived with his parents. The most important grown-ups in his life were his mother, his father, and his uncle. Like many Woodland Indians, Cokoe's people were divided into *clans*. When a child was born, he became a member of his mother's clan, not his father's. Cokoe and his mother and his

14

uncle (his mother's brother) all belonged to the same clan. His father belonged to a different one.

Cokoe's Uncle Soningo was sagamore (chief) of the village. The sagamore was like a father to everyone. He saw that they all did as they were supposed to do. He was especially interested in Cokoe. He wanted Cokoe to grow up strong and brave and wise. This was important because when Soningo died or retired, the nearest male relative in his clan would become chief. And that, of course, would be Cokoe!

I WONDER

I wonder how Cokoe and his family built their wigwam homes.

I wonder what kinds of food Cokoe's mother prepared for her family.

I wonder if I would like to dress like Cokoe and his friends.

I wonder how the Indians traveled from village to village, and how news spread from one tribe to another.

I wonder why a guardian spirit was so important to Cokoe.

WORDS WE NEED TO KNOW

Algonquin	dugout canoe	Mohican	tribute
breechcloth	guardian	mortar (a strong container) and pestle	wampum
ceremonies	Iroquois		wigwam
char	Lenni-Lenape	quest	Woodland
clans	Mohawk	quiver	Indian
		storage	

Cokoe jumps quickly from his bed of furs, for this is a very special day.

1: Cokoe Starts the Day

Cokoe awoke with a feeling that something special was about to happen. He was lying on his own little bed of furs. His feet were stretched toward the fireplace in the center of the room. Opening his eyes he looked around in the dim light. Cokoe's eyes were sharp, even in the dark. That's why they called him Cokoe the Owl.

Now, sitting up, Cokoe tried to think of what was special about the day. He couldn't remember. Everything looked the same as usual. Above him he saw the brown bark which shingled the walls and roof of his *wigwam*. The walls and roof were all in one and they were curved. It was like sitting under a big brown bowl turned upside down.

In the middle of the ceiling above his head Cokoe could see a round hole. Down through that hole came light from the sky. Out of the same hole went smoke from the fire directly below it.

That was the fire which had kept Cokoe's feet warm all night. Now he could see his mother stirring the fire. She was adding wood to it. As she poked at the fire, bright sparks went flying up and out the chimney hole.

Cokoe turned and looked toward his father's bed. Tamquid, his father, wasn't there. Had he left? It must be late. Just then Cokoe's mother spoke to him.

"Cokoe, our elder brother the sun is already up. Why aren't you? Don't you remember what's happening today? Uncle Soningo will soon be here to take you hunting with him."

That was it! His uncle was going to take him hunting today! Cokoe jumped to his feet, scattering his fur bedclothes in all directions.

"Oh, Mother, I must be ready when he comes," said Cokoe.

Cokoe hurried toward the door. Stooping low, he pushed aside the skin door flap and went outside.

It was a fine spring morning, but chilly. Cokoe was wearing nothing but a little deerskin *breechcloth*. Barefooted he ran all the way to the brook, which tumbled along just beyond the village. At the bank he paused a moment, shivering.

Perhaps, he thought, just this one morning he could sprinkle a little of the water over his head and run back to the warm wigwam. But, no, that would be cheating. Surely his uncle and even his mother would know, somehow. And Uncle Soningo would not want to take a cowardly boy hunting with him.

The very thought alarmed Cokoe! Before he could change his mind again, he took off his breechcloth and hung it on a willow bush. Then, taking a deep breath, he plunged head first into the water. Up he came again, gasping and snorting. The shock of the cold water had taken the breath right out of him.

Once more he went under the water. This time he turned a complete backward somersault with his feet in the air. When he came up the second time he decided that was enough. No one could call him a coward now!

With two strokes, Cokoe swam to the bank and scrambled up it. He was shivering again. His teeth were chattering. The morning breeze on his wet skin felt even colder than the water. But Cokoe knew how to warm himself.

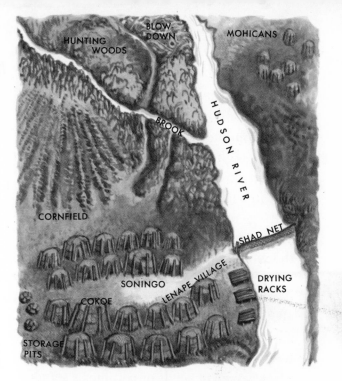

This is Cokoe's village. As you read his story, come back to this map to find the places he visits.

First with his hands he wiped the water from his arms and chest. Then he hurried over to the willow bush where he had laid his breechcloth. Here he broke off a newly leafed-out branch. With the willow branch he brushed the water from his back and legs. Then he switched himself lightly until his skin began to tingle with warmth. Soon he was dry enough to put his breechcloth back on. When he had tied it well, he started back toward home.

DO YOU KNOW—

1. How Cokoe felt when he woke up?
2. What sort of bed he was sleeping in?
3. How the inside of his house looked?
4. Who was going to take Cokoe hunting?
5. What Cokoe's mother called the sun?

THINGS TO DO

If your town has a Historical Society, a museum, or a library, find out from them what Indians lived in your area in olden times. Perhaps there is a collection of Indian things which you can look at.

17

2: Hunters Must Eat

Cokoe began to run again. Up the path from the brook he raced until he was within sight of the village. Then he slowed down to a walk. People seeing him in such a hurry might tease him for getting up late. So he walked lazily along as though he had all the time in the world.

Up ahead of him were the wigwams of the little village where he lived. They all looked much alike, small and round and close to the ground. Most of them were covered with gray-brown bark. Mats woven of reeds or cornhusks served as covering for a few of the houses. Each house had a low, arched doorway. The door flaps were made of deerskin or smaller animal skins sewn together. Over the doorway of one house hung a huge, gray wolf skin. That was Uncle Soningo's house.

Other people were stirring in the village. All of the other boys his age had already been down to the brook and back again. Some of them were playing a game on the open ground between the houses. With bows and arrows they were shooting at a moving target. The target was a small wheel of braided cornhusks. One boy started the wheel rolling

After his bath Cokoe walks home through the village. Everyone is awake and stirring, for there is always much work to be done in an Indian community.

away from them and gave the signal. The others all shot at it. Each boy's arrows were specially marked. When the wheel stopped rolling, they all ran to pick it up. It was easy to tell by the marked arrows which boy had hit closest to the center.

As Cokoe walked by, the boys called out to him, "Cokoe, come and play with us!"

But Cokoe answered, "No, I have something more important to do today. I am going hunting with my uncle."

By then Cokoe had reached his own doorway. The deerskin flap had been fastened aside. Cokoe stooped low to enter. The house was light with morning sunshine from the open door. Cokoe saw his uncle sitting by the fire, waiting for him.

As Cokoe entered, his uncle turned and spoke to him, "Well, how is the mighty hunter this morning?"

Cokoe said nothing. He was ashamed of having slept so late.

Then his uncle spoke to Cokoe's mother: "I see, my sister, that you let your son sleep late? Is he sick? Perhaps he is too weak to go hunting."

Cokoe's heart sank. He was going to be left at home!

Then Soningo laughed and spoke again, "But I also see, my sister, that his hair is well soaked with the cold water of the brook."

Cokoe laughed, too. His uncle was teasing him. Now he knew that they would go hunting together after all!

While Cokoe was putting on his moccasins and leggings, his mother busied herself near the fire. She had made corn meal cakes wrapped in dampened cornhusks. Now she was poking them out of the hot ashes where they had cooked. The hunters must have something to eat before they set out, and something extra to take along. They would be gone the whole day; perhaps even longer. She handed a warm cake to Soningo and another one to Cokoe.

Soningo spoke to her again. "Tamquid came over to my wigwam this morning, sister. Yes, he was there while the mighty hunter here was still dreaming in

19

his soft bed." He nodded toward the boy who was still struggling with his leggings. Cokoe couldn't find the thongs which would fasten them to his breechcloth. Then he discovered that he had the leggings on the wrong legs. No wonder he couldn't find the thongs. They should be on the outside, not the inside!

Soningo pretended not to notice Cokoe's struggles and went on talking to his sister. "Tamquid is going into the forest today. He is looking for a tree that will make a good, sturdy *dugout canoe*. He says he will go up along the river. There is a blow-down up that way, where the big wind blew down many trees last fall. Cokoe and I will go past the place, but we must go farther on. There will be no deer so close to the noise of canoe-making. All that hacking and scraping is bound to frighten the deer farther into the forest."

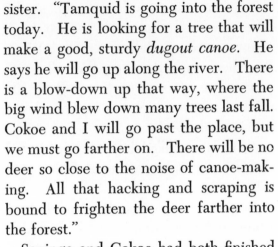

Cokoe's leather leggings will protect his legs from scratches when he hunts in the forest.

Soningo and Cokoe had both finished their corn meal cakes. Now Cokoe's leggings were on straight. His mother had packed the extra cakes in a little leather pouch. This was tied to the belt of Cokoe's breechcloth. His *quiver* of arrows was slung across his back. In his right hand he carried his bow.

Cokoe's mother saw that they were ready to leave. She wished them good hunting. She was proud of her son. As Cokoe followed his uncle down the path toward the forest, he was proud too.

DO YOU KNOW—

1. What the wigwams in the village were covered with? What the doors were made of?
2. What sort of game the boys were playing?
3. What breakfast Cokoe's mother gave him?
4. Where Cokoe's father had gone?
5. What extra clothes Cokoe put on to go hunting?

THINGS TO DO

Find out about some of the other games the Indian boys and girls played. Then choose one to play that the class can take part in.

The mighty wind giant has roared through the forest, tearing down bushes and trees!

3: The Canoe Makers

As Cokoe and Soningo walked on into the forest, the sounds from the village became fainter. They could still hear one or two of the dogs barking, and there was the steady thump of a *mortar and pestle* as some woman ground her corn into meal. Finally they were beyond even these sounds. They walked on in silence. The forest floor was soft and spongy with a thick layer of damp leaves and moss. Their soft deerskin moccasins made no noise.

For a while Cokoe forgot that he was a hunter and simply enjoyed himself in the fresh spring woods. He was looking for the little people who, he had heard, lived in the woods. He had never seen them, but he was told that was because they were so small and quick and clever. How tiny they must be to live under toadstools and ferns! He must ask Soningo more about them. But just as he

was trying to get up enough courage to break the silence, the woods suddenly brightened. Cokoe saw that they were no longer walking in the shade of trees. Now they were standing at the edge of a clearing.

Here was the blow-down his uncle had spoken of earlier in the morning. It was the place where the big wind had blown down so many trees. They were all lying on their sides in a tangle of branches and dead leaves. There were oak and maple, chestnut and birch, and here and there a giant evergreen. Some were completely uprooted. Others still had their roots in the ground, but had been snapped off halfway up the trunk by the force of the wind.

Cokoe said to his uncle, "It looks as though a giant had done it!"

Soningo answered, "It was a giant. Don't you know about the wind giant?

21

The log is held in place by stones. The bark is chopped away and a groove made.

He is as tall as the tallest tree in the forest, and his voice is as loud as the loudest waterfall. You know how a waterfall roars. That is how the wind giant roars. His hair is long and black, and his eyes are as bright as lightning."

"But how does he tear down the trees?"

"Well," said Soningo, "when he is angry he rushes through the forest walking on his hands. His long hair becomes tangled in the trees and pulls them up as he walks along."

Cokoe wondered if this were really so. Was his uncle just making it up? He looked at his uncle's face to see if there was a smile on it. No, the expression was serious and sober. Well, he thought to himself, there certainly are things in this world more powerful than people. He believed in the tiny woods-elves the grownups talked about, although he had never seen them. He believed in the Manito, the Great Spirit, who had power over everything and all people. He guessed, then, that he could believe in a wind giant. But he wished that just once

he might see one of these spirits. His uncle guessed what he was thinking and spoke to him.

"You do not have to see the wind giant to believe in him, Cokoe. You can see what he has done right here in the woods. Who else could have done it?"

Cokoe admitted he didn't know anyone else who could have done it. Then he changed the subject, for at that moment he heard a sound of chopping coming from the other side of the clearing.

"That must be Father making the canoe. Let's go and watch him." And Cokoe started off toward the sound, straight across the clearing. He had only taken a few steps when he tripped over some tangled branches and fell on his face. He almost let out a whimper as the dry twigs scratched his face and a hidden rock bruised his shin. But he picked himself up bravely and turned around to see what his uncle thought of him.

Soningo was standing there patiently waiting to show him the easiest way across the tangled clearing.

The men burn and scrape the log many times before their canoe is ready for use.

"Sometimes, Cokoe, the long way around is the shortest way to go. It will be easier to walk along through the edge of the woods where the wind giant hasn't made the going so hard."

Once again Soningo took the lead, and they walked quietly through the woods at the edge of the clearing. By the time they reached the place where Tamquid was working on the canoe, Cokoe's scratches no longer smarted and he had forgotten the bruise on his leg.

Cokoe's father was not working alone on the canoe. There were two other men helping him. Canoe-making was hard work and took a long time. The men had chosen the log carefully for soundness and size. Then they had dragged it to a place convenient for working—along the riverbank on the one open side of the clearing. When the canoe was finished, it could be rolled or slid into the water.

The log had been propped between stones so that it wouldn't roll while the men were scraping away the bark with sharp stone axes. The men had worked hard and already the log was fairly smooth. Now they were beginning to hack out a groove along the top. When that was finished, they would build a fire all along the groove, feeding the fire with dried moss, sticks, and leaves. They would have to watch it carefully so that it wouldn't burn where they didn't want it to. The fire would *char* the wood just enough so that they could scrape it away with clamshell scrapers. This would go on—burning and scraping, burning and scraping—until they had hollowed out the whole log and shaped it into a long, narrow boat.

DO YOU KNOW—

1. Why Cokoe and his uncle had to go far into the forest to hunt?

2. What Cokoe looked for under the toadstools and ferns? What a blow-down is? What tools were used in shaping the canoe?

THINGS TO DO

Make a model of a dugout canoe. You can use either soap or clay. Try carving the soap with a clamshell instead of a knife. If you use clay, work it roughly into shape with your fingers, and then finish shaping it with a shell.

23

These Lenape men are hard at work. One man is going to mend the shad nets. Can you tell what the other men in the picture are doing?

4: Off to the Woods Again

The three men working on the canoe were pleased to see Cokoe and Soningo. The visit would give them a chance to talk and rest. Tamquid was especially pleased to see his son walking toward him, straight and tall with his bow in his hand, like a brave hunter. Tamquid put down his stone axe and turned to greet them.

"Good morning, Cokoe. Good morning, Soningo." Then he spoke directly to Cokoe.

"Well, Little Owl, you really look tall now, as tall as that bow you hold in your hand. I'm glad to see you have grown since I left you asleep in the lodge this

morning. You didn't look nearly as tall lying down as you do on your feet."

Cokoe knew he was being teased again. Why was it that grownups so often teased children? It was one of the things he never could understand. He must try harder to do the things which pleased them. Then they wouldn't tease him. But right now he didn't know how to answer his father.

As Cokoe stood there, his father reached over and gently tugged his hair.

"How tall is a hunter when he's lying asleep, Cokoe?"

Cokoe felt the gentleness of the tug. The smile on his father's face told Cokoe that he wasn't really angry. It even gave him the courage to answer jokingly.

"A hunter must be well rested, Father, so that he may run swiftly."

"Ho, ho! That was a good answer," laughed Tamquid.

The other men laughed too. They liked to see a boy show some spirit.

While the men stood around talking, Cokoe turned to look at the work they had been doing. He wondered how long it would take to finish the canoe.

Tamquid guessed what he was thinking and answered his question. "It will be many days before we finish it, Cokoe. Perhaps two moons from now. Let's see, we are in the frog moon (spring) now. I should say by the moon of the first green corn (summer) the canoe should be ready."

"Such a long time and so much work!" said Cokoe.

"Yes," said Soningo, "so much work.

But our work for today is hunting, Cokoe. Let's go."

"Happy hunting," said Tamquid as they turned to leave. "Take a good look at us before you go, Cokoe. And don't be surprised if we look like strangers on your way back."

"What do you mean?" asked Cokoe, puzzled.

"We'll be covered with dust from the charred wood. You may not know us through the black soot."

Cokoe smiled at his father and answered, "I will know you, Father."

As he turned to follow Soningo once more into the woods, he called back over his shoulder, "What shall I bring for your supper, Father?"

"Anything covered with fur or feathers, Cokoe. Just see that the bears don't make supper of you."

Cokoe laughed and ran to catch up with Soningo.

The women work too. Curing hides is one of their jobs. What other work do they do?

"Laugh and chatter all you want to now," said Soningo. "As soon as we are beyond the sounds of the canoe-makers we must be quiet ourselves."

Cokoe had many questions to ask.

"Why do the bushes and low tree branches look so chewed up?" he wanted to know.

"Don't you remember that we had a very hard winter, Cokoe? The deer could not find food in the open places, because the snow was so deep. They had to stay in the deep woods where the ground was more protected. Here they ate the bushes which stuck out of the snow, and the bark and lower branches of trees. But there wasn't enough food for all, and many of them did not live through the winter."

"Why don't they just crawl in a hole and go to sleep when it's cold?" asked Cokoe. "Bears do."

"Yes, but deer are not bears. Deer must eat all winter long. They must also keep walking around when it's cold in order to keep warm. The more they walk around, the hungrier they get. But

Cokoe and Uncle Soningo must go deep into the woods. The deer have moved far into the forest away from the sounds of the village and the canoe-makers.

if they should lie down they would freeze. You see, they haven't much choice."

"Why do those blue jays make so much noise in the trees over our heads?"

"Perhaps they are warning the forest animals that Cokoe the mighty hunter is after them," Soningo joked. "No, Cokoe, I don't really know why they do it. That is just the way of blue jays. But they will get tired after a while, and leave us alone. We had better stop talking, too."

DO YOU KNOW—

1. Why the canoe makers were glad to see Cokoe and Soningo? How long a moon is?

2. How long it would take to make the canoe?

3. Why the canoe makers would be black later in the day?

THINGS TO DO

Go for a walk in the woods or in a park and see how many of the trees you know, how many animals, how many birds. If you know the birds by sight, close your eyes and see how many you know by their calls. This is the sort of wood lore that Cokoe knew.

5: A Hunting Lesson

The woods were changing now, becoming darker. Cokoe noticed that the trees were closer together. Looking above him he saw that the tops of the trees joined each other, making a roof of woven branches and pale green leaves over his head. Here and there were big, lacy holes where the twigs had not yet leafed out. Through these holes shafts of sunlight came slanting down to the ground. In some of these shafts of light there were tiny midges flying round and round each other. The blue jays had stopped screaming. All was quiet.

Suddenly Soningo stopped walking and stood silently listening. There was a faint sound. Cokoe heard it, too. It was a soft swishing of branches far ahead of them. The two Indians quickly dropped to the ground and listened carefully again.

Soningo whispered to Cokoe, "It is a deer browsing."

Cokoe nodded and answered, "He would have run off if he had heard us."

Soningo disagreed. "He has heard us. That's why he stopped for a while. But he isn't alarmed because he has not scented us yet. We are lucky. The wind is at his back."

"Shall we just wait here until he comes close?" asked Cokoe.

"No," answered Soningo. "He may change his direction, or the wind may turn. Listen and I'll tell you a better way."

Cokoe was so excited he could hear his own heart beat.

"Now," said Soningo, "you go, Cokoe, off to the left. Circle slowly toward the deer. Keep low. Crawl on your belly, if you must. And be very quiet. The deer must not hear you or scent you. When you are within sight of him, stand up behind a tree. If he sees you, stand perfectly still. Deer have poor eyesight and he may not know you are a human."

"When shall I shoot?" asked Cokoe.

"You will not shoot this time, Cokoe. While you are circling to the left, I will be moving toward the deer from the right. I will get as close as I can without alarming him. Then I will draw an arrow from my quiver and notch it to the bow string. When I am ready I will give you the signal to rush toward the deer. He will run away from you and toward me."

"What will the signal be?"

"It will be a bird call, the sound of a thrush. Do you know the sound?" asked Soningo.

"Yes," nodded Cokoe.

Cokoe raised himself to a crouching position and began circling toward the deer as Soningo had told him to. Soningo moved off to the right. They were both as silent as shadows.

Cokoe moved slowly and carefully. He placed every footstep so that it would make no noise. The crackling of a twig would be enough to scare the deer away too soon. It seemed a long time before he finally came within sight of the animal. Cokoe breathed faster when he saw the deer. It was a female, a slender doe

Cokoe rushes at the deer to chase it toward his uncle. Why doesn't Uncle Soningo kill the deer?

with wide ears and a white tail. She was feeding on the new leaves of a dogwood tree. Nearby was a clump of hemlock.

As Cokoe watched the doe, he heard the call of a thrush. The deer heard it, too, and raised her head. It didn't sound quite right to her, but she didn't know why. Cokoe knew. It was Soningo's signal for him to rush toward the deer. As soon as she saw him, the frightened doe turned and went crashing away through the forest.

Cokoe stopped when he saw his uncle step from behind a tree with his bow drawn. But Soningo didn't shoot! When he saw the deer, he dropped his bow and turned to watch her bounding away through the woods.

Cokoe ran toward his uncle. "What's the matter, Soningo? Why didn't you shoot?"

Soningo answered, "We don't shoot the does, Cokoe. They must be spared to raise the fawns. That one we just frightened may have a fawn around here somewhere. Go look in that clump of hemlock trees. That looks like a good bedding place for a fawn."

Cokoe walked over to the hemlocks. He raised one of the lower branches which touched the ground all the way around. It was cool and dark under the trees. The smell of the brown needles on the ground was good. Cokoe peered around in the gloom. At first he saw nothing but a tangle of branches. Then his sharp eyes saw two little forms. They were two speckled fawns lying side by side. They lay perfectly still and didn't even move an eyelash.

Cokoe called to Soningo, "They are twins, Uncle!"

Soningo came over to look. "They are twins all right. Now we had better go away from here, Cokoe. Their mother will come back when we leave."

"But she has left them!" cried Cokoe. "Couldn't we take them home with us?"

"No, Cokoe. Their mother can take care of them better than we can. She will be back. Let's leave them alone."

Cokoe was disappointed. Soningo explained that if the fawns were raised in the Indian village, they would not be afraid of humans when they grew up. Some day they might wander into the woods and be shot by a hunter. Then Cokoe would lose his pets.

DO YOU KNOW—

1. Why the hunters were lucky that the wind was at the deer's back?

2. What plan Soningo had for catching the deer? What Soningo's signal was to be? Was this a good plan? Why?

3. What Cokoe found in the clump of hemlock? Why Soningo said that fawns should not be raised as pets?

THINGS TO DO

1. Try making fire by twirling a stick of hard wood in a hole in a piece of soft wood.

2. Make corn meal by pounding dried corn in a wooden bowl with a wooden pestle.

Cokoe discovers two tiny fawns. Why can't he take them back to the village?

6: Alarming News

"Come, Cokoe," called Soningo as he moved away from the fawns. "The sun is already high over our heads and we haven't caught any supper yet."

Sadly Cokoe dropped the hemlock branches over the hiding place of the fawns.

"Cheer up," said Soningo. "There are many deer in the woods. We will find a buck yet."

"I am not sad because we didn't get the doe," said Cokoe. "I only wish we could take the fawns home."

A little farther along in the woods a huge buck came bounding toward them. Before Cokoe could think what to do, Soningo had sent an arrow into the animal's chest. The shot brought the buck to his knees. In a few seconds Soningo had rushed to the side of the wounded deer. He gave one thrust of his knife and the animal was dead.

Cokoe stood watching as Soningo spoke to the deer he had just killed. "I am sorry to take your life, my brother. But the Lenape have had a hard winter, too. Last year's corn is almost gone, and the new corn is just planted. I thank you for giving your life so that we may eat."

When Soningo had finished speaking, they heard another sound in the woods. It was a footstep. In another moment an Indian came into view. When he saw Cokoe and Soningo, he stopped.

Soningo spoke to him. "Greetings, friend. I see by your weapons that you are hunting. Have you had any luck?"

The young man answered, "If it weren't for you, I would have had luck. That was my deer you shot. I have been trailing him since the sun came up this morning. I did not come so far to help you make the catch. Now I will take the meat and go home."

The young man spoke their own language, and he looked like a Lenape. But Cokoe had never heard anyone speak so rudely to his uncle. After all, Soningo was a sagamore, the chief of his village!

Right away Soningo knew what was wrong. He laughed and spoke to the young man. "You are a Lenape, my brave, but what clan do you belong to?"

The young man answered boldly, "I belong to the Turtle Clan. One day I will be chief of my village. My uncle is old and ailing. Soon I will take his place."

"You started out hunting this morning in Turtle country," said Soningo, "but now you are in Wolf country."

The young man nodded. He understood.

Cokoe was puzzled. He did not understand.

Soningo turned and spoke to him. "You know that you belong to the Wolf Clan, don't you, Cokoe?"

Cokoe nodded. Yes, he knew that very well.

Soningo continued, "And this brave has said that he belongs to the Turtle Clan. Then it is very simple. The woods on one side of his village belong to the Turtle Clan for hunting. When he started out this morning he was in his own territory. But he has come a long way since then. He has tracked the deer all the way across his own woods and into ours. Now he is in Wolf Clan territory."

Cokoe asked in wonder, "You mean the woods don't belong to everybody?"

"Yes, the woods belong to everybody, Cokoe. But the right to hunt in certain woods belongs to certain families. Each clan has its own area."

"Then who owns the deer we shot?" asked Cokoe.

"That is a problem," answered Soningo. Then turning to the young brave he said, "I think the best way would be to divide it in two."

But the young man was more friendly, now that he understood. He answered, "No, I will have other chances on my way back home. You take it to your wigwam. I know of a brook where the deer go for water at sundown. I will surely find one then, if not earlier."

In 1600 there were two great groups of Indians in New York State. Cokoe's people, the Lenni-Lenape, belonged to the Algonquin group. The Mohicans, Mahicans, and other tribes along the east coast were Algonquins too. The Iroquois lived to the north and west of the Algonquins. The most important Iroquois tribes were the five nations you see on the map.

Indians
in
New York State ~ 1600

"We thank you," answered Soningo. "And I'm sure the young hunter with me has learned a lesson in courtesy."

"It is nothing," said the young man. "By the way, I think I saw signs of a *Mohawk* war party back there in the forest."

"In that case," said Soningo, "hadn't you better come back to our village with us? We would be glad to shelter you at our fire."

"Oh, no. I am not afraid for myself," said the young man. "One Lenape can outwit a dozen Mohawks. I only thought it would be better to get the boy home. The Mohawks are treacherous. Instead of attacking us, they might prefer to capture the boy and make him work for

The Mohawks are near the Lenape village! They have stopped along the way to eat and paint their faces for the big meeting.

them. Anyway, I would probably be safer at my own fire than at yours. I think they are heading in your direction."

"Yes, I have been expecting a visit from them," said Soningo. "But I didn't expect a raid. It should be a *tribute* party on its way to us. Are you sure it was a war party?"

"No, I am not sure. There were about six in the group. I saw where they had slept in a pine grove. A small fire was still smouldering. Scattered nearby were six green twigs with charred ends. They must have divided some game and roasted it over the fire. A Lenape would not have left a single live spark."

"No, neither would a Mohawk in his own woods," said Soningo. "They don't care if our woods burn down. But it is spring now. There is not much danger."

"The reason I thought it was a war party," continued the stranger, "was that I found a bark tube of red paint that one of them had left. It was lying under a fern beside a little spring at the edge of the grove. Probably it fell from some Mohawk's pouch and rolled out of sight when he stooped to drink."

DO YOU KNOW—
1. What Soningo said to the killed deer?
2. How hunting grounds were divided?
3. By what signs the stranger knew there were six in the Mohawk group? What made him think it was a war party?

THINGS TO DO
Although we no longer get most of our meat food by hunting wild game, there are rules we must follow when we do hunt. These rules are made by the Conservation Department of our state. Write and ask them for printed information about the rules. Compare these rules with those of the Indians.

7: A Mohawk Raid

Cokoe gave a start when he heard these last words. The thought of the red paint sent a chill down his spine. Perhaps the Mohawk warrior had been sitting beside the spring painting his face! He knew that warriors painted their faces before going into battle. And he remembered something terrible that had happened long ago when he was a little boy.

One dark night when everyone was asleep, the Mohawks had raided his village. First one of them had raced from house to house with a torch setting each one on fire. The dogs began to bark and the sleepy people stumbled out of their wigwams, but it was too late. Already the other Mohawks were running in from the woods, killing and capturing as fast as they could. Cokoe remembered the high, bloodcurdling war whoops of the raiders. He remembered the terrifying sight of their painted faces. They looked even more frightening in the light of the blazing wigwams. He had only a glimpse of them as his mother hurried him and his older sister out of the house.

His father had already snatched up his war club and was out the door before them. Women and children were screaming. One of the screams was so close it hurt his ears. It was his sister. A Mohawk had struck his mother's arm and dragged the girl away. Cokoe never saw her again.

Somehow his mother and he got away into the woods. Their dog had followed them. He had come whimpering along, his tail between his legs.

His mother had found a safe spot for the night. They heard only faint sounds from the village. Cokoe's mother sat up the whole night. The dog curled up beside her feet, and Cokoe fell asleep in her arms. He was hardly more than a baby then. But even a baby can remember terror.

Soningo glanced down at his nephew and saw the fright on his face. "What is the matter, Cokoe? Is it the thought of the red paint that bothers you?"

Cokoe didn't answer, and Soningo said to the stranger: "The first time he saw red paint it was on the faces of Mohawks raiding our village. I remember the time well. We fought and made a peace with them, but not until the whole village had been burned. We had to promise to pay them tribute of corn and *wampum* to keep the peace."

Turning to Cokoe he said, "You have seen red paint since then. You know that we paint our faces for important *ceremonies*. The Mohawks paint themselves for their ceremonies, too. They paint themselves when they come to pay a tribute visit. It is like wearing your best clothes for special occasions."

When Soningo spoke like that, Cokoe's fear disappeared. How was it his uncle always knew what he was thinking?

The Indians have many ceremonies. They give thanks to the Great Spirit and to the animals, sun, rain, and all things in nature, which they call their brothers.

Perhaps it was because grownups had longer memories. They had lived a longer time. They could remember way far back to the time when they were little children. Probably the same things had happened to them. The thought comforted Cokoe. If the same things had happened to grownups, then what had happened to him was not so bad after all!

The young warrior said to Soningo, "I didn't mean to frighten the boy. I only thought I had better tell you what I had seen."

To Cokoe he said, "I didn't know you were scared. I didn't see it on your face."

Cokoe was pleased. It was important that a young man ten years old should not show fear!

"I think the red paint was just to decorate themselves with," said Soningo. "It wasn't war paint. It would be silly for them to raid us now. What could they take? Our winter supplies are almost

Cokoe is hungry after hunting many hours. The two hunters rest as they eat their corn meal cakes.

gone. Our cornfields have just been planted. If they raid us now, there will be no harvest for them to share later. No, I don't believe it is a war party."

"Well," said the young man, "if I am to bring home any game tonight, I had better get back to my own hunting grounds." He said good-by to Soningo and Cokoe, and walked off into the woods.

Cokoe and Soningo watched until he had disappeared. Then both of them turned to the deer Soningo had brought down.

"Now," said Soningo, "we have work to do. Do you know what the next step is, Cokoe?"

"Yes," said Cokoe, "we must hang the game for a while until it has bled. Then we carry it home and let Mother take care of it."

Cokoe found a piece of grapevine. Soningo tied the deer's hind legs with it and hung the game from the limb of a tree. This work was too heavy for Cokoe. He just stood and watched.

When Soningo had finished, Cokoe asked, "Now can we sit down and eat something, Uncle Soningo?"

Soningo looked up at the sun and laughed. "There is our elder brother the sun only halfway across the sky, and you already want to eat. But since we have had such good luck hunting, I guess we have earned some food."

"I know a better reason for eating," said Cokoe.

"What is it?" asked Soningo.

"I am hungry!" answered Cokoe.

DO YOU KNOW—

1. What red paint made Cokoe think of? Why Soningo thought it wasn't a war party?

2. How Soningo hung the deer? What time it was when Cokoe and Soningo ate in the woods?

THINGS TO DO

You have already begun to look back into the history of your own community. Find out how recently Indians have lived in the area. If there are Indians living among you now, find out if they came from somewhere else, just as your ancestors did.

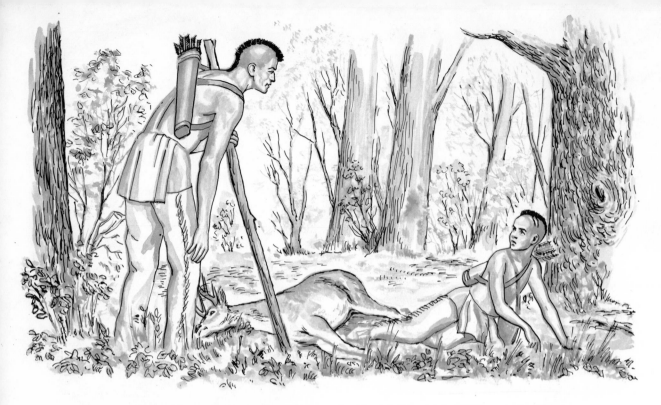

Cokoe learns by making mistakes. Soningo lets him figure out how to carry the deer.

8: The Hunters Return

The two hunters finished their lunch in the woods and got ready to return home. Cokoe was eager to have his friends in the village see him carrying the deer. Soningo could easily have carried the deer, but Cokoe wanted to help.

He found a sturdy sapling, which he cut down with Soningo's stone axe. The deer's hind legs and forelegs were tied up and the sapling was slipped between them. Soningo lifted the front end of the pole to his shoulder. Cokoe lifted the other end to his. That way the weight of the deer did not bother them. But Cokoe soon discovered that this was an awkward way to carry the load. Soningo's shoulder was so high up and Cokoe's was so low down. Of course the deer slid right down the pole and banged against Cokoe's chest!

Soningo smiled as he heard his nephew grunt. He had known this would happen, but said nothing. He wanted Cokoe to figure out what to do.

Cokoe thought he knew. He spoke up and said, "Let's change places, Uncle Soningo. You take the back end and I'll take the front."

This time as soon as they shouldered the load—wham!—the deer slid down the pole again and hit Cokoe in the back, knocking him down.

Cokoe picked himself up from the ground. This blow had sent him sprawling head over heels in the leaves. He wasn't hurt, only a little ashamed of himself. Imagine a mighty hunter falling on his face!

"What now, Little Owl?" asked Soningo, trying hard not to laugh.

Before he made another suggestion, Cokoe thought for a while.

"There is one more way we can try," he said. He spoke slowly, trying to figure ahead as he talked. "I will carry the front end on my shoulder. You carry the back end in your hand, down at your side. Don't lift it to your shoulder. Do you think it will work that way?" he asked hopefully.

"We'll see," said Soningo, as he raised his end of the pole.

It did work better than before. The deer stayed in the middle and didn't slide either way. But it was not very easy for Soningo. To keep the pole level he had to bend his elbow and raise his arm a little. Cokoe didn't notice this because he was in front. He walked happily along. How the other boys would envy him when he came home from the hunt carrying a deer!

After a while Cokoe's shoulder began to get sore. He was glad when Soningo said, "Let's rest awhile, Cokoe."

When they started on again, Soningo threw the deer over his own shoulders. Cokoe was afraid he was being left out. He felt easy again when Soningo said, "Be sure to bring that sapling along, Cokoe. We will carry it your way again when we get closer to home. I want you to be fresh and strong. What will they say to me if I wear you out on your first deer hunt?"

Sure enough, when they entered the village Cokoe was walking proudly in front and Soningo behind. Between them swung the deer on a pole.

The other boys Cokoe's age came running up. They were all excited.

"Did you shoot the deer, Cokoe?"

Before Cokoe could answer another one asked, "Where is the bloody arrow, Cokoe?"

When Cokoe told them that his uncle had shot the deer, they were disappointed. If Cokoe had shot it, there would have been a party to celebrate. But the boys still ran along with the

Cokoe's friends run to greet him, as he proudly returns to the village.

hunters. They admired the size of the deer, and they admired Cokoe for helping his uncle on the hunt.

At Cokoe's house they dropped the deer outside the door. "Tell your mother it is hers to divide," said Soningo, as he left for his own house.

Cokoe went inside. His mother was sitting by the fire weaving a basket. When Cokoe came in she looked up smiling. "You are back early, Cokoe. You must have had luck."

"Yes, Mother, we had luck. There is meat outside the door. Uncle Soningo says you are to divide it."

"I will, Cokoe. But first tell me about the hunt. Did you get the first deer you saw?"

"I didn't get any deer at all, Mother. But I helped to carry it home. The first deer we saw was a doe. The Lenape don't take does, Mother," said Cokoe, remembering the lesson he had learned.

"And I saw two spotted fawns, Mother. They were the babies of the doe we didn't shoot. I found them in a hemlock thicket."

"You have sharp eyes, Cokoe," said his mother. "You left the fawns where you found them, didn't you?"

"Oh, yes. But they were very pretty, Mother. You would have liked them."

"Yes, I'm sure I would have liked them, Cokoe. But I have enough to take care of with you and your father. You are still a fawn yourself, you know. Now run along and play. You have been a hunter long enough for one day."

Cokoe ran out of the house again. He still had much to tell the other boys. Wait till they heard about the party of Mohawks in the woods!

DO YOU KNOW—

1. What sort of pole the hunters used to carry the deer? Why it was hard for Cokoe and Soningo to carry the deer together?

2. How Cokoe's first plan for carrying the deer worked out? How the second worked out?

THINGS TO DO

1. Choose partners and carry something on your shoulders the way Cokoe and Soningo did.

2. Another way the Indians sometimes carried heavy loads was by a strap across the forehead. Indian women often carried their babies on cradleboards this way. Try it and see how it leaves your hands free to do other work.

Cokoe tells his mother about the hunting trip and the twin fawns that he had to leave in the woods. What is his mother doing?

Before the shad swim up to the Lenape village, the great nets must be mended.

9: Trouble in the Cornfield

The next day Cokoe awoke early. He wanted to be up when the Mohawks arrived. They had not come the night before, so Cokoe thought they would get to the village early in the morning. Before he was out of the house, however, his mother asked a favor of him.

"Cokoe, I want you to watch the cornfield for me today," said his mother. "If we want a good crop, we'll have to keep the crows from eating the seeds."

Cokoe's heart sank. His mother knew that he didn't like the work. He felt that he was too old for it. But she knew that she didn't have to coax him, either. He was old enough to understand his part in family work. If they had no corn crop, he too would go hungry.

Cokoe started off for the cornfield, thinking about his duties. This didn't make him any happier. His mother didn't know his real reason for wanting

to stay in the village that day. He hadn't told her about the Mohawks.

Cokoe decided to go past his uncle's house on the way to the cornfield. He could ask Soningo if he had heard anything about the Mohawks yet.

On the way Cokoe met his uncle coming along the path. Soningo was carrying a fish net. Other men following behind were also carrying nets. Cokoe thought the shad must be running up the river. He was going to miss another bit of excitement!

"Good morning, Cokoe," said Soningo. "Where are you going in such a hurry today? I see you didn't let the sun find you in bed this morning."

"Good morning, Uncle," said Cokoe. "I was coming to ask you about the Mohawks. Have they come? Are you going fishing? What do they want?"

"Wait a minute, Little Owl. Which

Cokoe angrily throws rocks at the thieving crows.

question do you want me to answer first?"

"About the Mohawks," said Cokoe. "Are they here?"

"No, they are not here. I don't know when they are coming. When they do come, they will have to look for us. We can't wait around all day with so much work to be done."

"And the shad, are they running?" asked Cokoe.

"No, they haven't come either. But we are taking the nets down to the river-bank to mend them. The shad will be running soon, and we must be ready for them."

"I am going to watch my mother's cornfield today," said Cokoe sadly. "The seeds haven't begun to sprout yet, and the crows may still get them."

While they were speaking, a flock of crows went flying overhead. They were cawing loudly and heading in the direc-

tion of the cornfield. Cokoe watched their flight. Without another word, he dashed off in the same direction as the crows.

Cokoe was breathing hard when he reached the open field, but he saw that he couldn't rest. It had rained during the night. Some of the bright yellow kernels his mother had planted so carefully were lying on the bare ground. The crows were busily pecking at all they could find.

Cokoe saw in a flash that if he didn't stop them, there would be no corn to harvest later. Or at least his mother would have to come again and plant the field. Quickly he grabbed up a handful of pebbles and ran toward the birds. As he ran he flapped his arms and yelled, "Caw! Caw!" as loudly as he could. When he was close enough he began throwing the pebbles one by one. Cokoe's aim was good. He hit one of the big birds. The others, hearing all the noise, flew off.

The crows did not go far. They simply flew up to a tall, scraggly pine which grew at the edge of the field. From the pine tree they watched Cokoe. Maybe he was just having fun and would go away soon. Their bright eyes could still see the kernels of corn just waiting to be picked up!

But Cokoe was not having fun. He didn't even stop to rest. Busily he set about putting the seeds back into the ground. The earth was soft where his mother had dug it for planting. And the night's rain had made it even softer. This made the work somewhat easier. He dropped a few seeds into a hole he made with a stick. Then he hilled the earth up around the seeds and went on to the next one.

It took quite a while before he finished the whole field. Once, when he stood up to straighten his back, he saw

that the crows were still watching. Cokoe shook his fist at them and called, "Thieves! Robbers! There is plenty of food in the woods for you! Go and find it, you good-for-nothing corn stealers!"

The crows seemed to understand that there was no chance of stealing any more food. With a loud cawing they all rose from the tree and flew off. Cokoe watched them go over the tops of the trees until they were out of sight. Then he went back to replanting the seeds.

DO YOU KNOW—

1. Why Cokoe wanted to be up early?
2. What work Cokoe had to do first? Who usually tended the cornfields?
3. What Soningo and the other men of the village were getting ready for?
4. How Cokoe replanted the corn?

THINGS TO DO

Discuss the work of the Indians in growing their crops. Compare it with the growing of crops on a small American farm, and on a large farm where they use machinery.

Cokoe quickly replants the kernels of corn.

Cokoe's eyes close slowly in the warm sun. Soon, in a dream, he is swimming with a shad.

10: *Cokoe Has a Dream*

By the time Cokoe finished the job, the sun was at the standing-still place (noon). He was tired, but pleased with what he had done. A ten-year-old boy could be proud of saving his family's corn crop. He sat down at the edge of the field to rest. It was pleasant to sit there in the warm sunshine. The air was soft and fresh. Mingled with the smell of the woods and the earth was the faint smell of flowers. Looking down by his feet, Cokoe saw some wood violets which he had almost stepped on.

The warmth of the sun, the smell of the flowers, and the weariness of his back and arms made Cokoe drowsy. At first he dropped his head between his knees. Soon he was too sleepy even to sit up. He lay back on the moss and leaves. He crossed his arms over his eyes to shield them from the sun. Soon he began to doze. Half awake and half asleep, he began to think of the things he might be doing. If only he didn't have to stay in the cornfield!

If he had gone with his father this day, Cokoe thought, he would be helping to make a dugout canoe. If he had stayed at home, he could be playing with other boys. Or he might be watching his mother clean the hide of the deer they had brought her. He might have learned how she changed stiff rawhide into soft buckskin. If he had gone with his Uncle Soningo, he would now be helping to mend the nets. They were long brown nets of Indian hemp. Sometimes they stretched all the way across the big river.

Cokoe thought of the river flowing endlessly along. How could so much water keep coming and coming and coming? And so many fish! In his mind's eye he could see the silvery bodies of the shad slicing their way upstream. By now Cokoe was no longer even half awake. He was fast asleep!

Cokoe's mind had slipped from thinking into dreaming. In his dream he still saw the shad, but now he was under wa-

ter swimming along with them. It didn't seem strange to him. The light under water was dim and greenish, but he could see quite well. The water seemed to wash his eyes clear. On either side of him he could see the shad swimming. There were many of them, more than he could count. The river was crowded with them. Sometimes they passed so close to Cokoe that he could feel the fluttery touch of their fins and tails. They paid no more attention to him than if he had been a fish himself.

In his dream Cokoe began swimming across the path of the fishes on his left, and moving over toward the bank. He didn't know why. Perhaps he just wanted to see what it was like over there. He had a feeling it might be dangerous, and this was exciting. But when he reached the side of the river it didn't look much different from the middle. There was the brown, muddy bank. Here and there a rock stuck out which Cokoe had to swim around.

All of a sudden a bright, furry face came close to his under water. Cokoe saw the neat little ears and the open mouth set with tiny, white teeth ready to strike. With a quick stroke Cokoe brought his arms down to his sides and darted under a rock. That was an otter!

A shad who had been following Cokoe swam up beside him under the rock. He was a big fellow, bigger than any of the others. Cokoe was still breathing fast from his scare when the shad spoke to him.

"Little Brother," said the shad, "you mustn't swim so close to the bank. You were lucky that time. The otter can't get under this rock. But there are other enemies waiting for your next mistake."

Cokoe thought how kind it was of the shad to warn him, but he said nothing.

The shad, a little annoyed with Cokoe for not answering, went on talking.

"What do you think the heron is going to have for his next meal? Or the hawk, or the kingfisher, or the man? Yes, there may be a man-child just like you standing on the bank now. He may be waiting to throw a spear at you, or to pull you in with a hook. He may just scoop you up out of the water with a net!"

Cokoe shuddered to think what might have happened to him! With a swish of his tail the shad was gone, leaving Cokoe to get over his fright as best he could. Cokoe hadn't even thanked him for his advice. Finally he got up enough courage to swim out from under the rock and back toward the middle of the river. He looked around for the big, friendly shad, but couldn't find him.

Back in the middle of the river Cokoe felt safe once more. There were fish on all sides of him. When he looked up he could see their white bellies. Below him their shiny backs moved steadily forward. And on either side of him their fins were stroking the water just as his arms and hands were doing. He felt safe, as though nothing could happen to him. But again something did happen.

Up ahead of them Cokoe's sharp eyes spotted a long, brown net blocking their way. Well, they would have to swim around it. But, looking both right and left, Cokoe could see no way around it. There was no end to the long net swaying in the current. It was a giant net tied to poles stuck in the mud of the river bottom. And it stretched all the way across the river!

The shad in front of Cokoe were darting here and there. They were trying to find holes in the net big enough to squeeze their bodies through. Cokoe swam up to the net with some of the others and tried to find a way through. The closer he came to the holes, the smaller they looked. Then he tried leap-

Cokoe and the shad are trapped! They dart back and forth looking for a way through the great net.

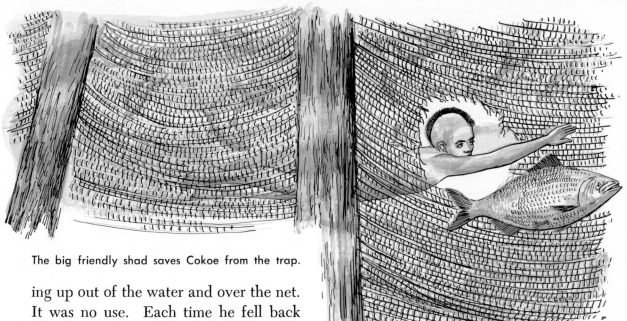

The big friendly shad saves Cokoe from the trap.

ing up out of the water and over the net. It was no use. Each time he fell back into the water on the wrong side of the net.

Cokoe was getting very tired. All of a sudden he heard a strange song. The big, friendly shad had come up beside him singing. It was a watery kind of music that Cokoe had never heard before. He listened to the words, but they didn't make any sense to him. They were not Algonquin words. (They were dream words, of course, but Cokoe didn't know he was dreaming.)

The big shad moved up close to the net and turned sideways to look at Cokoe. He was still singing, and his song seemed to invite Cokoe to come up beside him. Cokoe moved closer. He noticed that, as the shad sang, one of the holes in the net was growing wider. As soon as the hole was wide enough the shad led Cokoe through. On the last notes of the shad's song, they were both safe on the other side.

This time Cokoe wanted to thank the shad before he disappeared. He opened his mouth to speak, but the shad was talking to him.

"Little Brother," said the shad, "you may have my song. It is yours. It will give you strength when you are weak. It will give you courage when you are afraid. And it will show you a way out when you are trapped."

"But how can I learn the song?" asked Cokoe. "I don't understand those words. Would you please sing it for me again?"

But once more, with a swish of his tail, the shad was gone.

DO YOU KNOW—

1. What time it was when Cokoe finished replanting the corn? Why he was so sleepy?
2. Why Cokoe didn't think it strange to be swimming with shad? What an otter looks like?
3. What was blocking Cokoe's path on his way up the river? What was the shad's magic way of helping Cokoe?

THINGS TO DO

1. Tell some of your dreams to each other.
2. Find a picture of a shad. Do not copy it, but draw it so that people will know it is a shad and not a trout or a salmon.

11: The Mohawks Have Come!

Cokoe felt unhappy and lost when the shad disappeared. Suddenly the water seemed dark. The strong current of the river pushed and shoved at his shoulder. While he was fighting to keep from being pushed downstream again, he heard his name spoken.

"Cokoe, Cokoe! Wake up! How can you sleep with the sun in your eyes?"

Cokoe awoke with a start. He blinked his eyes and looked up. It took him a few moments to realize that he wasn't still dreaming. The pushing and shoving on his shoulder was not the river current. It was another boy Cokoe's own age, a friend from the village. The boy was speaking to him.

Cokoe races from the cornfield to his wigwam, for the Mohawks are in the Lenape village! He must hurry up and dress for the meeting.

"Your uncle says I am to tend the cornfield for you. The Mohawks have come and he wants you to listen to the meeting. I wish I were you. Will you tell me all about it later, Cokoe?"

Cokoe thanked the boy and promised to tell him every word he could remember. Then he raced off to the village.

As he ran, he noticed that the sun was casting long shadows. He must have slept a long time! Could the crows have come back and robbed the field while he was asleep? No, he surely would have heard their cawing. And what was that strange dream he had had? Something about a shad and swimming under water. And the shad had sung a song! He must try to remember it later and tell his mother and father. Perhaps they could explain it to him. But now he must hurry and get to the meeting.

First he stopped at his mother's wigwam. He must appear as a handsome young warrior before the Mohawks. (Well, in a few years he would be a warrior.)

His mother saw him coming. She knew he was in a hurry and didn't question him about the cornfield. That could wait until later.

"Cokoe, your knife is hanging from the rafters above your bed. And there is a little packet of blue jay feathers tucked into the bark beside it."

"Oh, thank you, Mother," said Cokoe. "I have something to tell you about the cornfield. Remind me later. I am in a hurry now."

"I know, Little Owl," said his mother. "Can I help you? Shall I braid your hair?"

For several moons now Cokoe had been letting one lock of hair from the top of his head grow long. The sides of his head were shaved clean all the way to the top, where a crest about an inch long stood up like a brush. The front lock, from his forehead halfway back to the crown of his head, was the part he was allowing to grow. It was just barely long enough to braid. Cokoe had a difficult time trying to braid it himself.

"It would be a help, Mother, if you would braid my hair while I tie on my knife."

Cokoe reached up to the rafters and took down his knife while his mother was braiding his hair. As he brought the knife down, he saw that it was in a new case. His mother must have made it for him. It was a beautiful leather case embroidered with porcupine quills. The design was worked out in red, yellow, and blue. Cokoe smiled up at his mother in thanks. It was so pretty, and it fitted his flint knife just right.

When Cokoe's mother had finished the braid and tied the feathers to it, Cokoe felt of it to see if it was all right. It was even better than all right. His mother had surprised him again by braiding in a lock of her own hair which she had saved from long ago. Added to Cokoe's own hair, it made a fine-looking braid which reached all the way to his shoulder.

Cokoe was handsome indeed when he entered the wigwam where his uncle was sitting with the Mohawks. He stood

Cokoe's mother helps him dress. He must look very neat and handsome when he meets the Mohawk warriors, so that Uncle Soningo will be proud of him.

very straight and tall in the doorway until his uncle nodded for him to sit down. The Mohawks looked him over carefully. They knew that this wasn't just another little village boy. This was someone special, probably the chief's nephew.

Cokoe moved back toward the wall and sat down. The Mohawks were sitting cross-legged in a half-circle around the fire, opposite the door. Soningo sat facing them. No one spoke. Soningo had crumbled a few dried tobacco leaves in his hand and packed them into the bowl of his long-stemmed pipe. Now he lighted the pipe with a burning twig from the fire. After a few puffs he passed it on to the nearest Mohawk brave.

Cokoe watched the pipe carefully as it went from hand to hand. Each warrior took only a few quiet puffs and then

Cokoe stands straight and tall as he enters Uncle Soningo's wigwam. The Mohawks, with their painted faces, look very stern. Cokoe wonders why they have come.

passed it on to the next one. It was a beautiful pipe, with a bowl of dark stone carved in an elbow shape. The wooden stem was long and straight, and where it flattened out to meet the bowl it was decorated with dyed porcupine quills.

Cokoe knew that Soningo and his friends sometimes smoked the pipe just for pleasure. But this time there was a special meaning to it. If each Mohawk warrior took the pipe and smoked, then they had come on a friendly visit. But if one of them refused, it might mean something else.

Veils of bluish smoke hung in the quiet wigwam as Cokoe watched each warrior take his turn. Five of them had taken the pipe, and now it was passed to the

last one. Would he take it and smoke? Cokoe held his breath until he thought he would burst. The Mohawk had taken the pipe but he wasn't smoking. He sat looking into the fire, the pipe in his hand. Finally he raised the stem to his mouth. As the first puff of smoke left the Mohawk's lips, Cokoe let his breath go in one big sigh, "Whoo!"

The sound of Cokoe's sigh was so startling and funny that all of the Mohawks began to laugh. Cokoe reddened in shame. Everyone was looking at him. Even Soningo couldn't help laughing at his nephew.

When the others had finally quieted down, Soningo spoke to Cokoe, half joking. "You are pretty good at holding

your breath, Cokoe. The next thing you should practice is hiding your feelings."

Hearing Cokoe's name, one of the Mohawks turned to the others and said something in Iroquois. They all began to laugh again. Cokoe felt very uncomfortable at being the object of a joke he couldn't understand. Seeing his troubled face, the Mohawk who had first laughed now took pity on him. Speaking in Algonquin, he said to Cokoe, "I told them we should have known your name was Owl by the way you said, 'Whoo!'"

Cokoe tried to explain that he was called Little Owl because of his sharp eyes. They wouldn't listen. All they did was laugh at whatever he said. Cokoe didn't think it was as funny as all that.

However, he was glad that everyone was relaxed. Now they could get on with the meeting.

DO YOU KNOW—

1. How Cokoe's mother helped him get ready for the meeting?
2. How Cokoe wore his hair?
3. What Cokoe's mother had made to surprise him? Why Cokoe went to the meeting?

THINGS TO DO

Begin collecting things that the Indians used in decorating themselves: feathers, shells, paints, porcupine quills, deer and moose hair, turtle shells, and so forth. Do not collect anything made of metal. Remember that in Cokoe's time the Indians did not know the use of metal. You can get these things in the woods, at the seashore, from people who tame birds, or at the zoo.

49

12: Everybody Is Hungry

It turned out that all of the Mohawks understood Algonquin a little bit. But the one who had first laughed at Cokoe's name spoke it the best. And so it was he who talked with Soningo about the purpose of their visit.

The winter had been a long and hard one for the Iroquois as well as for the Lenape. Snow had drifted deep around their villages. The bitter cold had driven the deer into far-off sheltered places where the hunters could not find them. Sitting with empty stomachs, the people listened to the howl of wolves on the cold north wind. They knew that where the wolves howled there must be game. Some of the bravest hunters had gone out to follow the sound. Some of them came back with food for their people. A few brought no food but were lucky to come back alive. Others did not come back at all.

By spring the young warriors had become very restless. The village chiefs had said there were to be no war parties. They knew that the young men were not strong and healthy after such a hard winter. Making war would be too risky. Instead, they sent the young men out on tribute-gathering journeys. Now that spring had come, they could live off the land on the way. They would bring back tribute goods. And to show their good faith, they would even take along some furs to trade.

"And so here we are," said the Mohawk, as he finished his speech.

Soningo looked quietly at the six war-riors, but said nothing. He was thinking: They don't look so poor and hungry now. They must have taken their time coming down the river. They probably spent more time hunting, eating, and sleeping than paddling their canoes. However, they seem friendly enough now. And it is better that they should come this way than on the warpath.

Cokoe was too busy admiring their handsome looks to think of much else.

At last Soningo spoke. "I have heard your story, Mohawks," he said, "and it sounds honest to me. I recall that we have promised yearly tribute in exchange for peace. Our supplies are low, too. But we will give you what we can spare."

When Cokoe heard his uncle speak of spare supplies, he wondered what he could mean. Only a few days before he had seen his mother take the last of their corn out of the *storage* basket. She was already looking around for fresh greens and roots. Yesterday they had eaten a meal of fiddlehead ferns.

Cokoe was even more surprised when his uncle spoke to him directly. "Cokoe, go to your mother and ask her to bring the extra stores of corn and smoked shad here to the Mohawks."

Quickly Cokoe got up from his place and went out the door. Once outside, he ran as fast as he could along the path to his mother's house. He noticed that the villagers were going about their business in spite of the important visitors in his uncle's house. Although Cokoe didn't know it, the men were ready to

"We must give food to the Mohawks," Cokoe tells his mother. But he is worried.
Where can there be extra food, for they have had hardly enough for themselves?

sound the war cry if necessary. Each one had seen to it that his knife or war club was within reach, though he might be mending a net or shaping a canoe paddle at the moment.

Cokoe found his mother outside the house. She, too, was busy. Chatting with some friends, she was sitting in front of a row of little clay dye pots. She was dipping bundles of porcupine quills into the colored waters, and then spreading them out on pieces of bark to dry. When she saw Cokoe come running up, she put down her work and waited for him to speak.

"Mother, Uncle Soningo says you are to bring the stores of corn and smoked shad to the Mohawks. Where are you going to get them? We don't have any more, do we?" asked Cokoe.

"Oh, yes, we do, Cokoe," said his mother. "We have them for just such times as this. Then the Mohawks won't take you away and eat you instead," she added laughing.

She led Cokoe around to the back of the house and off a little way to the edge of the woods. They came to a small pile of stones. Cokoe had seen this many times, but had never paid any attention to it. Now his mother stood beside the pile of stones and took three steps in the direction called "where the daylight appears" (East). She turned again and took three steps in the direction called "winter place" (North). Then she began poking around in the dead leaves and grass. Soon she found what she was looking for—the lid to an underground storage pit.

"Come, Cokoe, help me lift the stone," she called.

Cokoe helped his mother lift the heavy flat stone which had been completely hidden with old leaves and grass and sticks. Underneath, he saw a large basket of dried corn. When he and his mother had removed the heavy basket, they located another pit filled with smoked shad. There was still a third basket filled with beans!

Cokoe knew that winter supplies were often stored in ground pits like this. But he was surprised at how much there was. Most of all, he was surprised that he hadn't known about these particular pits at all. His mother saw his eyes getting bigger each time they lifted a basket from its hole.

"Are you wondering why we haven't been eating these things ourselves, Cokoe?" she asked. "We would have

Cokoe is surprised at the secret storage pit.

eaten them if the village had been starving. But it was important to have something to give the Mohawks, too."

"There are so many things the grown-ups must plan ahead for, aren't there, Mother?" said Cokoe.

DO YOU KNOW—

1. Why supplies of food were low in the Indian villages in spring?

2. What language the Mohawks spoke?

3. Why the Mohawks came to Cokoe's village? Why Cokoe's mother had stored away extra supplies of food? Where the food was stored?

4. What wild food the Indians ate is mentioned in this chapter?

THINGS TO DO

Discuss the word *tribute*. Your teacher can explain its meaning, but to understand it better your class might hold a contest or play a game. Any game in which the class is divided into two teams will do. It may be a tug-of-war, a race, or any ball game. The losers must then pay a forfeit, or tribute, to the winners' greater strength or better teamwork.

The Lenapes bring their goods down to the Mohawk canoes. There is great excitement in the village, for there will be much trading of furs, jewelry, and weapons.

13: *Trading*

Some other village women helped Cokoe and his mother lug the baskets of food over to Soningo's wigwam. The Mohawks were pleased to see how much there was. They were especially delighted with the smoked shad. This would be an unusual treat for people living so far up the river.

Many of the Lenape children and young women offered to carry the baskets down to the river where they would be stowed in the Mohawks' canoes. They had heard that there was to be trading and they wanted to be the first to see what the Mohawks had brought with them.

Those who did not go down to the river ran to their wigwams to see what treasures they had stored in the rafters. Some had boxes of feathers, others had beautiful sea shells. Cokoe's mother

knew she had more dyed porcupine quills than she could use up in a long time. One old man of the village was a skilled wampum maker. His pearly white and dark blue beads would bring a high price.

Down at the river Cokoe saw that the Mohawks' canoes had been pulled up under some sheltering bushes. First the Mohawk trade goods were taken out of the canoes, and then the Lenape food was stowed away. Cokoe wondered how the light, graceful elm bark canoes could carry so much weight. They were very pretty, but they certainly didn't look as sturdy as the Lenape dugouts.

Bundles of furs, tanned skins, turtle shells, and deer hooves for rattles were among the things the Mohawks had brought to trade. Cokoe's mother exchanged some of her fine porcupine quills for dyed moose hair which she could use in embroidery. Cokoe traded a bundle of blue jay feathers for a small turtle shell. It looked just the right size to make a dance rattle for a ten-year-old boy. Soningo and Tamquid were looking over some finely chipped flint arrowheads. They knew they could make just as good ones themselves. They bought them, however, thinking it was better to get them this way than when shot from a Mohawk bow!

The Mohawks had been invited to spend the night in the Lenape village. With the trading, eating, story-telling, and joking, it was very late before anyone was ready for bed. Even the babies had stayed up, laughing or fretting in their cradle boards. Sometimes the cradles were swung from the rafters and sometimes held in the mothers' laps.

Cokoe's eyelids finally grew too heavy to stay open. Quietly he crawled over to his own little bed and curled up in the furs to sleep. A little bit later he awoke, thinking there was something he had forgotten to tell his parents. It was dark in the wigwam, but the fire was still glowing. Cokoe heard his parents stir and knew they must be just getting to bed. Softly he spoke to them.

"I had a dream today."

Drowsily his mother answered, "What did you dream, Cokoe?"

It was his father's voice that asked, "When were you dreaming today, Cokoe? Do you mean just now?"

Cokoe was ashamed to answer that he had been asleep in the middle of the day. His mother's voice came out of the darkness again to answer for him.

"Cokoe has had a long and exciting day, Tamquid. I heard that he had to replant our whole cornfield before the sun was at the standing-still place. Probably he was tired and fell asleep after that."

"What was your dream about, Little Owl?" she asked him again gently.

"It was about a shad," said Cokoe. "He tried to teach me a song. He said it would help me when I was in trouble. And it did help, too. It made a big hole in the net so I could swim through and not get caught."

Cokoe got so excited telling his dream that he had to sit up in bed. At first his parents couldn't make head nor tail of it, but they were very much interested. Both of them got up, and Tamquid went over to poke up the fire as they listened. When Cokoe finished telling his dream from beginning to end, they were all three sitting around the fire. For a while

Here are some of the things that the Lenapes and Mohawks traded. There are spoons and a stone axe in the picture. Can you name some of the other things?

Cokoe tells his mother and father about his dream.

they were silent, and then Tamquid spoke.

"There is sometimes great power in dreams, my son. Not everyone is so lucky as to have them. Yours was a good dream, but only a sign. You don't remember the words of the shad's song. Perhaps you are still too young. But the shad will come to you again in a dream. Maybe this year, maybe not until next. When he comes the next time you will remember the song. Then the shad will be your *guardian* spirit all your life long."

"He called me 'Little Brother'," said Cokoe.

"We are all brothers, Cokoe," answered his father. "All things in nature are brothers, the wind, the deer, the shad, the stars."

"Yes," said Cokoe, "I remember that Uncle Soningo called the deer he killed the other day 'brother'."

"Our animal brothers give us their lives so that we may eat," said Cokoe's mother. "Sometimes in dreams they give us their strength or their swiftness. We must always remember to thank them.

"And we must always get enough sleep or we won't remember anything," she added laughing. "Come, Cokoe. If we don't get to bed soon, one of our brothers, the sun, will be up before us again."

DO YOU KNOW—

1. What the Mohawks brought to trade? What the Lenape gave them in exchange?
2. Why the smoked shad were a treat for the Mohawks?
3. What the Mohawk canoes were made of?
4. Why it was so late before Cokoe got to bed that night?
5. What Tamquid told Cokoe about dreams?

THINGS TO DO

Find out all you can about Hudson River shad, and make reports to the class. If you can, talk to fishermen who catch them now. Write to the State Conservation Department.

Cokoe is happy. Today Tamquid lets him help work on the dugout canoe.

14: Tamquid Tells a Story

The next day the Mohawks left. After the excitement of their visit, Cokoe found life very dull. He wandered around the village wondering what to do with himself. He didn't feel like playing with the other boys. Their games seemed babyish to him.

One day his father said to him, "Cokoe, why don't you come out to the blowdown with me? I'm still working on that canoe. The other men can't come today and I could use your help."

Cokoe was eager to see how the boat was coming along, so he went with his father. Together they worked on the log, first burning the wood and then scraping away the charred spots. Tamquid showed Cokoe how to control the fire by placing damp moss on the areas they didn't want to burn. The log was beginning to look like a long, narrow tub.

It was hard work making a canoe. Cokoe discovered that it took patience, too, because it was so slow. Now and then the clam shells they were using as scrapers had to be sharpened. Tamquid showed Cokoe how to do this by rubbing them on a piece of sandstone.

At the end of the day, the boat looked much the same, but Cokoe and his father were blackened from head to foot. On the way back to the wigwam they stopped at the brook to wash the soot from their bodies. Their arms and backs ached from bending and scraping.

The water of the brook was cold, but it felt good to them. Cokoe jumped in head first and came up with a handful of sand. He was going to use it for rubbing off the soot.

Tamquid, sitting on the bank, called out to his son, "You look like Muskrat!"

"What do you mean?" asked Cokoe.

"I mean Muskrat who helped to make the earth," answered Tamquid. "That's just how he did it."

"Is that a story?" asked Cokoe, wading toward his father.

"It is a story," said his father, "but if it hadn't happened, you and I wouldn't be here."

"Wasn't it the Great Spirit who made the earth?" asked Cokoe.

"Yes, it was the Great Spirit," answered Tamquid. "But after he'd made it once, he had to make it all over again. It was Muskrat who helped him. I'll tell you about it while you are washing yourself.

"It was a long, long time ago that the Great Spirit first made the earth. Then after he had made it there was a great flood. There was so much water that the whole earth was covered. Not even the tallest tree on top of the highest mountain stood out. You couldn't see anything but water anywhere.

"The Great Spirit wanted to make a new earth, but he couldn't find any dirt to start with. Finally he called all the water animals to him. One by one he sent them down into the flood to see if they couldn't find a little bit of dirt.

"Beaver went down and came up with nothing. Otter went down and came up with nothing. Finally Muskrat went down all the way to the bottom. When he came up he had a little pawful of dirt.

"The Great Spirit took Muskrat's pawful of dirt and put it on Turtle's back. As soon as it was placed on Turtle's back, that little bit of dirt began to grow. It grew bigger and bigger and bigger. When it finally stopped growing it was the earth, as big as it is now. That is the end of my story."

The Great Spirit takes the pawful of dirt Muskrat has brought from the bottom of the sea. He puts it on Turtle's back. This is how Muskrat helped make the earth.

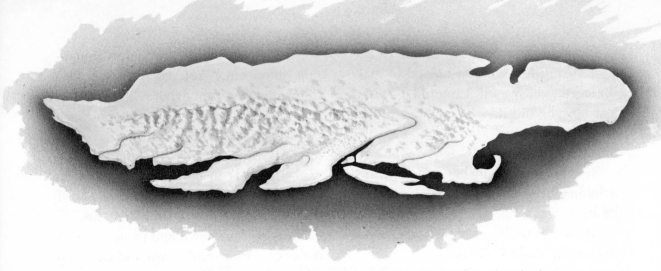

The Indians believed the world was a large island. Can you tell why they thought this?
Do you see anything that looks familiar to you?

"Is that true?" asked Cokoe. "Is the earth a big island floating on water?"

"I will not tell you whether it is true or not," answered Tamquid. "I will ask you a question. How many directions are there, Cokoe?"

"There are four," answered Cokoe. "First there is 'where the daylight appears' (East)."

"If you go 'where the daylight appears' all the way until you come to the edge of the earth, what do you find?"

"You find the ocean," answered Cokoe. "And the next direction is 'warm place' (South). I know that if you follow the river down that way you come to the ocean, too."

"Even if you go to the edge of 'where the sun goes down' (West) you find the ocean," said Tamquid. "It is a long way off, and you would have to cross many rivers to get there, but at the edge I am sure you would find the ocean."

"There is still another direction," said Cokoe. "What about 'winter place' (North)? Isn't that where the Mohawks and all the other Iroquois live?"

Tamquid laughed. "Yes, that's where they live. But they only live in the woods, as we do. If you go beyond their villages to the edge of the woods, you will still come to the ocean.

"Does that answer your question, Cokoe?"

"I guess so," answered Cokoe.

On the way home he kept thinking about it. There was one thing that bothered him. He kept asking himself over and over: "How does anyone know what lies beyond the Mohawk villages? Who would dare to go there and find out?"

DO YOU KNOW—

1. Why Cokoe was bored after the Mohawks left the village?

2. How Cokoe learned to sharpen clamshells?

3. What Cokoe used to scrub the soot from his body?

4. Why Tamquid said Cokoe looked like Muskrat?

5. What Cokoe called the direction North? East? West? South?

THINGS TO DO

Act out the story of Muskrat and the earth.

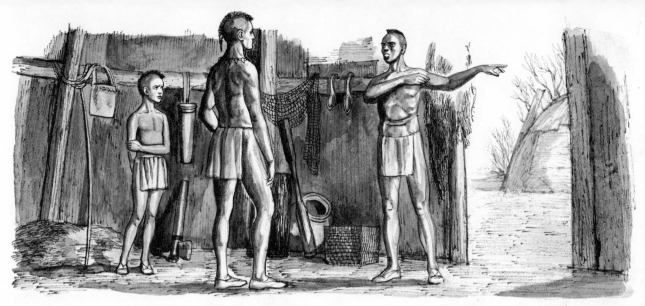

"The shad are running!" a messenger cries. This is a big event for the village.

15: The Shad Are Running

A few days later that same spring there was excitement in the Indian village once again. An Algonquin runner came panting in to say that the shad were beginning to come up the river. The message was brought to Soningo first, but was soon around the whole village. Cokoe sped out to the cornfield to tell his mother and then to the blow-down to tell his father.

Everyone left what he was doing to go fishing. Of course all of the children wanted to help. Shad fishing was more fun than any of their games. It was Soningo's job as chief of the village to direct the fishing. However, all but the youngest children knew exactly what to do. They had been through at least one season of shad fishing before.

The older men had been getting the nets ready for some time. There was one long one which would be stretched across the river, like the one Cokoe had seen in his dream. This would be held in place by upright poles and left in the

river overnight. By morning it would be so loaded with fish that it would take many hands to haul it in.

The smaller nets were taken out onto the river and dragged behind the canoes. For this kind of fishing someone had to paddle the canoe while others spread the net. The weight of the net told the handlers when it was full.

Cokoe was about to get into one of the canoes with his father when Soningo came along.

"Cokoe, there is an extra dugout up the bank a way. It's a small one. Do you think you and a couple of your friends could manage it?"

"Oh, yes, Uncle Soningo," answered Cokoe. "I'm sure we could. But who will help Father?"

"Never mind, Cokoe," said Tamquid. "Run along. It's time you big boys began to do a few things on your own."

Soningo pointed out the dugout and Cokoe dashed off to ask two friends to work with him. The three of them

59

would work as a team, just like the grownups.

As they watched the boys, Soningo said to Tamquid, "The shad run won't be very heavy these first days. Better let them get some practice while we are not too busy to keep an eye on them."

"That's a good idea," answered Tamquid. "You know Cokoe is getting to be a pretty big boy. He surprises me sometimes. Did he tell you about the dream he had the other day?"

"No," said Soningo, "but I've noticed how serious he is lately. Are you think-ing of sending him on a dream *quest* soon?"

"Yes," answered Tamquid. "Your sister and I thought we would send him out before the harvest moon. Because of his dream we are sure that a guardian spirit will take pity on him. He is going to be one of the lucky ones."

Just then there was a loud splash out on the river. Tamquid and Soningo turned to see what was the matter. It was Cokoe and the other two boys who had overturned their canoe. The three heads were bobbing up and down in the water. Cokoe still held the paddle. His friends were clutching the net. The canoe was floating near them upside down.

Everyone on the bank was laughing, but the boys didn't think it was so funny. They were good swimmers, but the wa-

Everybody helps fish for shad. Some of the shad are smoked on racks so there will be food for winter.

ter was cold and the river current strong. Tamquid, Soningo, and the father of one of the boys jumped in to help them. The men soon had them safe on the bank. There the boys stood like three wet and shivering puppies. Cokoe had swallowed a little water and the back of his nose stung.

People were still laughing and making remarks about the clumsy boys. One old man came up and pinched the boys' arms and legs. Then he turned to Soningo and said: "Those are three nice, fat shad you just caught. Are we going to eat them fresh or shall we smoke them first?"

Soningo laughed and answered, "I don't know that smoking will do any good, but a little fire to warm them won't hurt."

Cokoe's mother called the boys to come over by the smoke racks to dry off. She and her friends were building racks on which to hang the fish while they were being smoked. They had finished one and had already started a fire under it. Each rack looked like an arbor, or the framework of a house. Four poles had been set in the ground to make a square. The tops of these poles were forked so that two other poles could be laid across them to form frames. Across the two frames more poles were laid, making a rack. When the fish were hung on the smoke racks they looked like clothes on a line.

Cokoe and his friends soon dried off by the fire and were ready to try the canoe again. This time they decided who was going to paddle and who was going to handle the net before they pushed off from the bank. It was because they had tried to change their seats that they had tipped over earlier. No one had scolded them for this mistake, but they surely had been teased.

Later that day there was a feast of shad for the whole village. But before anyone was allowed to touch a mouthful,

61

a prayer of thanks was spoken. The prayer was said by Soningo. All who could crowd into his wigwam were there. The others stood quietly outside. Cokoe sat inside beside his mother. After the prayer, Soningo threw a pinch of tobacco into the fire. He asked Cokoe to do the same. The smoke of the fire was to carry their prayer of thanks to the Great Spirit.

The first fish was cooked over the same fire. The people waited while Soningo tasted it. When he told them it was good, they all went home to their own fires to feast.

While the shad season was on, Cokoe became expert at handling a dugout. Before long he even grew tired of it.

As the year wore on into midsummer, the little Indian village began to bake in the hot summer sun. During the day the village looked empty. Everyone found some reason to leave it. The open ground between the houses was bare and dusty. No children played there. They found cooler places at the edge of the woods or near the brook. The women went out to the cornfields. Some of the girls went berrying together. First there were the wild strawberries to pick, and later wild cherries and then blueberries ripened.

Many of the men went on long hunting trips and didn't come back for days. At night they slept in the woods, wherever they found themselves. It was on one of these trips with Uncle Soningo that Cokoe shot his first deer. There were not many people in the village to help him celebrate his first big game, but all those who were there had a taste of it. And they praised Cokoe for his skill in shooting with bow and arrow.

On some of the hot summer nights the men took Cokoe and his friends torchlight fishing. This was really fun. After dark they would all gather on the riverbank. They brought along sticks of pine wood and long shafted fish spears. The pine sticks were lighted and carried into the canoes. Out on the water the bright torches attracted the fish to the surface. When they came up, they were speared by the men sitting in the boats.

There was much splashing and laughter. Cokoe fell into the water a few times, but he wasn't the only one. Sometimes two men would aim at the same fish. Their canoes would bump together and everyone would land in the water. On a hot summer night no one minded at all.

After a night's fishing the Indians usually slept on the riverbank. It was cooler under the stars than in the hot, stuffy wigwams.

DO YOU KNOW—

1. How the Indians used the nets in shad fishing? What happened to Cokoe and his friends in the canoe? Why?
2. Why some of the shad were smoked?
3. What the Indians did before the feast?
4. What Cokoe and the others did during the hot midsummer days?

THINGS TO DO

1. Make a model smoke rack.
2. Visit a fish market and look at both fresh and smoked fish. Find out where the smoked fish came from and how old they are. Discuss the Indians' ways of preserving fish and our own modern ways.
3. You may imitate Cokoe in some of the following ways: sleeping outdoors, going barefoot, marking trails, cooking over an open fire.

Tamquid smears Cokoe's face with ashes! He wants to drive Cokoe away from home.

16: Cokoe's Dream Quest

One day along toward harvest time, Cokoe saw his father getting ready to go on a hunting trip. He asked Tamquid if he might go with him.

Cokoe was surprised when his father said, "No! You are getting so big that you make a lot of noise. You will scare away the game. Go off by yourself!"

Cokoe couldn't believe his ears. What had he done to make his father so angry?

Over at Soningo's wigwam, Cokoe found his uncle just as unfriendly as his father. Soningo was chipping flint arrowheads. Cokoe asked if he would teach him how to do it. Soningo said he didn't think he could ever learn.

Finally Cokoe went looking for his mother, to see if she could tell him what was the matter with everybody. He found her coming in from the cornfield with some of the fresh green ears. He asked her if they were going to have some of them for the evening meal.

"You are not going to have anything, you lazy boy," answered his mother.

Cokoe swallowed hard to keep from crying. Something must be wrong, he thought. Why were the three people he loved best in all the world being so unkind to him?

He followed his mother back to the wigwam. Tamquid was about to leave on his trip. When he saw the boy come in, he said to Cokoe's mother, "Can't you get rid of that good-for-nothing?"

Cokoe's mother answered, "I don't know what to do with him. I don't think he's ever going to grow up. Look at him. I think he's going to cry just like a baby!"

Cokoe threw himself down on his bed and hid his face in his arms. He had never felt so miserable in all his life.

Tamquid continued, "Our son is a sorry sight. Do you suppose that if we chase him off into the woods, some Manito will take pity on him?"

Cokoe didn't want the pity of the spirits. He wanted the love of his parents. He didn't know what was going on. He

Cokoe runs crying into the woods. He thinks the whole village hates him.

didn't know that his parents were only pretending to dislike him. They wanted him to run off in the woods by himself. They thought that after a few days of being alone and hungry he would have another dream. The shad would come to him again and this time he would learn the song.

After a few days of his parents' unkindness, Cokoe stayed away from home a while. He tried begging food from other houses. He didn't have much luck. No one seemed to want him around.

One day he sneaked back to his parents' wigwam to look for food. He was about to poke a corn cake out of the ashes when his father caught his wrist. With his other hand Tamquid smeared Cokoe's face with a handful of dirt and ashes.

Crying and wiping his face, Cokoe ran off into the woods. He kept running, past the cornfield, across the brook, and far on into the woods before he stopped. He thought he could never get far enough away from those people who were so unkind to him.

Cokoe stayed in the forest for several days. When it was daylight he wandered around looking for berries to eat. At night he slept on the ground. He had slept out many times before, but now the woods seemed frightening to him. In the darkness every sound was louder. Once, when he was sleeping, a porcupine came snuffling up to him in the dark. Cokoe awoke with a start and flung out his arm. The porcupine ran squealing away, but he had left two quills in Cokoe's hand.

The next day Cokoe was weak and tired and hungry. He had pulled the quills out of his hand, but the palm was sore and puffy. He stumbled through the woods looking for some cool water in which to bathe his hand. He knew that his mother would have picked some mullein leaves to put on the wound. If he hadn't been so dizzy, he would have remembered what they looked like. Now he was too tired to think.

He heard the sound of a waterfall and headed toward it. On the way he stumbled as he was crossing a patch of sunlight. Instead of getting up, he just lay there and closed his eyes. The whole world seemed to be swimming around him. Cokoe was asleep.

Once again in a dream Cokoe was swimming under water. The cool, green light seemed to clear his dizzy head. The soft water washed his feverish hand. Everything was peaceful and quiet. Then the big, friendly shad appeared once more. He swam up beside Cokoe, singing the same watery music he had sung before.

The shad spoke to Cokoe, "Little Brother, you look very unhappy. What is the matter now?"

"I don't know what is the matter," answered Cokoe. "At least I can't remember now."

"Are you getting along all right at home?" asked the shad.

"That's it," said Cokoe. "Everybody hates me. They say I am a baby and a good-for-nothing."

Cokoe has found a guardian spirit! His happy family welcomes him home.

"Have you used the song I gave you?" asked the shad.

"No," answered Cokoe. "I forgot the words."

"Then I will sing it to you again," said the shad. "And so that you will not forget, I will leave something with you."

This is the shad's song:

*"From salt water into fresh
      water I come.
In the frog moon I come.
In the time of planting I come.
Ee—yee—he—yee—e!"*

Cokoe heard the words clearly this time. He asked the shad, "What are you going to leave with me to remind me of the song?"

The shad didn't answer. With a swish of his tail he was gone.

Cokoe awoke with the sun full in his face. He felt better now. As he stood up he noticed something shiny on the ground beside his foot. Stopping to pick it up, he saw that it was a tiny round fish scale. That was what the shad had left!

Slowly Cokoe began to understand why his parents had driven him into the woods. They wanted him to have a guardian spirit. But the spirits came only to those who were suffering. Cokoe had suffered in the woods. He had been hungry, sick, tired, thirsty, and lonely. The spirit of the shad had come to make him strong again.

Cokoe soon found the trail leading back to the Indian village. He had been wandering in circles so it wasn't really far away. He wanted to show the fish scale to his parents. His mother would sew it into a little buckskin bag, and he would

wear it around his neck. There it would always be to remind him of his guardian spirit.

Soningo and his parents were waiting for Cokoe when he got home. They knew by his face what had happened. They were glad. He was given all the food he could eat, and his mother fixed his sore hand. Everyone was kind to him.

Later in the evening, as they sat around the fire, Tamquid tugged gently at Cokoe's forelock. Turning to Soningo he smiled and said, "You don't have to worry about the next chief, Soningo. Your nephew has a guardian spirit. He will be strong and brave and wise."

Cokoe found it hard to think about the faraway time when he would be chief. He was still only ten years old. For the moment he was happy. Everyone loved him and he had a guardian spirit.

His mother asked, "What would you like now, Cokoe?"

Cokoe answered with a yawn, "Most of all I would like to sleep," and he went once more to his own little bed of furs.

DO YOU KNOW—

1. Why Cokoe's family and friends were being unkind to him?
2. Why Cokoe didn't understand their meanness?
3. What finally drove Cokoe off into the woods by himself?
4. What animal left his quills in Cokoe's hand?
5. Why Cokoe didn't know what to do for his sore hand?
6. Where Cokoe was going when he fell down?
7. Who appeared to Cokoe in his dream?
8. What it meant when the shad gave Cokoe his song?
9. What the shad left Cokoe to remind him of his guardian spirit?

THINGS TO DO

1. With the things you have collected, dress yourselves up as Woodland Indians.
2. Act out Cokoe's second dream.

3. Plan a meal using only Indian food. If you have a place to cook and serve the meal, invite your parents to it. Tell them some of the things you have learned about the Indians of your state.

A New Look at Cokoe's Community

THINGS TO TALK ABOUT

1. Was Cokoe's life so very different from your own? He lived long ago before you were born, before your parents were born, before your grandparents were born, and even before that.

So there you have one difference, the difference of time. Cokoe lived long ago and you are living now. But while time was passing, between 1600 and now, people were doing things. From time to time their ways of doing things changed. Now you will find that Cokoe's people (American Indians) no longer live the way he did, anymore than you live just like your ancestors of 1600.

2. What about the difference in language between you and Cokoe? Cokoe spoke Algonquin, one of the many American Indian languages. You speak English. Can you remember **when you** first learned it? Probably not, be-**cause you** were so very young then.

Cokoe was about the same age when he learned Algonquin. He learned it at home like you, too. But you can read and write your language. Cokoe could not do that. He learned everything by listening and watching and imitating. How do reading and writing help you?

3. Did Cokoe live in a different part of the world than you? No, he didn't. He lived in New York State. He knew the same rivers and woods and valleys and hills that you know. There are even some trees standing today which were alive in Cokoe's time.

What things are there in your state that Cokoe couldn't have known? Had he ever seen a city? When the family needed food, did his mother send him to the grocery store for it? Had he ever seen an airplane, a horse, a dollar bill, a steel axe? How many other things can you think of that would have been strange to Cokoe?

HOW TO FIND OUT MORE ABOUT INDIANS

1. The Department of the Interior of our government in Washington, D.C., has a branch called the Indian Service. This branch keeps track of all the Indians in the United States. You might write and ask them for a map of the Indian Reservations.

2. Your state government in Albany can tell you about Indians living in New York State now. Find out from them where the Iroquois Indians are, and what has happened to the Algonquins.

3. Museums and libraries are good places to look things up. If there are any names of places in your neighborhood that sound Indian, look them up. Find out what they mean and what language they come from.

4. If there is an Indian Reservation near you, find out when there is to be a festival of some kind. Ask if you may watch it or take part in it. That way you may get a chance to hear some Indian language and music. And you may see some old-fashioned Indian costumes.

5. You can play one game like the Indian boys, even without bows and arrows. This game is called Hoop and Pole. First you need a hoop about a foot in diameter. A wooden embroidery hoop will do. Tie two cords across the hoop, from rim to rim, so that they cross in the center. This divides the circle into four equal parts. Paint each one of these sections a different color—red, yellow, blue, and green.

Each child who is going to play the game should have a stick or pole about four feet long. The ends of the poles should be painted in four six-inch bands of red, yellow, blue, and green, like the hoop.

You can play this game by twos or in teams. A starter rolls the hoop, and the other players throw their poles at it. A pole that goes through the hoop and stops it makes a score for the player. The red sections of both the hoop and the pole count four, the yellow three, the blue two, and the green one. If the red band of the pole is touching the red section of the hoop when it stops, the score is eight for the player who threw the pole. The most points wins the game.

Remember to mark the poles so that you know your own. And be sure all the poles are alike so that the game will be fair.

6. If your class has a place to garden, plant some Indian crops. Go on a berry-picking or nut-gathering trip.

7. Write to some Indian children. You will find that they are Americans, and read and write English just like you do.

8. Many of the Indian children's toys were similar to your own. They often played with tops, dolls, string (cat's cradle), stilts, balls, and hoops. One of the toys they played with you may be able to make for yourself. It is called Ring and Pin. The pin is a wooden stick about ten inches long. It should be tapered at one end like a drum stick. The ring can be made of a hollow bone (a marrow bone from the butcher) about an inch long. Tie the ring to the pin with a cord about sixteen inches long. To play the game, toss the ring from the pin and try to catch it back on the pin again.

BOOKS TO READ AND LOOK AT

Bleeker, Sonia, *The Delaware Indians*, Morrow, 1953.

Keelor, Katherine, *Little Fox*, Macmillan, 1944. This is the story of an Indian boy on Manhattan Island long ago.

Lorant, Stefan, *The New World*, Duell, Sloan and Pearce, 1946. This is mostly a picture book for adults. You might like to look at it, too.

Marriott, Alice, *Indians on Horseback*, Crowell, 1948. This book is about Indians of the Plains.

Thompson, Hildegard, *Coyote Tales*, U.S. Indian Service, Haskell Institute, Lawrence, Kansas. These are stories of the Navaho Indians.

RECORDS TO ENJOY

Music of the Sioux and Navaho, Ethnic Folkways Library (Series No. 1401), Records 1420A–1423A (78 rpm) or Folkways 401 (LP), Folkways Records and Service Corp.

Recorded in Indian communities by Willard Rhodes in co-operation with the U.S. Office of Indian Affairs.

Songs from the Iroquois Long House, Record No. AAFS26 (78 rpm). Recorded and edited by William H. Fenton, Smithsonian Institution, for the Library of Congress.

These are Seneca songs of dances, of dreams, and of boasts.

Songs of the Chippewa, L22 (LP) or 5 records (78 rpm), Library of Congress, Reference Dept., Music Division, Recording Laboratory. From the Smithsonian-Densmore Collection.

These are dream songs, war songs, and songs used in treatment of the sick.

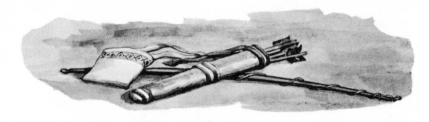

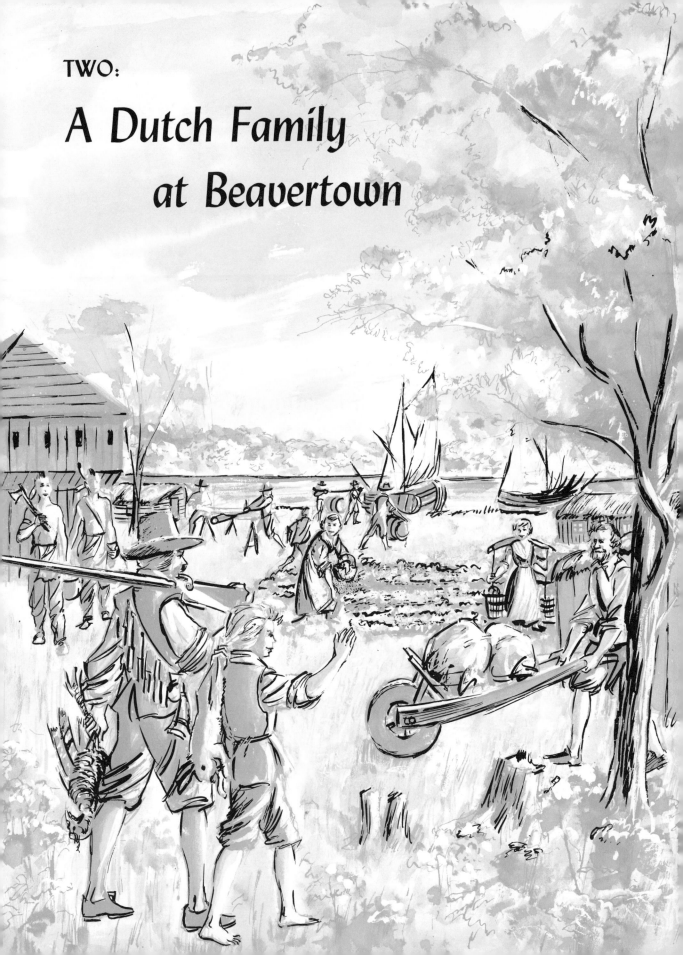

TWO:

A Dutch Family
at Beavertown

A Dutch Family at Beavertown

Cokoe was only a few years older when something new happened. A ship from far across the ocean sailed up the great river near his home. Nobody knows whether Cokoe saw this ship. Probably he did, because the Indians were excited about it. Some of them thought the ship was a huge bird. Others thought it was the biggest fish in the ocean.

This ship, the *Half Moon,* had sailed from the Netherlands, a country in Europe. This was the country of the Dutch. Henry Hudson was the ship's captain. The Dutch claimed the land where Cokoe lived. They called it New Netherland.

The Dutchmen who came here traded with the Indians. They bought furs. Some Dutchmen became trappers, because the Indians showed them how to trap fur-bearing animals.

In the Netherlands a group of businessmen started a trading company, called the Dutch West India Company. They sent ships and traders to New Netherland. But they were worried about keeping New Netherland for the Dutch.

Then somebody had a good idea. The Company should send families to live in New Netherland. People from England and France would not try to take the land away from the Dutch settlers. But how could the Company get Dutch families to go to this wild, strange country? These people were quite happy

at home. They had a good government. Most of them made enough money to live on.

"Well," said the men of the Company, "we shall offer families free land for homes. We shall carry them across the ocean. We shall give them food on shipboard, and even in New Netherland until they have their own gardens. We shall give our best workers jobs in our fur-trading posts. We shall pay them more money than they could earn here."

Would anyone go? Yes, some parents decided to take their families there, and that is what our next story is about.

I WONDER

1 wonder how I would feel if I had to leave my home and travel to a new land.

I wonder how long it would take today to make the trip Lisbet and Teunis made more than 300 years ago.

I wonder if I would like to help build my own home, grow my own food, and make my own clothes.

I wonder how the Dutch families kept in touch with their friends in the Old World and the New World.

WORDS WE NEED TO KNOW

baptize	felt	leeks	sloop
crullers	featherbed	mortar (*a building material*)	suppawn
dill	gourd	pewter	trencher
duffels	guilder	porthole	Walloon

1: Exciting News

"O Teunis," cried Lisbet, "we're going to the New World! Father and Mother just told me. Come on home. Let's find out about everything. Hurry!"

Teunis was playing beside the canal with his friend Joost. The boys were floating little toy boats. They walked along, beside the canal, guiding their boats with long sticks.

These children lived in the city of Amsterdam, more than three hundred years ago. In this city, many of the streets were canals with sidewalks on each side. People used boats in going from one part of the city to another.

Teunis did not speak for a minute. He was busy steering his toy boat. At last he said, "I don't want to go to the New World. I like Amsterdam. I like to play with Joost and my other friends."

"Come on home, Teuni!" cried Lisbet. She always was more excited about things than her brother.

As the children walked toward home, Teunis said, "What is the New World, Lisbet?"

"It isn't really new. Father told me that the New World has been waiting for us always, but people in the Old World didn't find it till lately."

"Doesn't anybody live there?" Teunis wanted to know.

"Indians live there," said Lisbet. "Some people call them the *wilden*, because they live in the wilderness."

Inside the house, the children stood waiting politely for their parents to speak. Even Lisbet, excited as she was, waited politely. This was the custom in Dutch families.

Before long their father, Kip Teunissen, turned to them. "Sit down," he said. He looked as if he found it hard to go on. Mother looked strange, too, as if she had been crying. At last Father said, "Well, children, we have decided to take a long,

Lisbet rushes to the canal to tell Teunis the news! They are going to the New World! Teunis and Joost are sailing their toy boats on the canal as she arrives.

long trip. We shall sail far away, across the Atlantic Ocean. We are going to live in a new land."

"What about the *wilden?*" asked Teunis.

"They will be fair to us if we are fair to them," said Father. "They were kind to many of the first Dutch people who went to the New World."

"It will be fun to meet a new kind of people," said Lisbet.

"We aren't going just for fun," said Father. "We're going so that I can make a better living.

"The Dutch West India Company will pay me more than they do now. I have worked for them a long time, so they trust me. They are giving me an important job, buying furs for the Company."

"Well, I suppose it is good to have more money," said Lisbet. "But I never thought we needed more. Teuni and I have been happy. Haven't you, Mother?"

"Yes," said Mother, "but I would like to have a larger home. Amsterdam is so crowded. Our house is squeezed in between other houses. We have only a small garden.

"We shall have more land in the New World. We can have a larger house. And when you grow up, who knows what will happen? Maybe you will each have a big farm. Maybe you will be important people in a big new city."

DO YOU KNOW—

1. Where Lisbet and Teunis lived? What the New World was? Who the *wilden* were?

2. How Father said the Dutch settlers should treat the *wilden?* Do you agree?

3. What company Father worked for? Why the company trusted him? Why Mother was willing to move to the New World?

THINGS TO DO

1. Make a picture of the children waiting politely for their parents to speak.

2. Make a model or a picture of the New World as the children thought it would be.

Even Mother's big trunk couldn't hold all they'd need for the trip to the New World.

2: The Last Days in the Fatherland

The next days were busy ones for Kip Teunissen's family. Lisbet and Teunis helped Mother pack a huge chest. They packed quilts, blankets, sheets, small straw mattresses for the children, and a big one for their parents. They packed a *featherbed*, too, for the grownups.

This huge chest was Mother's very best one. Father had made it for her wedding present. It was carved in pretty shapes of flowers and birds. The shapes had been painted red, blue, and yellow. "This will be the best piece of furniture in our new home," said Mother.

"Why don't we take the rest of our furniture?" asked Lisbet.

"Our ship will not have room for much furniture," said Mother. "Many families will be sailing when we do. We shall leave our furniture with Grandpa and Grandma."

"When we get rich, maybe we can buy Grandpa and Grandma some new clothes," said Lisbet.

"That's a sweet thought, dear," said Mother, "but there are no clothes to buy in the New World. There aren't any stores there."

"Where shall we get our clothes, then?" asked Lisbet.

"We'll take every bit of clothing we have," said Mother. "I shall take some woolen and linen cloth to make more. We shall pack our second biggest chest with cloth."

Lisbet looked thoughtful. This would be strange. No stores. What would they do when they needed to buy food?

"Will the *wilden* have food to sell us?" asked Lisbet.

"I don't know," said Mother. "We shall plant a garden as soon as we can."

"Can't we take some food with us?"

"We can take some vegetables and fresh meat for the first days on the ship," said Mother. "Food like that can't be kept very long, you know."

"Won't we have anything to eat after that?" Lisbet asked.

"The ship will carry food for us," said Mother. "It won't be as good as the food you are used to. But you're my brave girl. You and Teunis will be cheerful about it.

"You are going to have a wonderful adventure. Very few children in all the world are as lucky as you. People who have new adventures often have to give up some things they like."

"Shall we take our *trenchers?*" asked Lisbet.

"Of course," said Mother. "How could we get along without them? We'll pack them just before we sail."

In those days, most people ate from trenchers. A trencher was a wooden tray about a foot long and three or four inches deep. Often two members of the family ate from the same trencher. Mother and Father ate from one. Lisbet and Teunis ate from another.

The spoons and knives were to be packed at the very last, too. The spoons were made from wood or *pewter.* The knives were made of steel. Only very rich people had silver knives and spoons. Hardly anybody had forks of any kind. Most people used their fingers in place of forks.

At last everything was packed. "We're all ready," said Teunis. "Why don't we go?"

"I thought you didn't want to go, Teuni," said Lisbet.

"I don't mind," said Teunis. "It will be exciting. Joost and his family are going, so I shan't be lonesome."

"It's all right for you," said Lisbet. "Your best friend is going. But how about me? Annetje isn't going. I love her better than any other friend. I shall have nobody to play with."

"You will make new friends," said Mother. "There will be other children on the ship."

"When will the ship sail?" asked Teunis.

Father said, "It will sail tomorrow if the weather is good and the wind is right."

Lisbet packs the wooden trenchers last. The family will use them on the boat and in the New World.

He did not tell the children all that he knew. He did not tell them how dangerous weather could be. There were often bad storms on the Atlantic Ocean. Sometimes ships were lost or destroyed.

In those days ships were small and light. They were made of wood. They had no motors to drive them through the sea. They were driven by the wind blowing against their sails. If there was no wind, the ships would not move at all. If there was too much wind, they might be driven far from their course. They might be wrecked in storms. Everybody who sailed the seas in those days had to be brave.

DO YOU KNOW—

1. What the family packed before starting for the New World? Why Mother took only one fine piece of furniture?

2. Why Mother took material for new clothing for the family?

3. Why the trip was going to be a wonderful adventure for the children?

4. What trenchers were?

5. Why Lisbet thought she was going to be lonesome in the New World?

6. Why the ship had to wait for good weather before sailing? Is this true today?

THINGS TO DO

1. What special things would you pack if you were going on a long trip and could not take everything? Make a list.

2. Make a model of a trencher.

Off to the New World! As they row out to the *New Netherland*, the Dutch settlers wave good-by to the families and friends they may never see again.

As they near the big ship, Teunis and Lisbet think of the adventures ahead.

3: All Aboard for the New World

The next day was clear and sunny, with a brisk March wind. It was just the right kind of day for a ship to sail.

Kip Teunissen took his family to the harbor in a rowboat. The big chests had already been put aboard the ship. The family had only the small chest with them. Lisbet carried her baby doll and Teunis had his favorite toy boat. Grandpa and Grandma went in the rowboat, too. They wanted to be with the family as long as they could.

Before long, the rowboat reached a point of land called Cryers' Hook. Here people came to say good-by to their friends who were going far across the seas. You can guess how Cryers' Hook got its name. Mother's parents were very brave. They did not cry as they kissed their children and grandchildren good-by. They waved as the rowboat took the family toward the ship.

Teunis made believe that he did not care, but Lisbet's eyes were full of tears as she waved at Grandpa and Grandma. Mother squeezed her hand. She felt just as sad as Lisbet did. "Look at our ship," she whispered.

There ahead was the *New Netherland*. "Our ship was named for the land to which we are going," said Father.

The *New Netherland* soon towered above the children in their little boat. She looked huge to them, but to you she would look small. In those days, there were not many ships bigger than the *New Netherland*.

The rowboat that carried Kip Teunissen's family came close beside the *New Netherland*. Lisbet looked at the ladder hanging from the deck high above. "We can't climb all the way up there!" she cried. "Isn't there a door down low that we can go through?"

"No, dear," said Mother. "We're all going to have to climb up a rope ladder to the deck. It's all right. I'll go first." She sounded brave, but Lisbet knew that Mother was scared.

A kind soldier went up the rope ladder right behind Mother. He put out a hand to steady her as the rope swayed. From the deck she smiled down at Lisbet.

Then the soldier came down to help Lisbet. In almost no time, she was safe on deck beside Mother.

Father and Teunis were soon there, too. Then the soldier helped them take their small chest to the cabin, where all the families would sleep.

Lisbet and Teunis looked around the cabin. At each side were double-decker bunks. Curtains were hung in front of each. In the middle of the room was a big table, with benches at the sides and a chair at each end. Here the families would eat. All the furniture was fastened to the floor, so that it would not slide when waves rocked the ship.

"Is this all the room we'll have for weeks and weeks?" Lisbet cried.

"You'll get used to it, dear," said Mother, but she seemed as sad as Lisbet.

The soldier tried to cheer them up. "You won't have to stay here. When the weather is good, you will be on deck."

"We'll see you, won't we?"

"Of course you will," said the soldier. "I like children. I have a little sister about your age. If you don't see me, just ask somebody where Rem is. Most of the sailors know me. I've sailed with Skipper May before."

"To New Netherland?" asked Lisbet.

"Yes, indeed," said Rem. "I've been a fur trader there. I made friends with many of the *wilden*."

"Please tell us about them!" she teased.

"Later, when I'm not so busy," Rem promised.

DO YOU KNOW—

1. How Cryers' Hook got its name?
2. How the ship got its name?
3. How the family got aboard the ship?
4. Why the furniture of the cabin was fastened to the floor?

THINGS TO DO

Visit a museum to see models of sailing ships in the days of the Dutch settlers.

Lisbet looks back, glad to have reached the deck.

"How small it is!" Lisbet thinks when Rem shows them where the families must stay.

4: Life Aboard the Ship

As soon as the voyage started, the children began learning about everybody on the ship. The captain, Skipper May, was in charge of the ship and of everyone on it. He had sailed his ship to the New World many times before. When the wind blew hard, the sailors said, "Skipper May knows how to cross the Atlantic Ocean. Our ship will be safe."

Skipper May had two officers who helped him sail the ship. They were the first and the second mate. They took their turns at steering the ship. This was a task that needed great care. If a ship was steered in the wrong direction, it went off its course. Then it might sail for hours before getting back to its course.

Lisbet and Teunis became friendly with the other girls and boys on the ship. Many of these children spoke French. They knew the Dutch language, too. Lisbet made friends with a girl who spoke French. Her new friend was called Marie. Teunis and Joost liked Marie's brother, Pierre, very well, too. They also met two Dutch children, Maritje and her younger brother Jan.

"Why do so many of our friends on this ship speak French?" Lisbet asked her father one day.

"It's a long story," said Kip Teunissen. "To understand it, you must know the kind of country our Fatherland is. It is the best country in Europe for common people like us.

"Our laws are fair. They give everybody the right to worship God in his own way. The laws help men to earn a fair living. Our country has more schools than other countries have."

"I know," said Lisbet. "We're all proud of the Fatherland."

"People from other countries know about our good laws," said Father.

"That's why so many of them have come to live with us.

"In some countries, people of our religion are badly treated. Flanders is one of these countries. For this reason, many people from Flanders have come to live in the Fatherland. These people speak French. They are called *Walloons*."

"But why are so many Walloons going to the New World?" asked Lisbet. "They were treated fairly in the Fatherland."

"That is true," said Father, "but they don't want their children to forget Flanders. The children are learning the Dutch language. They are learning Dutch customs. The Walloons like our customs, but they like their own better. They want their children to learn the customs of Flanders. They think that in the New World everyone can have his own customs. In New Netherland, the laws of the Fatherland will be used. Everybody can have freedom to live in his own way."

"I understand," said Lisbet, "but I do not think the Walloon children are very much different from us. We have fun playing with them."

"People are very much alike," said Father, "whether they speak Dutch or French. I am glad you like the Walloons. I do too. There will be many Walloons in our new home."

The children soon got used to everything on the ship except the food. There was no fresh meat. The only fresh vegetables were carrots, turnips, beets, and cabbage.

In those days, there were no refrigerators. The ships did not have room enough to carry ice to keep food from spoiling. Beef and pork were salted so that they would not spoil. Herring and other fish were kept in salt, too. Dried peas and beans were often cooked. And there was always cheese.

At first, the passengers on the *New Netherland* shivered in the strong sea breeze. They wore their warmest clothes. Soon, however, the weather became warmer. The *New Netherland* was sailing south, toward the Canary Islands.

One morning, everyone was looking at the beautiful trees and flowers of these islands.

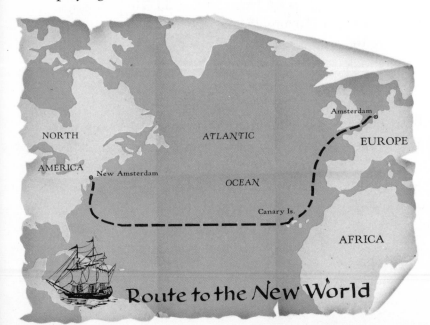

NORTH AMERICA

New Amsterdam

ATLANTIC

OCEAN

Canary Is.

Amsterdam

EUROPE

AFRICA

Route to the New World

This is the route the *New Netherland* took to the New World. When the Dutch settlers left Amsterdam, they sailed southward to the Canary Islands to pick up favorable winds and currents. There they turned west toward the New World. After several weeks on rough and stormy seas, their ship arrived in New Netherland.

Great storms rock and toss their ship.

Then the ship turned west. The weather was still warm. Most of the time it was pleasant. But sometimes there were storms. The wind blew hard and the waves were rough. The *New Netherland* bobbed up and down like Teunis's toy boat in the canal on a windy day.

Many of the passengers stayed in their bunks all day. Some of them were seasick. When they got up, they could hardly keep from falling down. They staggered from table to bunk and back again to hang on to the table.

"Oh, when shall we ever get to the New World?" Lisbet cried.

"Cheer up!" said Rem. "We're a little closer to New Netherland every day. This storm isn't too bad. I've been in worse ones. You will be all right."

And, sure enough, they were. After a while the sun came out. The waves were gentle and the sea was blue. The children could play safely on the deck again.

The ship sailed west for two weeks. Then one warm morning, Skipper May said, "Now we shall turn north. The weather will get cooler. Before long, you will see New Netherland."

DO YOU KNOW—

1. Why the Fatherland was a good country to live in? In what ways it was like our country today?

2. Who the Walloons were? Where they had come from? Why they wanted to go to the New World?

3. What the passengers on the ship ate? Why they did not have more kinds of food?

THINGS TO DO

Talk about Father's idea: "People are very much alike." What did he mean? Is his idea true in our time?

"What is the country like? Where are the *wilden*?" the settlers wonder.

5: New Netherland at Last

"I see green ahead!" cried Lisbet.

"That's just the ocean," said Teunis. He was tired of the ship and tired of the ocean. He felt like teasing his sister.

"No, it's land," Lisbet said. "I can see the shapes of trees."

"Of course it's land," said Rem, with a wide smile. Soon the children were leaning on the railing, with the grownups right behind them. Everybody was watching the land. It seemed to be coming to meet their ship.

"So many trees!" said Teunis. "They seem to grow wherever they want to. They're not in straight lines the way they are along our canals and roads."

"I don't see any canals at all," said Lisbet.

"That's because there aren't any," said Father, with a smile.

"What shall we skate on here?" asked Teunis.

"You'll find some good ponds for skating," said Rem. "And you'll love to slide down the snowy hills in winter."

The children had never lived where there were any hills. The hills of Staten Island looked huge to them.

"We can't grow food on hills," said Mother, a little worried.

"Crops will grow on hills that aren't too steep," said Father. "And there is a lot of level land, like this you see on your right." The ship was now sailing near Long Island. To Teunis and Lisbet, the flat land looked a little like home.

"But I don't see any farms or gardens," said Teunis. "Don't the Indians grow food, Rem?" he asked his friend.

"Indeed they do," said Rem. "They have gardens, as you shall see, but they have no farms. They move from place to place. When the land in one place gets worn out, they move to another."

"I haven't seen one house," said Lisbet. "Don't the *wilden* have homes?"

"Of course," said Rem, "but they're not like our houses. If I see an Indian home, I'll point it out to you."

The *New Netherland* was now sailing through a narrow passage. This passage is called the Narrows nowadays.

On the right side was low, level land. It looked so close that the children said, "We could jump ashore if we wanted to."

On the left side was Staten Island. It was hilly and covered with trees and bushes. Looking at the high, bushy shore, Joost whispered, "Look! The bushes are moving. Maybe the *wilden* are watching us."

"Of course the *wilden* are watching us," said Rem. "They've watched our ship ever since she came into sight. They're a little frightened, I think. Most of them have seen ships before, and people from Europe. Still, they don't know what's going to happen."

"I hope there will be Indians where we are going," said Lisbet. "Maybe they will sell us some milk."

"I'm afraid not," said Rem. "They don't raise cows or any other animals but dogs. For meat, they shoot wild animals in the woods."

"But what do they do without milk?" asked Lisbet. All the way across the ocean she had been wanting milk. All the children hoped to have as much milk as they wanted when they reached the New World.

"The *wilden* have other good things," said Rem. "You will like the fine geese and ducks. And you'll have your own garden vegetables by August."

"I wish we could start planting tomorrow," said Lisbet.

"We shall have to wait awhile," said Father.

"Why must we wait?" asked Lisbet. "This land looks good for gardens."

"It is," said Rem, "but most of the families are going farther up the North River." He took a piece of paper from his pocket and drew a small map. "Right here," said he, making a cross, "is where we are now. This big bay is the mouth of the North River. Farther up the river is the place where we are going. I'll put a star there. At this place, another river flows into the North River. This river is called the Mohawk. Along this river runs an Indian trail. Many Indians who trap fur-bearing animals use this trail. They bring fine furs from the west.

Why was Manhattan so important to the Dutch? Why was Fort Orange a good place for a trading post?

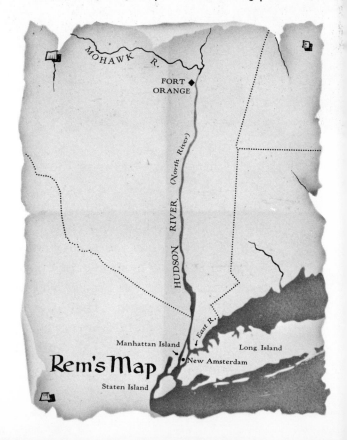

Other Indians bring furs from the land near the big lakes to the north.

"The Indians have found that Dutch traders pay them well for their furs. The Dutch pay better than the French, who live farther north. The place that I have marked with the star has become an important fur-trading post. That is why most of the families on this ship are going to live there. Your father will work at this trading post."

"Are you going to buy furs, too, Rem?" asked Teunis.

"No," said Rem. "I shall be one of the soldiers at the new fort."

"You'll keep us safe from the Indians, won't you?" asked Lisbet, shivering.

"Don't worry," said Mother, patting Lisbet's hand. "The Indians up there are friendly, I hear."

"Then why are we going to have a fort?" asked Teunis.

Rem answered, "We may have trouble with the French or the English. They would like our good trading place on the North River. But they almost never attack a place where settlers are living."

Teunis and Lisbet listen eagerly as Rem tells them of the fur-traders' huts and the unfinished fort.

The next morning, before the passengers were on deck, the *New Netherland* was sailing up the bay toward Manhattan. She sailed close to a small island covered with nut trees. "That's Nut Island," said Rem.

The children were more interested in the larger island lying right ahead of the ship. They saw a few huts that fur traders had built. They saw tumble-down walls of earth, too. "Those walls look like part of an old fort," said Father.

"A fort was started here," said Rem, "but it was never finished. I think it will soon be rebuilt. At any rate, eight soldiers are going to stay here to guard Manhattan Island."

"Why should they, if no families live on Manhattan?" asked Mother.

"It's an important island," said Rem.

Again he drew a little map. "Ships must pass Manhattan Island to sail up the North River or the East River. Suppose people of another country wanted to take New Netherland away from us. First of all, they would have to take this island."

DO YOU KNOW—

1. What the children saw as they sailed through the Narrows? What they thought about the land they saw?

2. Why the *wilden* were watching the ship? Why the children didn't see them?

3. Why there was no milk in the New World for the children to drink?

4. Why most of the families were going up the North River to live? Why there would be a fort and soldiers there? Why Manhattan Island was important to the Dutch?

THINGS TO DO

The children were going to find the New World different from their Fatherland. Talk about all the differences you can think of.

85

6: A Visit from the Wilden

Next morning, a strange little boat came close under the *New Netherland*. People rushed to the rail of the ship to get a look at this little boat. It had rounded sides, like half a tree trunk, and its ends were curved and pointed. It moved quickly over the water.

Three men sitting in the tiny boat were making it move. Each of them held a paddle. The men dipped their paddles in perfect time together. Each time they dipped their paddles the boat shot forward a little faster.

The men were even more exciting than their little boat. They wore no clothing above the waist, and their skin was very dark, as if they had spent much time in the sun.

"The *wilden!* The *wilden!*" cried everybody.

The Indians' canoe stopped right under where the children were standing. One Indian held up a string of fish. From a *porthole* lower in the ship, the first mate began talking with the Indians. The children couldn't hear what he said, but soon an Indian handed him the string of fish. Then he handed the Indian a small knife. "I wonder why he didn't give him any money?" asked Teunis.

Father answered, "The Indians would rather have things they can use. They need things made of iron. They have no iron mines. Their only knives are made from shells and sharp stones."

Other *wilden* came later. Some brought wild geese and ducks to sell. One of them brought two big birds. The birds were blacky-brown, with bars on their feathers.

"I never saw such big birds before," said Teunis.

"They are turkeys," said one of the sailors. "What a feast we shall have! Now we can say good-by to salted beef and dried herring."

The sailor was right. That day everybody sat down to a fine meal of roast turkey. How good it tasted!

"It's like chicken," said Father.

"It's like goose," said Mother.

"It's like duck and chicken and goose," said Lisbet, "only better."

DO YOU KNOW—

1. What the little boat of the Indians was called?

2. Why the Indians came close to the ship?

3. Why the Indians were not paid in money? What they wanted as payment?

4. Why the children were glad the Indians had come? Why the sailors were glad?

7: A New Friend

It was quite a while before the *New Netherland* sailed away from Manhattan. Skipper May had many things to do.

First, he had to send ashore the eight soldiers who were to guard Manhattan. They would be ready for anyone who might want to take the island from the Dutch.

Then he had to plan for three forts. There was to be a fort on the Connecticut River, called Fort New Hope. Two families on the *New Netherland* were going to live near Fort New Hope. Of course, some soldiers would be sent to protect them.

Other families were going to live on the Delaware River. The fort there was to be called Fort Nassau.

The *New Netherland* picked up some passengers before leaving Manhattan. One of these was a soldier named Daniel Van Krieckebeeck. People said that he would be in charge of the soldiers at Fort Orange.

"I hope not," said Rem. "The man is brave, but he hasn't good sense." The future was to show how right Rem was.

Another new passenger was much more interesting to the children. His name was Bastiaen Krol. His wife and children had sailed with the other families from Amsterdam. How glad they were to see him again, and how glad he was to see them! However, he found time for other people, too.

He was very fond of children. Sometimes he was joking, and sometimes he was serious. But he always spoke with the children as if they were his own age. He listened to them seriously, too, and never laughed at their ideas.

He had many things to do for the passengers on the *New Netherland*. Every morning and every evening he led the people in prayers. On Sunday, he read to them from the Bible and from a great book of sermons. He sat with people who were sick or in trouble. He gave them words of cheer and comfort that made them feel better.

This map shows the earliest Dutch settlements in the New World. The area shaded in gray shows what land the Netherlands claimed in her years of greatest power. Can you tell what states this land is part of today? In which community did Kip Teunissen's family settle? Do you live in or near any of these communities?

Bastiaen Krol leads the settlers in prayer. In what other ways will he help the settlers?

Lisbet asked him one day, "Why don't we call you Domine?" Domine was the Dutch word for preacher or minister.

"I'm not a domine," said Bastiaen Krol. "I haven't enough education to be a preacher. I can't hold a real church service. I can't marry people or *baptize* babies."

"I think you are just as good as if you were a domine," said Lisbet. "You help us all so much. Will you stay with us in our new home?"

"Yes," said Bastiaen Krol. "I came here to help the settlers and the Indians, too. I have always wanted to bring people the word of God. But I was taught to be a silkworker.

"The Church Council in Amsterdam could not send a real domine to a small settlement. So they let me come instead.

They gave me the name of Krankenbezoeker, which means Comforter of the Sick. I can help the settlers in some of the ways a domine does. Perhaps I can teach you children to read the Bible. Most of all, I hope that I can bring the word of God to the Indians. I have been learning the Indian language while I was waiting for the *New Netherland* to come."

DO YOU KNOW—

1. Where the three Dutch forts in New Netherland were to be built?

2. Why Lisbet and Teunis had to part from their new friends, Marie and Pierre?

3. Who Daniel Van Kreickebeeck was?

4. Who the children's new friend was?

5. The meaning of these two Dutch words: *Domine* and *Krankenbezoeker?*

THINGS TO DO

Talk about Bastiaen Krol and the things he did. Why did the children like him?

8: Sailing Up the North River

At last the day came when the *New Netherland* set sail up the North River. This was the river that Hudson had discovered. Later it was called by his name. On the right was Manhattan Island. On the left was land that is now part of the State of New Jersey.

There were no high hills to be seen on either side of the river at first. Farther on, the left shore became steep. The cliffs went straight up like great walls. On the Manhattan side, the shores were not so steep. But everywhere there were deep, dark forests. "Ghosts and fairies and giants might live in those dark woods," said Lisbet.

Farther up the North River, the shores were lower. There were smaller hills and places where the trees had been cut. Once in a while the passengers saw an Indian garden. "When will we have plants coming up?" asked Lisbet. "We'll be ever so late with our garden."

Every day the children went on deck early to see what was new. One dark morning, they found mountains towering over them. From behind the mountains on the left came a low growl of thunder. Lightning flashed above its peak. "Oh, a *donderberg!*" cried Lisbet, using the Dutch word for Thunder Mountain.

The thunder kept on growling from behind the mountain, and soon the rain poured down. There were thunderstorms nearly all morning long. Between showers, the children would scamper out on deck.

"Look at the sugar loaf!" cried Jan, pointing to a cone-shaped mountain.

"You're right, Jan," said Lisbet, for in those days, sugar came in high, pointed loaves.

"What steep cliffs!" cries Teunis. Today we call these cliffs the Palisades.

Later, the sun came out. Its golden rays shone on a high mountain. The bright mountain looked like a huge lump of butter. "Oh, a *boterberg*," cried Joost. For years afterward, the Dutch called this mountain *Boterberg*, or Butter Mountain. Now it is called Storm King.

Donderberg and Sugar Loaf still keep the names given them by the children long ago. The Dutch settlers made up a story about *Donderberg*. They said that the goblins who caused summer showers lived in this mountain.

The days were long and peaceful as the *New Netherland* sailed up the North River. There were no more thunder showers. The sun shone. A warm breeze blew from the shore. It brought the sweet smell of wild flowers. The trees had their new leaves, clean and shining.

How happy everybody was! No more wild winds to drive the ship off her course. No more rough waves to bring

sickness and fear. Spring was here and summer was coming. Soon the families would build their own homes on dry land. What a fine life they would have!

One afternoon Teunis was fanning himself. "How warm it is!" he said.

"This country has warmer summers than the Fatherland," said Rem. "It has colder winters, too. But you'll have plenty of furs to keep yourselves warm."

Soon the children forgot all about the weather. Rem was pointing to a small island right ahead of the ship. On the island were the ruins of a fort.

"When the Dutch first came here," said Rem, "they found the walls of an old fort on that island. The fort was built by French fur traders years and years ago. The Dutch decided to build a new fort in the same place. This they did, but the fort had bad luck. A flood came one spring. The water was so high and so strong that it tore away part of the fort. It flooded the rest. So we shall not build our fort on this island."

"You mean we're going to live near here?" asked Lisbet, her eyes shining.

"Yes," said Rem. "Skipper May will soon drop anchor. Then we can go ashore."

Rem shows the children ruins of an old fort. Now a new fort must be built near the new settlement.

"You will build your homes here," says Skipper May.

The passengers all looked at the green and pleasant shore. There was sandy, level ground near the riverbank. A little farther back from the shore were hills with dark woods covering them.

"What a beautiful place to live!" said Mother.

But Lisbet couldn't say a word. She could hardly get her breath. "So this is our new home," she was thinking. "We're here at last. Will the Indians be waiting to make friends with us? Will they be waiting to fight? How can we live in those dark, dark woods? We'll never feel safe. Or maybe we'll live on the shore of this beautiful river. What kind of house shall we have? Maybe we'll have only tumble-down huts like the fur traders on Manhattan. I'm scared, but I'm happy too. Oh, I can't wait till we get there!"

Skipper May came out on deck. Everyone was silent as he spoke. "You will soon walk on the land that will be your new country. You may live on the ship until you get your homes built. You may have food from our stores until you can grow your own. I shall be your governor. I will help you in any way I can. When I leave you, I shall place a good man in charge.

"Now God bless you in your new land. Krankenbezoeker Krol will say a prayer before we go ashore."

Skipper May and all the others knelt as the Krankenbezoeker prayed. He thanked God for bringing the settlers safe across the ocean. He asked God to help and protect them in the New World. "Amen," said everyone solemnly.

DO YOU KNOW—

1. Why the passengers on the *New Netherland* were so happy as they sailed up the North River?

2. How the climate of the New World was different from that of the Fatherland?

3. How Skipper May planned to help the settlers while they were making their new homes?

THINGS TO DO

Make believe you are going to live in a new land, as Lisbet and Teunis did. Write a little story about what you would expect and how you would feel about the new land.

9: On Dry Land

Soon the longboat was lowered into the water. The soldiers were the first to go ashore. They had put on armor over their leather jackets. They were wearing their steel helmets, too. Every soldier carried a gun, but they had swords or pikes besides. It was slow work loading an old-fashioned gun, so the soldiers liked to have an extra weapon that they could get at in a hurry.

Some of the fathers went with the soldiers. Two sailors rowed the longboat.

As the men stepped ashore, they were ready for anything. But nothing happened. There was not an Indian in sight. Where were the *wilden*?

Now the longboat was coming back toward the ship. Lisbet heard someone say, "I don't think the children should go ashore now. The *wilden* might kidnap

Wearing steel armor and helmets, the soldiers climb down into the longboat. They are the first ashore.

them. Anyhow, they'd only be in everyone's way." Her heart sank with disappointment.

Mother spoke up at once. "The children need to stretch their legs," she said. "The trip has been harder for them than for us. There are enough soldiers to protect them. Let them get off next."

Lisbet was standing near the rope ladder. She wanted to be the first child to step upon this pleasant land. The longboat was now beside the ship. Rem, who had come back with the sailors, was holding the rope ladder steady.

Lisbet was the first one down. Soon there was a boatload of children, and the sailors began rowing. On shore, the fathers were walking around, looking at the new land. Kip Teunissen was waiting to help the children ashore.

Rem was the last to step out of the longboat. The sailors started rowing toward the ship to get the women. Lisbet and Teunis, Father and Rem began walking along the shore. Lisbet sniffed the fresh air, sweet with the smell of wild flowers.

"We'd better go back and meet Mother now," said Father. "She'll soon be coming ashore."

Her family was there to meet her. "Oh, it's good to be on land again!" she cried. "But what shall we do first? There's so much to do."

"You can't do much this afternoon," said Rem. "Wouldn't you like to take a walk? There's something pretty I'd like to show you."

"It's beautiful!" exclaims Mother, as they all gaze in wonder at the waterfall.

"Well," said Mother, "what do you think, Kip?"

Father looked at the other families strolling along the shore. "Maybe we should find a place for a home first," he said. "We must be near the fort."

"There will be plenty of room for all of you," said Rem. "With only eighteen families, our new little town will not be crowded."

"All right, then," said Father. "We'll start working tomorrow. Today, let's do what Rem says."

Rem led the way into the woods. How dark and cool—almost too cool. "In the summer," he said, "you will come here to cool off. Now we're going to climb a little hill."

Kip's family had never climbed a hill before. Soon everyone was panting. "Keep on just a bit," Rem said, giving Lisbet and Mother each a hand to help them climb.

The new leaves rustled in the soft spring breeze. A few birds were twittering. Now and then a crow cawed. Then a new sound reached the children's ears —a soft steady splashing. "What's that?" asked Teunis.

"You'll see," said Rem, as he pushed aside some leaves and branches. The family came out into a little clearing around a pool. Above the pool hung a soft white veil, swaying a little. "Come nearer," said Rem, walking toward the veil. As the children drew near, they felt tiny drops of water sprinkling them. "Oh, I know!" cried Lisbet. "The veil isn't a veil. It's water falling from the rocks above."

"That's the splashing we heard," said Teunis.

"Yes," said Rem. "This is called a waterfall. Isn't it pretty?"

"Oh, it is!" cried Mother. "We don't have any waterfalls in the Fatherland."

Kip Teunissen wonders if he could build a wigwam for his family to live in.

"We couldn't," said Father. "There are no rocks and hills for the water to fall from."

When it was time to start down the hill toward the ship, Rem said, "Let's take a different path. This will take us past a deserted Indian village. You can see the wigwams the Indians used to live in."

"Don't any Indians live in this neighborhood now?" asked Father.

"Yes," Rem answered, "but they are shy. They know everything we do, but they don't want us to see them yet. They'll make friends, in time."

Father was looking carefully at one of the deserted wigwams. He looked inside and out. After a while, he spoke. "Rem, couldn't I make a wigwam? It wouldn't take as long as building a log house. Then we could bring our things from the ship and sleep at home."

"You could build a wigwam quickly," Rem agreed. "Of course, it wouldn't do at all in cold weather."

As Rem and the family came out on level ground, Lisbet said, "I hate to go back to the ship for supper. Those tiresome gray peas! Isn't there something we can eat here?"

"Not tonight, I'm afraid," said Rem. "Soon I'll show you how to cook some food that the Indians like."

The family was tired. The long walk had been a great change from the quiet days on the *New Netherland*. The other people on the ship were tired, too. After an early supper, they were all soon asleep, dreaming of the day to come.

DO YOU KNOW—

1. How the settlers went ashore? How the soldiers got ready to protect them?

2. Why none of the *wilden* were in sight when the settlers went ashore?

3. Where Rem took the family for a walk? What Father saw that gave him a good idea?

THINGS TO DO

Talk about the children's mother. What kind of person was she? What has she said or done so far in the story?

10: A Good Breakfast

Lisbet was the first to wake up. "The cabin seems different," she thought. "Why's that?"

"Oh, I know," she answered herself. "The ship isn't moving at all. We're here, in our new land. What's that lovely sound? Oh, birds, of course."

Now she was wide awake. She dressed quietly and quickly. Soon she was out on deck, looking at the beautiful shore. The other children came out one by one. Before long they were all scampering around and chattering about their new homes.

"We started ours yesterday," said Joost.

"You did?" asked Lisbet. She had hoped that her home would be the first.

"Well, we picked out a place for our home," said Joost, "and Father cut down some trees."

This news worried Lisbet. Would there be a good place left for her family's home? Maybe she had better wake up Father, so that he could start building right away. She forgot her worries as she heard a voice call, "Lisbet! Teunis!"

The voice came up from under the side of the ship. The children looked down. There was Rem. He was in the longboat, and he had hold of the rope ladder. "Who wants breakfast?" he called.

All the children shouted, "I do."

"Bring your trenchers, then," Rem called, "and don't forget your spoons."

The children scattered to the cabin.

When they were on deck again, Rem called to a tall sailor, "Brom, please tell the folks where their children are. They can see us from the deck." Then he held the rope ladder for the children. They

Breakfast is cooking on the shore as Lisbet climbs down to the longboat.

all climbed down into the longboat. As he rowed to shore, they wondered what they would have for breakfast.

On the shore, a fire was crackling cheerfully. Over it hung a big iron kettle. The children peered into it. Something smooth, yellow, and thick was puffing up in a huge bubble inside the kettle. Then the bubble would burst and the yellow mass would lie still for a minute. "What's that?" asked Lisbet.

"It's food that the Indians call *suppawn*," said Rem. "It is made of corn meal." With a big wooden spoon, he began dishing the suppawn into the children's trenchers.

Lisbet took a tiny taste of the hot suppawn. "It's good," she said, "but I'd like it better with milk."

"You shall have milk someday, when the Company sends us cows," said Rem. "Now you'll have to be happy with something else I have here." He reached into his leather pouch and brought out some pieces of something crumbly. It had a

light brown color. He shaved a piece with his big knife and sprinkled the shavings on Lisbet's suppawn. She smelled a delicious new smell as she tasted a delicious new taste. "Oh, it's good!" she cried. "What is it?"

"It's maple sugar," said Rem. "This is the only sugar the Indians have."

The children liked the maple sugar so well that they couldn't think of any better sugar.

It was fun to wash the trenchers and spoons under the water flowing from the rocks. It was such fun that Lisbet said, "Give me your trencher, Rem. I'll wash it for you." She was careful to get the trenchers clean. She wiped them on big burdock leaves that she found growing near the spring.

When the trenchers were all drying in the sun, Rem said, "Now, children, how would you like some fresh fruit?" Every child looked up with joy. It was a long time since any of them had eaten fresh fruit.

Lisbet and Teunis are delighted with the suppawn that Rem has cooked for them.

How good the wild strawberries taste to Lisbet and Teunis! It is their first fresh fruit in weeks.

"What kind?" asked Maritje.

"You'll see," said Rem, with a grin. "Let's go to that little meadow across the brook."

The crowd of children trooped gaily at Rem's heels. They all jumped over a small, gurgling stream. A little farther on, Rem bent down. He lifted aside a branch of heart-shaped leaves. There was a bunch of small, pinky-red berries. "Oo-oo, wild strawberries!" cried Teunis.

"Go ahead, children," said Rem. "Eat all the strawberries you can pick. But don't eat anything else. Some wild fruits aren't good for people to eat."

It seemed only a short time until parents were calling from the shore: "Jan! Teunis! Maritje! Where are you?"

"That's enough for now," said Rem. "There will be lots more berries tomorrow." He gathered the children together and they all went back to the shore. Mothers and fathers were a little surprised as they looked down at their children's faces. Every face was smeared with the pink juice of the delicious strawberries.

As you may know, Dutch and Walloon mothers were very tidy. But when these mothers saw how happy their children looked, they never scolded a bit.

DO YOU KNOW—

1. What Rem got for the children's breakfast?

2. What Lisbet did for Rem?

3. Why the children were so happy when Rem took them to pick wild strawberries?

4. Why the parents were not cross about their children's smeared faces?

THINGS TO DO

1. Cook some corn meal. Try eating it with maple sugar. Try it with milk. Which way do you like it best?

2. Find pictures of wild strawberries. If you have ever picked them, tell where you found them. Ask your mothers if they have ever made wild strawberry jam, and how they make it.

The young trees have been bent and tied to make a frame for the wigwam. Now the family covers it with bark. It will make a good home for the warm summer months.

11: A New Home

Everybody was too busy to think about face-washing, anyhow. Fathers and mothers were picking out places for homes.

Before long, Rem began calling from a place farther along the shore. Kip Teunissen and his family hurried toward Rem. He said, "I think this would be a fine place for your home. There's a pretty little brook where the children can go wading. It comes from a spring of cool, clear water. Every home needs good drinking water nearby. Besides, there's a good big piece of level ground here for your garden."

Mother said, "I like this place very much, but what can we live in?"

"It won't take long to build a wigwam," said Rem. "I learned how when I was here before. First we'll make a frame of saplings."

"What are saplings?" asked Lisbet.

"They're little trees, so small that the trunks can be bent over," said Rem. "We'll bend the saplings over and fasten them together. Then we'll cover the framework with bark. Or maybe we'll use cornhusk mats. The Indians make them, and maybe they'll sell us some."

"Could I build a fire in an Indian house?" asked Mother.

"The Indians do," said Rem, "but it makes the house rather smoky. You could do it on rainy days, if you had to."

"Let's get started," said Father.

The work began early. Two days later, the house was done. Then Mother and Father went back to the ship to pack their chests.

Rem said to the children, "Your mother and father will be very tired when they get back. Shall we have supper ready for them?" Lisbet and Teunis thought Rem's idea was fine.

Rem had a large piece of meat wrapped in leaves. He took a knife from his pocket and began cutting the meat into small pieces.

"This is deer meat," he said to the children. "Some Indian friends gave it to me. Teunis, do you think you could build a fire? We'll have to heat some water while I cut up the meat."

Everybody helped, and soon a delicious smell of boiling meat was rising from the kettle. Then Mother and Father returned. With them were some sailors, carrying the two big chests. Father was carrying the small one.

The kettle kept bubbling as Father put the straw mattresses on the floor of the wigwam. On the big mattress he placed a featherbed. "I shall have a featherbed, too, when I grow up," said Lisbet. Mother spread the sheets, quilts, and blankets on the beds. Now the inside of the wigwam looked a little like a Dutch home.

Everyone gathered around the fire. "When will the meat be done, Rem?" asked Teunis.

"In another half hour," Rem answered.

Another half hour to sniff the delicious smell and get hungrier and hungrier! The children wandered off, to get away from the good-smelling steam. They sat down on the carpet of pine needles just inside the woods, and tried to forget how hungry they were.

What was that in the shadows? Was it a high rock? A man? A tall boy? Or was it nothing? It surely was something. Yes, and it was alive. It had moved away. It darted out of the shadows, and the children saw what it was—a tall Indian boy.

They sat very still. "Do you think he'll come back?" Lisbet whispered.

"I hope so," Teunis whispered back. "Oh, there he is again!"

The boy did not come nearer, but he did not run away again. He was wearing a little apron of deerskin. Around his neck was a string of wampum beads. He looked shy, but as if he would like to speak to the children. They too felt shy and couldn't think of anything to say.

At last the Indian boy pointed to the *New Netherland* lying at anchor in the river. "Big dugout," he said. "From big, big tree," and he spread his arms as if to hold a tree as big as the forest.

The children didn't know what he meant, but they smiled at him. Next he

99

pointed to the red ribbon in Lisbet's apron, and then to his braid of hair. His head was shaved except for a long lock in the center, which was braided.

Lisbet untied her red ribbon and pulled it through the eyelets. She handed it to the boy, who tied it to his braid. Then he looked at Lisbet as if he were puzzled. Suddenly he got an idea. He took off his string of wampum beads and held it out toward Lisbet. After a minute she took the string of beads and tied it around her neck.

Just then Father called to tell the children that supper was ready. Their new friend darted away into the woods, saying just one word—the Dutch word for tomorrow.

Teunis and Lisbet were doubly excited. They were excited about their

Lisbet gives their new friend her red ribbon.

new friend, the Indian boy. And they were excited about the new food they were going to have. Should they talk first, or eat first?

They sniffed the good smell of the deer meat. While Father heaped their trencher, they started to talk. Then they began to eat, and the food was so good that they forgot to talk for a while. At last Father said, "Now what were you saying about an Indian boy?"

"He called our ship a big dugout," said Teunis. "Then he talked about a big, big tree."

Rem laughed. "I know what he meant," he said. "The Indian makes his boat out of a tree trunk. He burns and digs out the wood to make the boat. That's why he calls it a dugout. The Indian boy thinks our ship was built the same way. So he thinks it must have been made from a huge tree."

Everybody laughed. Then Rem said, "Don't think this Indian boy is stupid. He doesn't know about our ships, but he knows many other things. If he is your friend, he will teach you a great deal about the New World. I think your new friend is Mokween. His uncle, a chief, is an old friend of mine."

DO YOU KNOW—

1. What a family must look for in finding a good place for a new home?

2. How the wigwam was built?

3. What the children's new friend thought about the *New Netherland?*

4. How the Indian boy could help the Dutch children in their new land?

THINGS TO DO

Make a small model of a wigwam like the one Kip Teunissen built for his family. Furnish it with models of the household things.

Why have the *wilden* come? The settlers listen as Skipper May talks to the Indians.

12: A Treaty with the Indians

The next morning dawned crisp and cool. After breakfast, Father and Teunis got their axes and went to work in the woods behind the wigwam. They had worked only a few minutes when Rem came hurrying up. Almost out of breath, he said, "All the men are to come at once."

"Where?" asked Father.

"To the place where we landed," Rem answered. "Some Indian chiefs have come to speak with Skipper May. We do not know what they want, so the Captain thinks all the men should be with him. The women and children may come too, because these Indians seem friendly."

"Oh, let's go, Mother," cried Lisbet. "I want to see the Indian chiefs."

"Since the Indians are friendly, it will be all right," said Father. So the family hurried along with Rem.

"What Indians are these?" asked Father. He knew that two tribes lived near Fort Orange. They were the Mohawks and the Mahicans. These tribes were often at war with each other. Father was worried. He was thinking, "If we make friends with one tribe, the other tribe may want to fight with us."

"We are lucky," said Rem. "Indians from both tribes are here. They both want to be friendly, I think. They want to sell furs to us."

Soon Rem and the family came to the meeting place. Skipper May stood near the shore. His officers and soldiers were standing beside him. The settlers gathered nearby.

The Indian chiefs were standing straight and tall before the Skipper. They looked stern and solemn, but friendly.

101

Every chief had a shaved head. A lock of hair had been left at the crown, and a feather was tied to it. Their faces were painted with bright colors. They wore robes painted in bright designs. The designs were so fine that Lisbet thought the robes were covered with lace.

"The chiefs are wearing their best robes," said Rem, in a low voice. "The robes are made of animal skins painted with fine designs. The fine robes and the paint on their faces are good signs. They mean that this is a very important day for the Indians."

"Why is it important?" asked Lisbet, but just then another voice was heard. An Indian who had come with the chiefs was speaking to Skipper May. This Indian knew some Dutch words, and his words meant this:

"Our chiefs bid the Dutch brothers welcome to our land. We wish to live in peace with our brothers. We promise not to make war on you if you will promise not to make war on us."

Skipper May nodded his head. He said, "We Dutch will live in peace with our Indian brothers. We will buy furs from you. We will pay a fair price for the furs."

The Indian who had spoken to Skipper May turned toward the chiefs. He told them in Indian words what the Dutch leader had said. The chiefs spoke to him again, and he then spoke to Skipper May.

"Our chiefs ask you to give them iron goods for the furs. Our people need steel. Our women need steel needles instead of fishbones for sewing deerskin. They need Dutch cloth to make summer

A promise of peace is made. The Dutch and the Indians exchange gifts to show their friendship.

clothes. But we must have a little wampum, too, for every fur that we sell to you."

"What kinds of fur will you sell us?" asked Skipper May.

The speaker turned to a pile of furs on the ground nearby. He picked up a soft skin of silvery brown. "We will sell you the skin of the beaver," he said. Then he lifted a smaller skin of light brown with a darker brown stripe. "We will sell you the skin of the mink," he said. He showed skins of otters and wildcats. "All skins are best in the winter," he said. "Then the fur is thick and long to keep our animal brothers warm. We will bring you good skins in the winter and in the spring.

"These skins are gifts for the chief of our Dutch brothers." He lifted a huge skin with long black fur. Great claws dangled from the four legs of the skin. Lisbet shivered. She wondered if animals wearing skins like this would come prowling around the settlement. "It's a bearskin," whispered Rem. "Bears don't usually bother people unless the people bother them."

The Indian who was speaking for the chiefs laid the skins at the feet of Skipper May. The Captain thanked the Indian chiefs for their gifts. Then he sent one of his soldiers with gifts for the Indians. There were good steel axes and long, sharp steel knives. After thanks and more polite words, the Indian chiefs gave a sign of good-by. All the Dutch people stood silent as the chiefs left.

Then everybody began talking at once. Some people asked, "Do the *wilden* really mean to be friendly?"

This Indian is giving a huge bearskin to Skipper May. The settlers are happy about the gifts because it means that the Indians are friendly.

A Dutch trader who had been in the New World before said, "The Indians never break a promise."

"This is a very good beginning," said Rem to Kip Teunissen's family. "We have a treaty of friendship. That will mean peace and good trading."

DO YOU KNOW—

1. What tribes of Indians lived near the new Dutch settlement?

2. Why the Indian chiefs came to visit Skipper May and the settlers?

3. How the Indian chiefs were dressed?

4. What kinds of furs the Indians brought to Skipper May?

THINGS TO DO

1. Make a painting of the kind of robe an Indian chief might have worn to the meeting with Skipper May.

2. Make models or drawings of the things the Indians wanted in payment for their furs.

13: Planting the Garden

The family walked happily back toward their wigwam home. Now everybody could get to work without worrying about the *wilden*. Mother and Lisbet were going to plant seeds in the level, sandy land between their wigwam and the river. Father and Teunis were going to cut down trees. The wood was needed for many uses. The cleared land would make room for a larger garden.

The job that Mother and Lisbet were doing did not take long. Soon they had planted beets and spinach, carrots and cabbage. "We'll have *leeks* and *dill* and parsley for seasoning," said Mother. "We'll plant melons, too. I brought plenty of seeds from the Fatherland."

"No flowers?" asked Lisbet, in disappointment.

"I brought a few tulip bulbs," said Mother, "but of course they won't grow until spring."

"There are beautiful flowers in the woods," said Rem. "You can dig up some wildflower roots and set them out in your garden when more land is cleared."

Teunis and Father were chopping down trees behind the wigwam. Rem helped when he could, but he was often busy with the other soldiers.

Teunis never forgot his first day of chopping. It was his job to chop down the smallest trees. When Father brought down a big tree, Teunis had another job. He cut the small branches from the fallen tree. These branches were to be used for cooking fires.

"What shall we do with the trunks of the bigger trees?" asked Teunis.

"We shall save those for the time when we build a real house," said Father.

Teunis worked so hard that before long he was tired and thirsty. He went to the little spring for a drink. Then he sat down to rest a minute. When he looked up, he saw his new friend standing near. Both boys smiled.

The Indian boy came nearer. He stooped down and looked at Teunis's axe. Carefully he felt its sharp edge. Teunis handed the axe to him. He tried it on a tree near the brook. How well he swung the axe! How strong his arms were! He had the tree down in almost no time. Then he handed the axe back to Teunis.

Mokween helps his new friends build their home in the New World. How quickly he works to clear the land for a house! Lisbet and Mother begin their garden.

The boy went a few steps away and came back with a stone axe. He began chopping another tree. It took him a long time to bring down this tree. Now Teunis knew why the Indian boy liked the steel axe. It could do a much better job.

It was time for Teunis to go back to work. As he started away, the Indian boy made signs. Teunis understood that the signs meant, "Shall I come and help?" Teunis nodded happily. The boy followed him, carrying his stone axe.

He began working beside Teunis and his father. He never seemed to get tired. The next time Teunis had to stop and rest, Mokween borrowed the steel axe.

When Kip Teunissen noticed this, he went into the wigwam. In one of the chests, he found a small steel axe. He gave it to the Indian boy. The boy was so happy that he worked twice as hard as before.

By the end of the afternoon, Teunis and his father were very tired. They sat down to rest. The Indian boy sat near them. After a while, he handed the axe to Teunis and started for home.

"Here! You've left your new axe," said Kip to the boy. He held the axe handle toward Mokween. Mokween understood, for he smiled and patted the axe. Then he started off happily into the woods.

For many days, Teunis and his father worked at chopping down trees. Sometimes Mokween came to help. First, he would give the call of an owl. Then Teunis would go to meet him in the woods.

When the choppers stopped for a rest, they would sit near the cool spring and talk. Mokween had already learned some Dutch words. His Dutch friends were learning Indian words every day.

Often Mokween asked Kip and Teunis if their backs and arms were sore. If they

105

said yes, he would rub them with bear's grease. "What strong hands you have, Mokween," said Kip one day. Mokween only grinned shyly.

"You have helped us so much with the chopping," said Father. "We are about done. Now we must spade up the cleared ground for a larger garden."

"But we have no more seeds to plant," said Teunis.

"Maybe Mokween can help us get some more," said Father.

And, sure enough, the next time Mokween came to visit the children, he was carrying two gourds full of seeds. One gourd had kernels of corn in it. The other had pumpkin seeds. Mokween told the children the Indian names for these seeds.

Rem said, "You must plant both kinds of seeds just as Mokween tells you to.

"Ugh!" Lisbet groans, as she holds away the fish.

Then you will have delicious food in August. In the winter you can grind up the dried corn for corn meal. Then you can make suppawn."

Mokween told the children to dig the ground and make little hills about a foot apart. Then he did something that seemed very strange. He handed Lisbet a spoiled fish. She held her nose, but Rem smiled and said, "Put it into this first hill. Then add a few kernels of corn. The fish will help the corn to grow."

Lisbet made a face. "The fish smells bad. Why doesn't Mokween do this job for me?"

"Indian men don't plant gardens," said Rem. "They think that job is for women."

After the corn was planted, Teunis asked, "What shall we do with the pumpkin seeds?"

"Plant them between the hills of corn," said Mokween. "Pumpkins grow best in the shade. The corn leaves will shade them."

Later, Rem helped Lisbet dig up the roots of wildflowers for her special garden. Next year she was proud of her violets and wild roses.

DO YOU KNOW—

1. What Mother and Lisbet planted in the garden near the river? What the wood from the trees was to be used for?

2. Why the Indian boy got bear's grease for his Dutch friends?

3. What kinds of seeds Mokween brought to the family? How the Indians made their soil rich for growing vegetables?

THINGS TO DO

Talk about the reason why Mokween did not plant the garden for his Dutch friends. Do people today have ideas about what is men's work and what is women's work?

The settlers build a fort. They will need it for protection if they are attacked.

14: At Home in the New World

All the Dutch families soon had homes. They planted their gardens. Then the men had another big job. They were to build a fort. Rem and the other soldiers helped. So did the sailors from the *New Netherland.*

Fort Orange was a small fort. It had four corners. Each corner was built out like a little pointed room. From these pointed rooms, soldiers could see all around the fort.

"The fort will be a good place to store food for you to eat until your gardens are grown," said Rem. "When trappers begin bringing us furs, your father will work at the fort. The furs will be stored there until ships are ready to carry them to the Fatherland. The goods we shall trade for furs will be kept there."

"Why do the Indians want to sell furs for goods instead of money?" asked Teunis.

"The Indians don't know about our kind of money," said Rem. "Their money is strings of wampum beads."

"I don't see why those little beads should be worth anything," said Teunis.

"They are worth something because they are hard to make," said Rem. "The white beads are chipped out from conch shells. The black or purple ones are made from the inside of the shells of hard-shelled clams. The black beads are worth twice as much as the white.

"It is hard work to make these tiny beads. You must remember that the Indians have only stone knives to use. Even when the beads are chipped out, they aren't done. Holes must be bored through them. Wampum is usually strung on leather strings and made into bands or belts.

"Indians wear wampum as rich people in the Fatherland wear jewelry. Besides, the designs made with the beads sometimes are like words in our books. They tell things that the Indians want to remember.

"The Indians feel that wampum is important. Of course, they want the iron goods and cloth we have to trade with them. But they like a little wampum added to every bargain. Then they think that the bargain is fair."

At this time Skipper May was the governor of the settlement. The settlers liked and trusted him. He stayed with them as long as he could. In July he got ready to sail away. "I must visit the people in our other settlements," he said. "Adriaen Tienpont will be your governor while I am gone. I will leave sixteen soldiers to protect Fort Orange. Daniel Van Krieckebeeck will be in charge of the soldiers and the fur trade.

"You have a fine settlement. I shall tell everyone how well your corn is growing."

The corn was growing well, and so were the other vegetables. When the corn in Kip Teunissen's garden was a foot high, Mokween brought another gift. It was a gourdful of beans. "You must plant them around the cornstalks," said Mokween. "Bean plants need something to cling to. They will cling to the cornstalks. You will have green beans later in the summer."

"Oh, how I wish we had some fresh vegetables now!" cried Lisbet. Mokween smiled, then he darted away into the woods. His quick goings and comings no longer surprised the children. They were getting used to Mokween's ways.

He came back as quickly as he had gone. He was carrying his mother's big basket woven of reeds. In the basket were ears of young corn. There were two large yellow vegetables with long, crooked necks. The Dutch children had never before seen this kind of vegetable. "It's summer squash," said Rem.

Mokween set down his basket and began building a fire near the shore. Teunis and Lisbet helped to bring large chunks of wood. As the flames died down, these large chunks kept burning slowly. Mokween pushed ears of corn under the glowing wood. The roasting ears were still wearing their husks. He left them in the hot ashes.

Then the children began playing tag and leapfrog on the sandy beach. Mokween could run faster than Lisbet or Teunis, but they were quicker and stronger than they used to be. "If you live here long, you will be strong as Indians," said Mokween.

Soon it was time to go back to the fire. The roasting corn smelled delicious.

The Indians used wampum and pretty shells as we use money and jewelry.

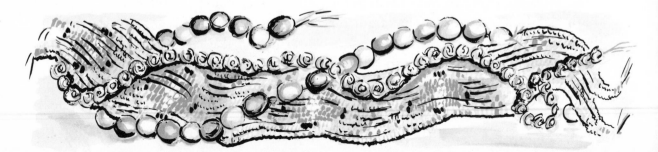

Mokween shows his friends how Indians cook. Do you know what vegetables he gave them?

"Now I will roast the squash," said Mokween. He put the squash into the hot ashes and added a little wood to the fire. Then the children had one more game of leapfrog.

"Call your father and mother," said Mokween. "We have a surprise for them." Father was chopping trees and Mother was knitting some blue stockings for Teunis. But they both came gladly to try the new food.

If you have ever eaten roast corn, you know how good it is. As the family had no butter, they sprinkled salt on the corn. They held the hot ears by the husks. The squash was harder to handle. But everybody thought it was so good that burnt fingers didn't matter.

"Why do you have corn to eat, while ours is still growing?" asked Lisbet.

"We planted ours in May," said Mokween. "Yours was planted in June."

"Is it too late to plant some squash?" asked Mother.

"Let's try it and see what happens," said Father.

Mokween was the children's best Indian friend, but not the only one. The Dutch and Walloon boys and girls had many Indian friends. They were learning Indian words, and the Indian children were learning Dutch words. The children could speak together better than the grownups. Bastiaen Krol and Rem were the only grownups who could speak easily with the Indians. The *wilden* trusted these men and came to them with their troubles. But Bastiaen was having trouble teaching the Christian religion to the Indians. They did not understand the Bible stories.

The Krankenbezoeker said to the children in the settlement, "I am glad you are friendly with the Indian children. They trust you and soon they will want to learn your religion. Then I will help them to learn. It is easier to teach children than grownups."

109

Sometimes he would sit near the children while they were playing. He often had a special treat for all the boys and girls. His wife made the kind of fried cakes that everybody in the Fatherland liked. The other women thought they could not make these cakes, because they had no lard to fry them in. But the Krankenbezoeker's wife used bear's grease instead. The New World fried cakes tasted different, but they were good all the same.

The big pockets of Bastiaen Krol's long black coat were often bulging with these good fried cakes. As he talked with the children, he sometimes said in a sad voice, "Oh, how I wish I had some fried cakes for you." Then he would make believe to look through the pockets of his coat. Of course, before long his hand would come out full of fried cakes. The

children learned to call these cakes *Krol-yers*. To this day we give them the same name, except that we spell it *c-r-u-l-l-e-r-s*.

With cruller crumbs on their mouths, the children would go back to their play. They played hide-and-seek just as you do. The woods had wonderful places for hiding. The trouble was that the Indian children knew the woods so well. They always knew where the Dutch children might be hiding. So the Dutch children always lost. One day Mokween said, "This is not fair. Let's have Indian children and Dutch children on each team. Then everybody will have a chance to win."

The Dutch girls loved to play with the papoose dolls the Indian girls made. These dolls were usually made of wood, and dressed in deerskin clothes.

"How I wish I had some fried cakes for you," Bastiaen Krol teases the children, as he reaches in his bulging pockets. Do you know what games the others are playing?

The Indian girls were interested in the dolls of the Dutch girls. They counted all the white petticoats these dolls wore. "Your dolls wear so many clothes, and so do you!" cried one little Indian girl. "Why do you need so many?"

"It's the way we dress in the Fatherland," said Lisbet. "That's all I know about it." Yet sometimes Lisbet wished that she did not have to wear so many clothes. She liked her red cotton skirt and her little blue jacket. But the weather was so very warm. She left her blue jacket at home now. Sometimes she even took off her little white cap, to let the wind blow through her blond hair.

Teunis wished that he could go without clothing, like the youngest Indian children. At least, he thought, he might dress like the older boys, with only a little apron of deerskin. But Mother said, "My children must keep the Dutch ways. You must wear your breeches, Teuni. You may leave off your jacket, but be sure you have a clean shirt. No, you needn't wear your hat or your shoes, except on Sunday. You will need them when winter comes."

As the days went by, the children from the Old World became more and more friendly with the children of the New World. They were happy as they played together in the hot sunshine and the cool shade.

By August, Kip Teunissen's family had corn to eat every day. Sometimes Mother put the ears into a kettle of water bubbling over the fire. Sometimes the children roasted the corn, as Mokween had taught them to do. Many other vegetables were ripe.

Father brings home enough meat for everyone.

As always, there was plenty of fish and meat. Perch and catfish could be caught in the North River. There were wild turkeys and ducks in the woods. Mokween's father had shown Kip the best places for hunting deer. When Kip brought home a deer, there was enough meat for everybody in the settlement.

There were blueberries and blackberries and red raspberries for dessert. What a fine New World this was!

DO YOU KNOW—

1. Three reasons why the men were building a fort?

2. Why wampum beads were worth so much to the Indians? What the beads were used for?

3. How Mokween helped the Dutch family have a meal of fresh vegetables?

4. Why Krankenbezoeker Krol thought the children could help him with his special work?

THINGS TO DO

Talk about differences in clothing worn by the Dutch and the Indian children.

The winter house must be built before the cold snows and icy winds of winter come.

15: Father Builds a Winter Home

It seemed strange when Kip Teunissen said, on one of the hottest days, "We must begin thinking about winter. We can't live in a wigwam when the snow begins falling and bitter cold comes. I have an idea for a big, strong house. But I'm afraid I can't finish it before winter. I'll get the cellar done, at least."

Mother looked shocked. "You mean we'll live in a cellar!" she cried.

"Don't worry, Johanna," said Father gently. "I'll make sure that we are all comfortable. You just wait and see."

The first thing Father did was to measure a large level place near the wigwam. He used stakes of wood to mark out a space twenty-four feet square. Inside this square he began digging a deep hole. Some of the other men helped him. Later he would help them build their homes. Rem helped, too.

Down, down, down went the hole. At last it was so deep that Father's head didn't show over the edge. Lisbet would go nearer and peer down into the hole with a worried look. But there was Father, in the far corner!

Before long, every wall was straight and smooth. Every corner was as square as square could be. "But how damp it will be!" said Mother, in a worried voice.

"Not at all!" boomed Father. "It will be lined with good stout wood. Here's where we use those fine tree trunks we cut down when we first came."

Father took the smaller trunks. He chopped away at them until there were four sides with square corners. He planed the sides to make them smooth and even. Then he and Rem laid one squared log beside another on the earthen floor of the cellar. The logs lay as close together as they could be. Now there would be a good floor for Mother to walk on. But what about the walls?

The same thing was done for the walls. Squared logs were placed side by side all along the walls. These logs reached about four feet higher than the edge of the cellar. Father left a space for a door at one side of the log wall. He put this opening in the south wall. "The Indians say that's where we should put it," said Father. "The cold winter winds don't often come from the south."

"But we'll have a door, won't we?" asked Mother.

"Of course," laughed Father, "but some cold always comes in around a door."

"How shall we get down into our cellar?" asked Mother.

"We'll jump, won't we, Father?" said Teunis. "It's just deep enough for a good, exciting jump."

"For you, Teunis," said Father, "but I don't think Mother would enjoy jumping. I'm going to build steps down into our new house."

"How about a roof?" asked Lisbet. "We haven't any tiles. What shall we use?"

"We shall use planks cut from the largest tree trunks," said Father. "Then I'll cover the planks with pieces of earth and grass, cut from the meadow. These will make a firm covering. They will soak up the rain, so that it won't drip in on us."

Soon Father had a good solid roof on the cellar home. Lisbet wanted to move in at once. "Not yet," said Mother. "It's still warm enough to live in our wigwam and cook outside. Father and Teunis will have to make us some furniture.

That fine big cellar needs more furniture than we now have."

"Did you say the cellar was fine?" asked Father, with a wink.

"Yes, I did," said Mother, smiling. "I'm sorry I said I'd hate to live in a cellar."

Father and Teunis went to work on furniture for the new home. They split and planed wood from the biggest trees Father had cut down. They built a fine, sturdy table for Mother to work on. The family would eat from this same table.

The next things they made were two benches. On these the family would sit while eating.

Mother liked the furniture, but she had one question: "Where will Father sit

Teunis and his father are making a table for their new home. Do you know what other things they made?

when he comes home tired? A bench without a back won't be very comfortable if he wants to rest."

Father and Teunis didn't say a word. They had a surprise for Mother. Two chairs with backs and arm rests had been made. Rem had them hidden at the fort.

Next Kip began sawing long, heavy planks for the beds. There would be a big bed for Father and Mother, and two small ones for the children.

At last the furniture was all done, or so Teunis thought. But Lisbet had an idea. "We need a little table for our Bible," she said. So Father and Teunis made a small, three-legged table for the big Bible that had been brought from the Fatherland.

By this time, the days were becoming shorter. The nights were cool, and sometimes there were days of cold rain and wind. The settlers began to worry about the long winter ahead. "We can get furs

Father helps Teunis cover the fireplace with mortar. It will be a kind of fireproofing.

for clothing before the weather gets really cold," said Rem.

"But how can we keep our homes warm?" asked Mother.

"Some of the men are building fireplaces of wood," said Father. "They daub the wood with clay to make it fireproof. But I don't like that idea. What if the clay should fall out? There might be a bad fire."

"I know what we can do," said Rem. "We can mix lime and sand with water. When this mixture dries, it's a very hard *mortar*."

"But where can we find lime?" asked Father.

"The Indians leave oyster shells in mounds. We can get lime by burning the shells. I know the Indians won't mind.

After this, the work on the fireplace and chimney went forward fast. Teunis learned how to mix just enough sand, lime, and water to make the mortar. It was his job to daub the mortar on the wood. This was as much fun as playing.

When the mortar dried, the wood had a strong, fireproof coating. The fireplace and the chimney were finished before the first cold little snowflakes began falling.

DO YOU KNOW—

1. Why the family couldn't live in a wigwam all winter? Why Father was planning a cellar home?

2. How the cellar home was to be kept warm and dry? How the roof was made?

3. What furniture Father and Teunis made?

4. How the fireplace was made so that it would be safe?

THINGS TO DO

Talk about all the ways in which the new home was different from yours. How was it like yours?

A new baby in the Le Roy home brings all the settlers out to visit and help.

16: Autumn at Fort Orange

Many pleasant and exciting things happened before the settlers' winter houses were done. In one of the Walloon homes, a baby boy was born. He was named Jean Le Roy. What a buzz of excitement went through the settlement! All the mothers brought food to the Le Roy house. The children begged for a look at the new baby. Quietly they tiptoed into the room where he lay beside his mother. They smiled at his little red, puckered-up face.

But now everybody had a worry. Who would baptize the baby? He must be brought up a Christian, and of course the first thing to do was to baptize him. People went to see Krankenbezoeker Krol. "I wish I could baptize the baby," he said, "but I cannot. The Church Council at Amsterdam gave me my orders."

Kip Teunissen thought a long time. Then he said, "Perhaps you should go back to the Fatherland when the *New Netherland* sails. You could ask the Church Council to let you baptize babies. There will be many children born in the New World."

Joost's father then spoke. "My oldest girl Ytie wants to get married. She and Evert Ryersen are engaged. You should ask the Church Council to let you marry young people, too."

Bastiaen Krol said, "Perhaps I ought to do what you say. But I couldn't get back here before spring. Would it be right to leave you without a comforter of the sick all that time?"

"I think so," said Kip. "Most of us are young and strong. We shall not have much sickness, I hope. We will say our own prayers while you are gone. We will read our Bibles."

"But who will teach the children?" cried Lisbet.

Krankenbezoeker Krol said, "When I come back, I will start a good school for you all. You can study twice as hard, to make up for lost time. Now I must do the best thing for the whole settlement. I will ask our governor if he thinks I ought to go."

A few days later, the *New Netherland* dropped anchor near Fort Orange. Everyone was glad to see Skipper May again. He and Bastiaen Krol had a long talk. They decided that Bastiaen should return to the Fatherland, to see the Church Council.

The ship lay at anchor off Fort Orange only a few days. Hundreds of furs were put aboard, to be sold in the Fatherland.

Some of the furs had been brought from far away by trappers the winter before. Others were skins of animals trapped by the settlers or the Indians nearby. There were people who would not wait until winter, when the furs would be best. They were in a hurry for the things they would get in payment.

Besides furs, the ship would take the settlers' letters to the Fatherland.

Mother wrote a letter to Grandma, and Lisbet added a note. It took her a long time to write this note. It was hard to learn in the schools of those days, because they were not very pleasant. Children didn't have interesting picture or story books. They had to treat the teacher like a king or a queen. Some teachers used cruel punishments.

In the Fatherland Teunis and Lisbet had gone to different schools, as boys and girls always did. They had been lucky in having kind teachers. In fact, they were lucky to have any education. Some of the children in the settlement could not read or write at all. Some of the grownups could hardly write their names.

The children of Fort Orange liked Bastiaen Krol so well that they all wanted

Furs are loaded on the ship, as Bastiaen Krol talks with Skipper May about returning to Holland.

The Krankenbezoeker is off to Holland! Everyone gathers to wave good-by to him.

him to teach them. They were sorry they could have no school until spring.

They all went to say good-by to him on the day the ship was to sail. Their parents were sad, too. There was even a sad smell in the air. "What is it, Rem?" asked Lisbet.

"It's smoke from a brush fire," said Rem. "The Indians are hunting. They build brush fires to try to drive the animals toward the hunters."

"I like the smell of the smoke," said Lisbet, "but it makes me feel all the more sad."

"Cheer up, dear," said Mother. "See how brave the Krankenbezoeker's wife and children are. Let's ask them to our home for supper. A good way to forget sadness is to do something helpful for other people."

DO YOU KNOW—

1. Why the settlers were happy when Jean Le Roy was born? Why they were worried?
2. Why Bastiaen Krol decided to go back to the Fatherland?
3. Why Mother and Lisbet waited so long before sending letters to the Fatherland?
4. What schools were like in the Fatherland in the days when the first Dutch settlers came here?

THINGS TO DO

1. Discuss and compare the different things we send to and receive from Europe today and the things the Dutch settlers sent to and received from the Fatherland.
2. Talk about ways of sending mail to Europe today, and in the days of the Dutch settlers. What is the greatest difference?
3. Visit a museum or a library to find out what letters looked like at the time about which you are reading.
4. Compare the schools of today with the Dutch schools that Teunis and Lisbet went to.

With the new sloop the settlers can easily visit their friends along the river.

17: Fort Orange Becomes Beavertown

After the *New Netherland* had sailed, the people of Fort Orange felt far away from everybody else in the New World and the Old World. Joost's father and two other men decided to make a small sailing ship. It was called a *sloop*. It could sail on the North River more easily than ocean-going ships could. Now the people could send goods and messages to Manhattan in four days or less, and bring goods from Manhattan whenever ships from the Fatherland came there.

Of course, the sloop could not be used in the winter. Then the North River might be frozen solid. Or ice cakes might be floating in the water. These ice cakes were sometimes big enough to wreck a small ship.

The other men kept on building their homes. These houses were made of logs or of split wood with the bark left on. They were thatched with reeds. Lisbet and Teunis thought their cellar home was going to be the best home in Fort Orange.

"It's a good thing that the house is almost done," said Kip one day. "Things are getting busy at the fort. I'll have to spend more and more time there."

"Why do you have to do so much of the work?" asked Mother. "Daniel is in charge of the goods at the fort."

"Daniel is in charge, but he doesn't want to work," said Father. "When I need help, he says he's in charge of the sixteen soldiers. I guess Daniel is a boss, not a worker."

"What do you do at the fort?" asked Teunis.

"I can show you better than I can tell you," said Father. "Would you and Lisbet like to go to the fort with me to-morrow?"

"Oh, yes," said both children.

Early the next day, the three went to the fort. The front room was used for buying furs. Here Indian or Dutch trappers brought skins of beavers, minks, and other animals. There were scales for weighing the skins.

In a storeroom there were goods used to trade for furs. Iron kettles were stacked up, one inside another. Sharp knives of different sizes lay in boxes on the shelves. There were axes in one corner.

Small boxes held fishhooks and needles. On a hook hung many strings of wampum.

There were huge rolls of cloth in the storeroom. This was a coarse cotton cloth called *duffels*. The Indians liked to wear duffels in summer, as it was cooler than deerskin. Besides, it was easier than deerskin for the Indian mothers to sew. Some rolls of duffels were red, some were blue, and some brown.

"Don't you have guns to trade with the Indians?" Teunis asked Father. "I should think they would want something better than bows and arrows."

"They would like guns and gunpowder," said Father, "but I don't think it's good to let the Indians have these things. It's all right as long as they are our friends. But suppose the Indians should get angry at us? They might use our own guns and powder against us.

"Some traders have given the Indians rum for their furs. I don't like this idea. Indians are not used to rum. When they drink it, they fight. They might want to fight us, and then where would we be?"

Father saw that Lisbet looked scared. "Don't worry, dear," he said. "The In-

The children visit the fort's storeroom. They see many furs. What else do they see?

dians are friendly. We just want to keep them that way. For this reason, we are fair in our trade. Some traders cheat the Indians. They say the furs weigh less than they do. They give bad goods in trade. They don't give good wampum to make the bargain fair. They give beads of glass or stone instead of the good sea-shell wampum. Sometimes they give loose wampum beads instead of strings. Perhaps the beads are not even pierced so that they can be strung."

Just then Father had to go into the front room. Two Indians had brought furs to sell. They had come from the north, where winter comes earlier. They had beaver and otter skins to sell.

Father weighed the skins carefully. He told the Indians how much the Dutch West India Company would pay for their furs. One Indian said he wanted his pay in fishhooks, needles, and a kettle. The other wanted an axe and some duffels.

Father went into the storeroom and brought out a big iron kettle. The Indian said, "I find out if it is good kettle." He went outside and filled the kettle with spring water. When he came back, water was dripping from a hole in the bottom of the kettle. "Kettle no good," said the Indian.

Father brought out three more kettles. At last, the Indian found one that did not leak.

Then Father went into the storeroom for a roll of red duffels. When the Indian saw it, he frowned and said," No, no. Not red. If I wear red, deer see me. My enemies see me. I must have dark color."

Father got some brown duffels, and the Indian seemed pleased. Then Father

"Kettle no good," the Indian tells Kip. He wants a good trade for the furs he brings to the fort and a string of wampum to make the bargain fair.

Dutch trappers brought their furs to the fort too.

gave each Indian the other things he needed. He added a string of wampum for each, to make the bargain fair.

Next, a Dutch trapper came in. He had lived with the Indians for three years. He had four beaver skins to sell. Two were golden brown and two were as dark as a chestnut.

"These furs are worth two *guilders* each," said the trapper.

A guilder was a silver coin, about the size of a fifty-cent piece. The Dutch used it as we use a dollar, but it would buy much more. Today these beaver skins might cost from twenty-five to forty dollars.

"The Company will not pay you two guilders each," said Kip. "These beavers were trapped while the weather was still warm. If you had waited until winter, the fur would have been better. I will give you a guilder and a half for each. That makes six guilders."

The man grumbled a little, but at last he said, "All right. I need a good skinning knife. I'll take the rest of my money's worth in gunpowder and wampum."

Gunpowder was sold by the handful. When a group of hunters needed more gunpowder, they always sent the man with the biggest hands to buy it. This trapper had big hands. "What are you going to do with so much gunpowder?" asked Kip. "I hope you aren't selling it to the Indians."

"I can do what I want with it," said the trapper. And with that, he was gone.

121

"Father," asked Teunis, "how do you know what to give the traders for the skins?"

"I have to think how much money our goods are worth. Then I give the traders enough goods to make a fair price."

Just then an Indian came in with four mink skins. One was pale brown, one yellow brown, and the others were almost black. Down the back of each skin ran a darker stripe. Lisbet touched the fur. "Oo, how soft!" she cried. "I like mink the best of all."

After Father had paid the Indian with an axe and some wampum, Lisbet asked, "Why do you pay more for beaver than for this lovely mink?"

"Beaver is a fur that the Company wants very much," said Father. "Much beaver fur is used in making men's hats. The fur is cut off and pressed into a kind of *felt*. Hats made of beaver are called beavers. They are worn by rich men, who will pay high prices for them."

Just then Daniel Van Krieckebeeck came into the room. The men went into a room that the children had not seen before. Here piles of furs were stored. These furs would be sent to the Fatherland the next time a ship sailed. The new furs were stored in their proper places. As the men left the room, Daniel locked the door behind him. "We have many guilders' worth of furs here," he said to Kip. "I am glad we have sixteen good soldiers to protect our storeroom. If these furs were stolen, the Company would blame you and me."

As the children walked home with Father late that afternoon, Lisbet said, "Where do beavers come from?"

"I know," said Teunis. "Mokween took me to see a beaver dam last week. Let's ask him to take us both tomorrow."

Mokween was glad to show the children a beaver dam. Off they went the next day to a stream in the woods. The beavers were building a dam across the stream.

Lisbet looked at the beavers, working so hard. "I like beavers," she said. "I am sorry we have to sell their fur. What can we do for them? I know—let's call our settlement Beavertown. The fort can still be called Fort Orange, but our town can be named for the beavers."

When Lisbet told her idea to her parents, they liked it. They told their friends. Soon the settlement was called *Beverwyck*, which is the Dutch way of saying Beavertown.

DO YOU KNOW—

1. Why some of the settlers built a sloop?
2. What goods were used in trade with the Indians? Why the Indians wanted each kind of goods?
3. What kinds of goods Father did not want to give the Indians for their furs?
4. Why beaver was worth so much?
5. Why the Indians who came to the fort did not speak as well as Mokween?

THINGS TO DO

1. Talk about the kind of man Kip Teunissen was. Was he a good man to be trading with the Indians? Was he a good father? Was he a good person to be a settler in a new land? Tell the reasons for your ideas about him. How was he different from Daniel Van Krieckebeeck? How was he different from the trapper who came to the fort?
2. Collect pictures of beavers and beaver homes. Try to get samples of furs of the kind that were sold at Fort Orange. Read about how beavers live.

122

The house is finished! Now Kip Teunissen's family will be snug for the winter.

18: St. Martin's Eve

The weather was getting chilly. Kip Teunissen's wigwam was cold in the morning. He and Teunis wanted to do the moving into the cellar as a surprise for Mother and Lisbet. One bright day they had their chance.

Lisbet and Mother had gone to Maritje's house for the midday meal. When they got back, late in the afternoon, Father said, "Come see your cellar home."

Mother stooped down and went through the opening. The door was just high enough for Lisbet. Down the steps they went. What a sight met their eyes!

The cellar room was warm and bright with the light from a roaring fire. Before the fire were two fine big chairs with high backs. A table stood in the middle of the room, with a bench at each side. Pots and bowls were in the cupboard near the fireplace. The big bed in the far corner was made up with the featherbed

and the large blankets and quilts. The children's smaller beds were neatly spread with smaller quilts.

Mother and Lisbet were too happy to speak at first. Father said, "Aren't you glad we got moved before St. Martin's Eve?"

St. Martin's Eve was a holiday that children of long ago enjoyed as you enjoy Halloween. Ghosts and goblins roamed the earth on St. Martin's Eve—or so people believed.

"Dutch ghosts won't cross the ocean to roam around in these woods," said Teunis. "It was fun trying to keep away from them in the Fatherland, but it was scary, too. I won't be scared here."

"Why not?" asked Lisbet. "There could be Indian ghosts behind all the big trees. Ghosts love crossroads, you know. They could be waiting where the Indian trails cross our path to the fort."

123

"I don't know about ghosts," said Mother. "I never saw one, but maybe I shall someday. I don't think they will hurt a good person."

"Are we going to have the special St. Martin's Eve foods?" asked Lisbet.

"Yes," said Mother. "I'll make pancakes and cook a fine goose. Mokween's uncle shot it and Mokween sold it to me. I paid for it with two big needles that his mother wanted."

On St. Martin's Eve the goose was roasting slowly on the spit over the fire. Suddenly Mother got an idea. "We must ask Rem to our feast. Teuni, will you run down to the fort and see if he can come?"

Teunis started up the stairs. Then sud-denly he stopped. Lisbet was watching him. "He's scared," she thought. "He thinks an Indian ghost might hurt him. Poor Teuni! I'll go with him. A ghost wouldn't hurt both of us, I'm sure."

"Wait a minute, Teuni!" cried Lisbet. "I'd like to go with you. May I, please?"

How happy Teunis looked! Sometimes he thought girls weren't much good, but now—anyhow, Lisbet was fine. They started out together, walking rather fast. The way was almost as dark as night. Everything was as usual until they got to the place where the trail to the river crossed their path.

As they drew near the crossroad, they saw something coming toward them.

The something moved silently. It was not so tall as a man. "Maybe ghosts are shorter than people," Teunis whispered. What should the children do? They couldn't turn back. They must take the message to Rem. So they went forward, hoping that the something would disappear. Instead, they heard Mokween's owl call.

Lisbet was so happy that she ran up and hugged Mokween. Teunis said, "I knew it was you all the time. Lisbet thought you were a ghost."

"Why should I be a ghost?" he asked.

"This is St. Martin's Eve," said Teunis. "It is a special night for ghosts in the Fatherland."

"We do not have special nights for ghosts," said Mokween. "Spirits of our great men are always near us. Spirits of birds and animals are here. They do not hurt us. Sometimes they help us."

"Is it a ghost?" the children wonder.

"How about spirits of the Dutch?" asked Teunis.

"I don't think they come here," said Mokween. "My mother and my uncle and all my family have never seen a Dutch ghost. If they had, they would have told me."

"Why have you come here tonight, Mokween?" asked Lisbet.

"I was coming to your house," said Mokween. "My mother made some moccasins for you. She used her new steel needle for sewing them."

Lisbet's moccasins had designs in red, showing stars and a sun. The ones for Teunis had deer painted in blue. The children sat down then and there to try on their moccasins.

"How pretty!" said Lisbet.

"How good they feel!" said Teunis.

"Come to the fort with us," Lisbet said. "We have to ask Rem for supper." Then she had an idea, "Why don't you come to supper, too, Mokween?"

Mokween shook his head. The chil-

What fun to go sledding down the snow-covered hills! The Dutch children had never seen such hills.

dren urged him, but he was too shy to come into their house. "We'll save you a piece of the goose, for tomorrow," Lisbet promised.

At the fort they found Rem. "We hope you're not on guard tonight," Teunis said. "You must have some of our St. Martin's goose."

Rem was free to go with the children, and soon they were in the cellar home. Later, when everyone was full of pancakes and goose, Teunis asked for the breastbone of the big bird. The breastbone was supposed to show what kind of winter was coming. A hard breastbone meant a very cold winter. A soft breastbone meant mild weather. If the breastbone was very white, it meant much snow.

Teunis scraped off the last bits of meat, and then felt carefully of the bone. This breastbone was hard and white.

The next morning, Teunis came clattering down the steps into the cellar home. "The goose was right!" he cried. And sure enough, the world was covered with a blanket of beautiful snow.

Kip Teunissen had an idea. "I will make sleds for Lisbet and Teunis," he said to Mother. "Then they can coast down the hills."

"How can you make a sled without iron for the runners?" asked Mother.

"I will use the trunks of saplings," said Father. "I'll take small ones that can be bent, so that the runners will curve up in front. I will take off the bark of the saplings, to make them slippery."

When the sleds were done, the children were excited. How they loved coasting down the smooth hillsides! Some other Dutch and Walloon fathers made sleds for their children. "It's better here than in the Fatherland," said Teunis. "There we had no hills for coasting."

He was quiet for a minute, looking at his father. Then he said, "Father, would you mind if I gave my sled to Mokween? He hasn't any nails, so he can't make one for himself."

"Of course you may give Mokween your sled," said Father. "I will help you make another for yourself, if you want me to."

Before long, the weather turned very cold. The Dutch and the Walloons had never known such cold weather. Some of the mothers had already made fur coats and caps for their families and themselves. The fathers had brought in furs, after the Indians had shown them how to trap the animals that lived nearby. The Indians taught the settlers about the ways of the fur-bearing animals and their hiding places.

The Dutch West India Company allowed its settlers to trap as many animals as they wished. They might use the furs for their families or sell them to the Company. Only the Company might send furs to the Fatherland to be sold. The profits were big and the Company was growing richer.

The settlers used the cheaper furs for their own clothing. They trapped the skunk with its clean white stripe. Often they trapped the small animal that the Indians called the musquash. We call this animal a muskrat today. The mothers in the settlement used this fur to make warm hats and gloves for their children.

Kip Teunissen had not done any trapping. He had been too busy at the fort. Now, few trappers came through the snow to the fort, so Father had time to go out trapping with the other men. But before he had caught anything, the family had a fine surprise.

One very cold day, Mokween came to his friends' cellar home with a big black bearskin. "It is for you," he told Mother. "My uncle shot the bear."

"He should sell the skin to the Company," said Father. "It is not fair for us to take such a fine gift."

"Please take it," said Mokween. "Mother can make warm coats for Lisbet and Teunis." And that is just what Mother did. The children looked like little black bears themselves, in their thick, furry coats. How cozy they felt!

DO YOU KNOW—

1. Why the children were excited about St. Martin's Eve?

2. Why Lisbet went with Teunis to the fort?

3. What Mokween brought for the children?

4. What Mokween thought about ghosts? Does his idea make you think of any of Cokoe's adventures?

5. How Teunis proved that he was a good friend of Mokween's? Is it more friendly to give away something you want or something you don't want?

THINGS TO DO

1. Teunis was scared on St. Martin's Eve. Was there ever a time when you were scared in almost the same way? If so, write about it. Did somebody else help you to get over your scare, or did you help yourself?

2. Talk about Lisbet. What kind of girl was she? Do you know a girl like her?

How big and warm the new bearskin coats are!

It's the first St. Nicholas Eve in New Netherland! The family is busy and happy.

19: *The Christmas Holidays*

A long period of holidays was drawing near. It lasted from St. Nicholas Eve, December 5, to Twelfth Night, January 6. St. Nicholas Eve was a favorite holiday of children. Then it was that they put their shoes by the fireplace for the Saint to fill with sweets. Bad children got nothing but a rod or a switch—at least so Lisbet and Teunis had heard. But they had never known a boy or a girl who was sad on St. Nicholas Day. Maybe their friends were all good. Or maybe St. Nicholas forgave bad children at the last minute.

There were people who believed that St. Nicholas did not decide about this question. These people said that he had a wife, called Mollie Grietje. She told

him what each child was to get for a St. Nicholas gift.

As you may know, St. Nicholas was the Dutch name for Santa Claus. Dutch children looked for him on December 5 instead of on Christmas.

Before the first St. Nicholas Eve in Beavertown, Mother said to Lisbet and Teunis, "My children have been very good ever since they came to the New World. I'm afraid, though, that St. Nicholas will not be able to bring you as much as usual. It may be hard for him to find us in our new home."

The other Dutch and Walloon mothers said the same to their children. Yet on the morning of St. Nicholas Day, every child found something good in his shoe.

The mothers had made maple sugar candy. It was soft and smooth, like fudge. Some squares had hickory nuts on top and some had black walnuts.

The fathers had made skates for their children. They had smoothed pieces of bone or deer horn for the runners. They had made straps of tough pieces of deerskin.

The children wanted to try their skates at once. Teunis remembered a frozen pond in the woods that Mokween had shown him. He and his friends went there right after breakfast.

Some Indian children heard the shouts of the skaters. They came running to the pond. These boys and girls had never before seen skates. They watched with wonder as their friends glided over the ice. They wanted to try skating too. But how could they fasten skates to moccasins?

Lisbet looked at Mokween. He was standing proud and silent, away from everybody else. He would not even look at his Dutch friends.

Lisbet whispered to Teunis, "Mokween's feelings are hurt. He thinks that we have something we have not shared with him. He has shared everything he could with us. Let him put on your shoes and skates, Teuni. You can wear his moccasins while he tries skating."

When Teunis told Mokween this plan, the Indian boy shook his head. Then he changed his mind. He smiled shyly and took off his moccasins. He pushed his narrow, brown feet into Teunis's shoes. When he tried to stand on the skates, he almost fell. He looked angry, but then he smiled again and let Teunis help him.

The other Dutch and Walloon children saw what Teunis had done. They too lent their shoes and their skates to their Indian friends. Then they all tried at once to teach the *wilden* to skate.

This was great fun. There was many a spill at first. The children from the Fatherland couldn't help enjoying their friends' spills. The Indian boys and girls could run faster than they. They could shoot arrows straighter and farther.

Merry laughter echoes through the woods as the Dutch children test their new skates on the frozen pond.

They could play longer without getting tired. They knew all sorts of things about the woods. But they had to be taught how to skate.

After a few hours of trying, the Indian children were able to stand straight on their skates. They could take long strokes as their teachers did. The teachers were pleased with themselves.

One day Father said, "I got a beautiful beaver today. This one I shall not sell to the Company. You shall have it, Johanna. It will make a fine muff for keeping your pretty hands warm. When we lived in the Fatherland, I never could afford a gift like this for you."

Perhaps this gift came at Christmas time, but Christmas to the Dutch was not usually a time of gift-giving. It was a quiet, holy day. Without Krankenbezoeker Krol, the people of Beavertown could not have a service of prayers and Bible readings. However, they met together in one of the larger homes and sang the holy songs of Christmas.

Both the Dutch and the Walloons missed their church. How glad they would be when their good Bastiaen Krol got back to them! Then the services would seem like church. And someday, when they had more time, they would build a little church.

New Year's Day also was a quiet holiday with the Dutch. It was a day of thanksgiving, and the Dutch were truly thankful. They were thankful for their safe voyage. They were thankful that nobody was sick, in spite of the cold, cold weather. They were thankful that they had enough to eat. They knew that the Pilgrims at Plymouth had nearly starved

during their first winter. Many had been very ill and had died. They were thankful that the *wilden* were friendly. Above all, they were thankful that their children would grow up in this broad, beautiful country. Here there was room enough for everybody.

The last holiday of the Christmas season was Twelfth Night, or Three Kings' Night. Father brought hemlock branches to decorate the cellar home. Mother made waffles for the children and their friends. Her waffle iron would hold only one waffle, so it took a long time to make enough for all the children.

As the last guest went up the steps of the cellar home, Lisbet said to her mother, "This has been a wonderful Christmas season. It has been as good as it was in the Fatherland. Thank you for everything."

DO YOU KNOW—

1. What the Dutch children got on St. Nicholas Day? Who Mollie Grietje was?

2. How long the Dutch Christmas season lasted? What the special holidays were?

THINGS TO DO

Discuss the difference between the Dutch Christmas and our holidays at the same time of year. Visit the library to find books that tell about holidays in other lands.

As the snow melts, many trappers bring their furs to the fort for trading.

20: *Spring in Beavertown*

The children, like everyone else in Beavertown, found the winter long and tiresome. The North River was frozen. No ships could come with news of the Fatherland. No sloops could come with news from Manhattan.

In early spring, there were days of pale sunshine. A soft wind blew from the south. Warm rain fell gently. "Spring is really here," said Lisbet, one rainy evening.

Then next morning, she went out and found a fairyland of ice. The weather had changed suddenly. A cold wind had come from the north. It froze the rain to the branches. It froze the drops into icicles. Now bright sunlight made the ice-covered trees sparkle like jewels.

In a day or two, all the ice had melted from the trees. The weather became warm again. The snow was melting. Under the snow arbutus began growing. Mokween showed Teunis where to find enough for a large bouquet for Mother.

Father was very busy at the fort, these days. Indian and Dutch trappers were coming from their winter camps. They were carrying great loads of skins. "I hope we shall get some ironware and cloth from the Fatherland soon," said Kip. "I have hardly enough goods left to trade for all the furs."

The ice in the North River had now melted. Soon sloops began sailing up the river from Manhattan to Beavertown. The sloops brought goods for trading. The goods had been brought on ships from the Fatherland.

The people on the sloops also brought news. "More people are coming from the

The big day arrives! Here is the ship with their Krankenbezoeker and news from home.

Fatherland," they said. "Most of them are settling on Manhattan. The settlement there is called New Amsterdam. It will soon be the largest settlement, we think. We are going to have a fort to protect us.

"Skipper May is no longer governor of New Netherland. We have a new governor. He will live at New Amsterdam and visit the other settlements. He is leaving Adriaen Tienpont as governor of Beavertown. Daniel Van Krieckebeeck is still in charge of the soldiers."

"But have you any news of Bastiaen Krol?" asked the people of Beavertown.

"Yes," said one of the men from New Amsterdam. "He will be with you soon."

Many of the settlers cried, "Thank God!" They had been afraid their Krankenbezoeker might never come again.

What a wonderful day it was when he reached Beavertown! Men, women, and children flocked to the shore to greet him. The others waited while his own family kissed and hugged him. Then everybody began talking at once. The men said, "God bless you," and some of the women were crying. Jean Le Roy's mother said, "Now at last our baby can be baptized."

Joost's father said, "Now my girl Ytie can be married. Come into our house, Bastiaen. My wife will make you a cup of tea."

In New Netherland, there wasn't much tea. The settlers drank it only on very important days.

"I will have some tea later, thank you," said Bastiaen Krol, "but first I must give people their letters." He began reading the names on the letters. The first one was for Johanna Teunissen. Lisbet took the letter and ran to give it to Mother.

The letter was from Grandma and Grandpa. It brought good news. They

132

were well. They were happy to know that their children and grandchildren were living comfortably in the New World. "Oh, how good to hear from our old home!" said Mother. Her eyes were wet, but she was smiling.

The other settlers had letters, too. Some of them could not read. They asked Bastiaen Krol to read their letters. He had a busy time for a while.

Lisbet could hardly wait to ask him, "Did your ship bring any cows?"

"No, but other ships did," said Bastiaen. "Each cow had a stall to herself and a special servant. Hogs and sheep will soon be coming, too."

"Where are the cows now?" Kip Teunissen asked. He knew how his children and all the others had missed the good rich milk they were used to.

"They're on Manhattan," said Bastiaen. "At first they were unloaded on Nut Island. But there was not enough grass there for so many cows—over a hundred.

So the cows were moved to Manhattan."

"Aren't we going to have any cows?" asked Lisbet. Every child looked as worried as she.

"I'm sure you are," said the Krankenbezoeker, "but I cannot tell you when."

DO YOU KNOW—

1. Why few ships came to the Fatherland in the winter? How the people of Beavertown got news when spring came?

2. What special treat Joost's father offered to Bastiaen Krol? Why everybody was so glad when Krol got back to Beavertown?

3. Why the people of Beavertown were so glad to get letters?

THINGS TO DO

1. If you have ever seen an ice storm, make a painting or a diorama to show how it looked.

2. Ask your mother to show you how to make a rice pudding.

How carefully the precious cows are cared for. On the boat each cow has her own stall and keeper.

21: Lisbet's Happy Birthday

Lisbet's birthday, her second at Beavertown, was coming on the sixteenth of September. "What would you like for a gift?" asked Mother.

"A cow," said Lisbet. "I'm still hungry for milk—or thirsty. I don't know which to say."

"Well, I think I can give you a cow," said Mother, smiling.

Lisbet looked at Mother. Surely Mother had no cow to give her. Yet Mother never said anything that wasn't true. Well, there was nothing to do but wait and see.

The morning of September 16 dawned bright and clear. Mother said, "Lisbet, you needn't do any work today. I will wash the trenchers and clean the hearth.

Lisbet loves her beautiful silver pitcher.

You may go out and play with your friends."

When Lisbet came home, the table was set for dinner. Mother had roasted bobwhites as a special treat. The birds were small, so Mother had roasted two for each of the family. "What you don't eat, you can have cold for supper," she said.

As Lisbet was finishing the last of her dinner, Mother said, "I promised you a cow for your birthday. Here it is." She handed Lisbet a little silver pitcher in the shape of a cow.

"It has belonged to our family for a long time," said Mother. "A rich lady gave it to your grandmother for an engagement present. Grandmother gave it to me when I got engaged. I meant to give it to you when you got engaged, too. But I thought you should have it now, since you wanted a cow so much!"

"Oh, I did, Mother, and I love it! I shall not use it at all until I have some milk to put into it."

"Well, I'm sure you will be able to use it before long," said Mother. "Now run outside and play; this is your day, you know."

As Lisbet stepped outside, she gave a sudden shout. "A ship!" she cried. "A big ship is sailing up the North River."

All the family came to look. Forgetting everything else, Mother and Father joined the other settlers hurrying toward the landing. The first men ashore had this story to tell. "We had bad luck with our cattle on Manhattan. Twenty of them died in the pasture. We think they

Cows arrive in Beavertown! How happy the children are, for now they can have milk and cheese again!

must have eaten some bad weed. So we have brought some of the cows to Beavertown. We think the pasture here will be better for them."

"How will you get the cows ashore?" asked Teunis. Lisbet didn't ask anything. She was too happy to speak.

"We open a door in the side of the ship," said the sailor. "Under this door the longboat is waiting. Then we drive the cows down a ramp into the longboat. We can bring only two cows ashore at a time. It will take hours to unload them all."

And so it did. But the children never got tired of watching. The Dutch and Walloon children were thinking of milk and cream, butter and cheese. The Indian children were too puzzled to think. They had never seen a cow before.

"They are bigger than bears," said Mokween. "They must be very dangerous. I will get my bow and arrow and my steel knife."

"Cows won't hurt you," said Teunis. He was glad that he knew more about something than Mokween did. "They don't eat people. They eat only grass and grain."

Lisbet looked at every cow that was driven off the ship. She asked herself many questions. Would Father buy a cow? Which one would be best? "Oh, please, Father," she whispered, "the little one with the black face and the white star on her forehead."

"All right," said Father. "She looks like a good cow."

And that was how Lisbet got two cows on the same day—and a very happy birthday it was.

DO YOU KNOW—

1. Why Lisbet didn't have to do any work on September 16?

2. What Mother gave Lisbet?

3. Why the cows were brought to Beavertown? How they were unloaded from the ship?

THINGS TO DO

1. Try modeling cows and other farm animals with clay or papier-mâché.

2. Write a story about a happy birthday you have had, or some other day when you were as happy as Lisbet was on her birthday.

The children learn quickly when Mokween's mother teaches them. Two girls are washing clamshells for dippers. Do you know what the other children are doing?

22: Trouble in Beavertown

The next winter began happily. The people had their Krankenbezoeker to read prayers and the Bible at their church meetings. New babies were baptized. Young people got married. The children were learning to read and write. Bastiaen was still trying to teach the Indians the Christian religion. They did not learn religion fast, but they did learn to trust Bastiaen.

The people in Beavertown learned ways to make themselves more comfortable. They used turkey wings to brush their hearths. The boys made brooms from hemlock branches. Mokween's mother showed the children how to dry *gourds* to make dippers and bowls. The girls scrubbed clamshells clean and set

them in the sun to lose the fishy smell. Then the shells were good for skimming the cream from the milk. They were good ash trays for the men, too. The men had learned about tobacco from the Indians. They smoked it in long pipes carved from brierwood.

Kip Teunissen's family now had a pig as well as a cow. The pig ate scraps from the table and the milk that the family couldn't drink. In the winter hungry deer sometimes came in from the woods and ate her food. She did not know how to scare them away. Instead, they scared her. In spite of this, she grew fatter every day.

The fur trade was good during the first part of the winter. Then the Mohawks began fighting the Mahicans. Their men did not have time for trapping. "In spring, things will be all right," said Kip. "The trappers from far away will come in with their furs. They are not at war."

Things were not bad, but everybody was worried. At night the settlers could hear the war whoops of the Indians. They shivered in their beds.

"It is their war, not ours," said Bastiaen Krol. "We can be friends with both sides."

Adriaen Tienpont had gone back to the Fatherland. He left Daniel Van Krieckebeeck in charge of the settlement. "I wish the new governor would come to visit us," said Kip. "I don't think Daniel is wise enough to take good care of Beavertown in wartime." But the new governor stayed in Manhattan.

When the second spring came, Kip said, "I must now put another story on our cellar home. You children are old enough to have bedrooms of your own. Besides, as you know, we'll need a new room before long for the new member of the family."

Before long, a baby sister was born. They called her Lammetje, which means "little lamb." Father made her a cozy cradle with a little roof over one end. Lisbet wanted to rock the cradle all day long, but Mother said, "Lammetje must learn to rest by herself sometimes."

Teunis made toys for the baby, but she was too young to enjoy them. "We'll keep them in the small chest until Lammetje is older," said Mother.

Mokween loved the new baby. Whenever he could, he came to see Lammetje. He liked to rock her cradle as well as Lisbet did. He brought her a cornhusk doll.

But he did not come to play with Lisbet and Teunis any more. He was old enough now to go hunting with his uncle. He had to learn the Indians' skills and secrets, for someday he might be a chief.

He was still friendly, but he seemed worried. He would not tell the children why. But they knew that Mokween's father and his uncle were often away from the village. Mokween had to be ready to help protect his family if the warlike Mohawks came.

The Dutch fur traders had always kept out of Indian wars. They wanted to be friendly with all the *wilden*. The soldiers at the fort were to be used only if the settlement was attacked.

Mokween brings Lammetje an Indian doll.

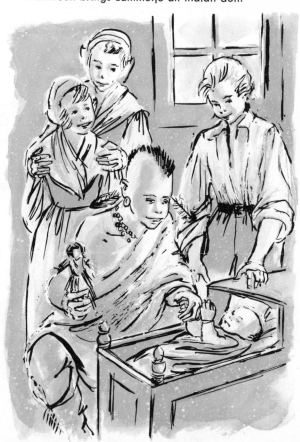

Now, however, Daniel Van Kriecke-beeck had a new idea. He said, "I have promised the Mahicans that we will help them in their war. They are not so cruel as the Mohawks.

"Today I shall take six soldiers and march against the Mohawks. Rem, you must be ready to follow us with the other soldiers. If we do not come back in two hours, bring the soldiers to help."

Rem shook his head sadly. He did not like this idea, but he had to obey orders. When Daniel and his six soldiers did not return, he started out to help them—but too late. Inside the woods, he saw three soldiers running toward the settlement. They were white with fear. "Daniel is dead," they said. "So are three of our men."

"Lead us to the enemy," said Rem. "We must try to get back our dead. We can at least bury them. Bastiaen Krol can say the prayers for the dead."

The three soldiers led Rem and his men to the place of battle. They could find no Mohawks. The fallen soldiers were nowhere to be seen. "The Indians have carried off our dead," said Rem.

There was nothing to do but return to the fort. The few soldiers knew they could not hope to fight a strong tribe like the Mohawks.

What sadness and fear in Beavertown that night! The women cried and held their children close. "Do you think the Mohawks will try to punish us for Daniel's act?" asked Johanna.

"I hope not," said Kip Teunissen. "The soldiers and the other men will try to protect Beavertown. We must have a meeting at once."

"Don't leave us alone," said Mother. She snatched up Lammetje, and said to the older children, "Come on. Hurry!" At the fort, they found all the other families huddled together in fear.

"The others have been killed!" cry the soldiers, as they run to meet Rem.

The Mahicans leave the peace meeting in anger. No gifts from the Dutch will help.

"This is very bad," said Father. "We must make peace with the Mohawks at once, but we have no leader to speak for us.

"There is one man that the Indians still trust. That man is Bastiaen Krol. He knows their language. He has tried to make Christians of them. Let him act as our leader."

Joost's father said, "I will sail my sloop to New Amsterdam at once. I will ask the governor to make Bastiaen our leader. But don't wait till I get back. He must hurry to save us all."

That is how the Krankenbezoeker became the governor of Beavertown. "I do not want to take such a hard task," he said. "But it is my duty. I will try to make peace."

And so he did. He met some of the Mohawk chiefs. He promised that the Dutch soldiers would never again fight them. He gave them gifts—axes and a huge roll of brown duffels and five large kettles. He gave them strings of wampum to prove that the bargain was honest.

Now the Mohawks were happy, but the Mahicans were not. Their chiefs came to see Bastiaen Krol. "Daniel promised to help us fight our enemies," they said. "You must do as he promised, or Dutch brothers are breaking their word."

Bastiaen Krol said, "You are our friends. We will help you in all peaceful ways. But we will not fight in Indian wars. We might all be killed. Then you would have nobody to buy your furs."

Mokween's uncle wanted the other Mahican chiefs to make a friendly answer. But they went away with angry looks. They would not take the gifts that Bastiaen tried to give them.

DO YOU KNOW—

1. How the people in Beavertown learned to live in more comfortable ways?

2. Who Lammetje was? What person outside the family loved her most?

3. Why Mokween was busy and worried these days?

4. How Daniel Van Krieckebeeck got Beavertown into trouble?

5. What happened when Bastiaen Krol spoke with the Mohawks? With the Mahicans?

"Beavertown is in great danger!" warns Mokween. "But do not say who told you."

23: The Last Days of Beavertown

Everyone in Beavertown was worried. What would happen? Although the days were bright and warm, people stayed in their homes. The Dutch and Walloon children did not play with their Indian friends.

One day Mother said, "We must stop acting afraid. If our old Indian friends think we do not trust them, they will be sad. Perhaps they will become angry. I shall keep Lammetje outdoors in her cradle while I work in the garden. Teuni, please come and help me."

After a while, Mother went into the house to start supper. As Teunis played with the baby, he heard a low call. It was like the call of an owl, but Teunis knew it was no owl. This was Mokween's old call.

"What shall I do?" Teunis thought. "I must trust Mokween. Mother would

want me to." Then he called in a low voice, "Lisbet, come and watch the baby."

In a second, Lisbet came. Teunis darted into the woods. There was Mokween waiting, very tall and strong. Without a word, he led Teunis farther into the woods. Then they came out on the shore, far from any houses.

Mokween said in a low voice, "I am your friend. I am the friend of your family. No harm must come to little Lammetje. So I will tell you something. My people are planning to kill everybody in Beavertown. My uncle said no, but all the other chiefs said yes."

"But how about the friendship treaty?" asked Teunis.

"My people say that your leader broke the treaty when he made peace with the Mohawks. There is no more friendship. Now I must leave you. I have gone against my own people to tell you this. They would kill me if they knew. Warn your leader, but do not tell my name. Now good-by." Quick as a flash, he was gone.

Teunis was frightened, but he knew he must act brave. He found his way back to the settlement. He did not stop at home, but went straight to Commander Krol's house. There he whispered the dreadful news. "I cannot tell you how I know, but it is true," he said.

"I will not ask your secret," said the Commander, "though I can guess. I will tell every man in Beavertown to be on guard all night. We must warn all the families to come to the fort."

The Commander called the men together. Teunis helped the families move into the fort.

When the Indians came, they found the houses empty. They knew everybody must be in the fort. They were not strong enough to attack Fort Orange.

Nobody knows to this day why they did not burn the houses. Perhaps Mokween's uncle asked them not to. The next day there was no sign of the Mahicans near the settlement.

The angry Mahicans attack Beavertown!

Before long, Mokween's uncle came to see Bastiaen Krol. Soon afterward, the Mahicans made a new treaty of friendship with the Commander. The people of Beavertown began to feel comfortable and happy again.

In the fall, a small sailing ship dropped anchor near the fort. Two men rowed ashore. They brought a message to Bastiaen Krol. "New Netherland has a new governor, Peter Minuit," they said. "He orders all families to leave Beavertown. There is a new fort on Manhattan. It is called Fort Amsterdam. It can protect people from the Indians. Everyone will be safe on Manhattan."

"I don't want to go," said Teunis.

"Oh, Teuni," said Lisbet, "that's just what you said about coming to the New World."

"I don't want to go either," said Mother, cuddling Lammetje. "I don't want to leave our cellar home. I don't want to leave my garden. The tulips were so pretty last spring. Now the corn and beans are getting dry. We shall have plenty of food next winter. Beavertown is our home."

"Listen to me, Johanna," said Father, in a strong, but quiet, voice. "You, too, children, are old enough to understand. We must go to Fort Amsterdam to be safe. The Mahicans and Mohawks are still fighting. We might get into trouble again."

"Will you work at the fur-trading post in Fort Amsterdam?" asked Mother.

"I don't know," said Father. "The Company will give me some sort of job, I am sure. But perhaps I'd rather make furniture for the other settlers. I hear that there are now two hundred people in New Amsterdam. Some of them will surely need furniture.

"Long ago," he told the children, "before I worked for the Company in the Fatherland, I used to make furniture and sell it. I can do that work very well."

"Will Rem be going with us?" asked Lisbet.

"I'm afraid not," said Father. "He will be left here with fifteen other soldiers to protect the furs. They will protect the Dutch traders who come here, too."

"Oh, dear," said Lisbet, "what shall we do without Rem?"

"You can write to him," said Father. "Maybe later he will come to the fort at New Amsterdam. Nobody can take Rem's place with us, I know. He helped us learn how to live in this new country. But you will have many friends in New Amsterdam. The families that went to Fort New Hope and Fort Nassau are being called back, too. You'll see your friend Marie, and Teunis will see Pierre again."

"I think we'll like New Amsterdam as well as Beavertown," said Lisbet.

"Well, maybe," said Teunis, "but I'll never forget Mokween."

And so Lisbet and Teunis and little Lammetje lived happily in New Amsterdam with their parents and their friends. The settlement grew bigger. Sometimes there were troubles. Some of the governors did not understand the Indians as well as Bastiaen Krol did. Some of the governors ruled well and some ruled badly. But Kip Teunissen's family lived on and were happy. When Lisbet was grown up, she married Teunis's old friend Joost. Little Lammetje grew up and married the Walloon who once was baby Jean Le Roy.

After a while, some people went back to Beavertown to live. Teunis married Maritje and they decided to make their home in Beavertown. There he often saw Mokween, who was now a chief of the Mahicans. Teunis never told anybody, not even Maritje, how Mokween had saved the settlement. But he put the story into a diary which was found a hundred years later. That is how we know about it today.

DO YOU KNOW—

1. How Mother showed that she was brave?

2. How Mokween proved his friendship for his Dutch neighbors?

3. How Teunis showed that he could be trusted?

4. Why the settlers had to leave Beavertown? Why Manhattan was a good place for them to go to?

5. How Teunis and Lisbet felt about going to Manhattan? Which of them liked new adventures best?

6. What old friends Teunis and Lisbet met in New Amsterdam?

7. Whether any of Kip Teunissen's family ever saw Beavertown again? How we know that Mokween saved the settlement?

THINGS TO DO

1. Make up a story about children saving grownups from danger, as the two boys did in this chapter. Your class might divide into groups, each to make up such a story. Then each group might act out its story for the class.

2. Look through story books or history books telling of other settlers in our country, and see if you can find stories of danger and bravery like the one you have just read.

3. There are many interesting books about life in New Amsterdam. Read them to find out what life was like when Teunis and Lisbet were living there.

4. Draw or paint pictures showing how you think Teunis, Lisbet, Lammetje, and Mokween looked when they grew up.

A New Look at Beavertown

THINGS TO TALK ABOUT

1. Talk about the reasons why the children's parents wanted to go to the New World. Would your parents like to go to a new country for the same reasons? If so, where would they want to go?

2. Talk about the way the Dutch children and the Indian boy made friends. Can you think of any better way?

3. Discuss Mokween's signal for telling Teunis when he was coming. Do you and your friends have any signals of this kind?

4. What did it mean to be a good citizen in Beavertown? What does it mean to be a good citizen in your town today? Is good citizenship different today from what it used to be in olden days?

5. Were the Dutch wise in wanting New Netherland for their own? Give reasons for your answer to this question.

6. In what ways are parents today the same as parents were in the Dutch days? In what ways are friends the same?

7. Talk about the ways neighbors at Fort Orange found to help one another. Think about ways in which neighbors today help one another. Decide whether neighbors helped one another more in the days of this story or today.

8. Discuss these questions: Are cattle brought to our country today? How do children traveling on ships get milk to drink?

9. What foods do you enjoy which the Dutch settlers did not have? How are your clothes different from those of Lisbet and Teunis?

10. How was an ocean voyage different in the days of the Dutch settlers from what it is today? Talk to someone you know who has crossed the ocean and ask about food on today's ships. Ask about sleeping aboard ship and about what happens during a storm. Tell the class what you find out.

Write letters to steamship companies or travel agencies asking for travel folders showing modern ships. Compare modern ships with the *New Netherland*. Visit a modern passenger or freight ship, at an ocean, lake, or river harbor. Find out all you can about life aboard such a ship.

HOW TO FIND OUT MORE ABOUT THE DUTCH SETTLERS

1. On a map of the eastern part of the United States, find what places the Dutch claimed, and which of these places are now part of New York State.

2. If the Dutch settled in your part of the state, visit any houses, landmarks, or other

relics they left. Wherever you live, libraries will have books or pictures about Dutch settlers. Museums may have things the Dutch used, or pictures of Dutch settlements.

3. Read about other settlers in the New World, and decide whether they had a harder or easier time than the Dutch settlers.

4. If you know anybody who speaks French, learn to say and write some of the words the Walloon children might have used. If you know anybody who speaks Dutch, learn some Dutch words, too.

5. Act out the story of the Indians and the *New Netherland.*

6. Try to get a large map of the Hudson River between New York City and Albany. Find the mountains that the children named. Draw pictures of the mountains as you think they looked from the river.

7. Ask your mother how she cooks dandelion greens. Is her way like Rem's? If dandelion greens are in season, try cooking some. If not, try to remember what the plant looks like and paint the leaves and flowers from memory.

8. Ask your parents or your doctor what people can do for sore backs and arms. Are the treatments used today at all like Mokween's treatment?

9. Plan a school lunch or a party for parents at which you will serve only foods that the Indians and their Dutch friends might have eaten.

10. Find out how mortar is made today. What is it used for?

11. Make a table model of the pond. Make stand-up pasteboard or paper dolls showing how the Dutch and the Indian children looked on the ice. If you prefer, make a diorama of the scene.

12. Make a puppet show to tell the story of the troubles with the Indians and Krol's meetings with the leaders.

13. Try to remember all the things you know about Daniel Van Krieckebeeck. Was Daniel a hard worker? Was he a wise man? Was he a brave man? How was he different from Bastiaen Krol?

14. Ask the librarian to help you find books that tell how the new settlers in other parts of the New World got along with the Indians. Read or tell some of the stories to your classmates.

BOOKS TO READ AND LOOK AT

Berry, Erick, *Tinmaker Man of New Amsterdam,* Winston, 1941, or E. M. Hale (Cadmus Books), 1948.

Coatsworth, Elizabeth, *First Adventure,* Macmillan, 1950. A story of the Pilgrims.

Coatsworth, Elizabeth, *Wishing Pear,* Macmillan, 1951. A story about two girls and a pear tree in New Amsterdam.

Dalgliesh, Alice, *America Builds Homes,* Scribner, 1939.

DeAngeli, M. L., *Elin's America,* Doubleday, 1941. The story of a Swedish girl whose family settled on the Delaware River twenty years later than Lisbet and Teunis settled on the Hudson River.

Dilliard, Maud Esther, *A Farm for Juliana,* Dutton, 1951. The story of a Dutch family who came here later than Kip Teunissen's family. This and the next two books will tell you some of the words the settlers used.

Dilliard, Maud Esther, *Twins of Old Flatbush,* Dutton, 1952.

Dilliard, Maud Esther, *Wishing Boy of New Netherland,* Dutton, 1950.

Duffe, M. L., *New Amsterdam: Colonial Days,* Row, 1942.

Follett, H. T., *House Afire,* Scribner, 1941.

Hart, A. B., and Hazard, B. E., *Colonial Children,* Macmillan, 1937. Information that will be interesting for those of you who are very good readers.

Maloy, Lois, and Dalgliesh, Alice, *Wooden Shoes in America,* Scribner, 1940.

Meadowcroft, E. L., *Ship Boy with Columbus,* Crowell, 1942.

Leetch, D. L., *Annetje and Her Family,* Cadmus, 1940.

Spoerer, G. R., *The White Man Comes,* Nelson, 1934.

RECORDS TO ENJOY

There are no recordings that tell of the Dutch in the New World, but there is one that tells about the Netherlands, where Teunis and Lisbet lived before they came here:

The Wonderful Windmills, Pacific, No. 505, one 10″ record. A trip to the land of windmills. Different members of the windmill family sing the windmill songs.

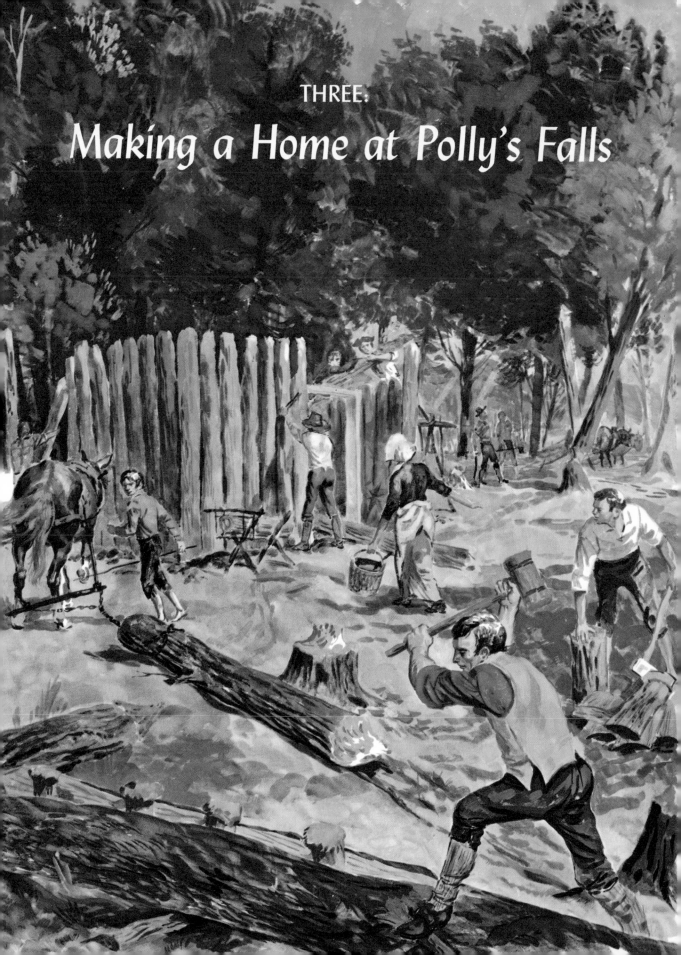

THREE:
Making a Home at Polly's Falls

Making a Home at Polly's Falls

As the years went by, more Dutch and Walloons came to live in New Netherland. People from England came, too. After a while, the Dutch gave their part of the New World to England. New Netherland became New York. The governors were now English, but not much else changed.

People moved back to Beavertown, which was now called Albany. The North River was named the Hudson. Some people settled land west of the Hudson, along the Mohawk and other rivers. But the settlers did not go very far west, because there was so much fighting.

First there was fighting between the English and the French. After the French were driven out, the colonists began fighting for freedom from England. They had to fight both the English and some Indians who were helping the English. This was all part of the Revolutionary War.

After the war, many fathers in the United States said, "Now we can take our families to western New York State. The Indians who lived there have sold most of their land to our state." Some fathers bought land. Others had land given to them, because they had helped fight for freedom.

The pioneers who went to western New York suffered more hardships than the first Dutch settlers. The pioneers had to

make their own way through the wilderness. (They traveled in small groups, often of only one family.)

The story you are about to read tells about a man who had been a soldier in the Revolutionary War. He and his family went to western New York to make a new home. They had hard work and they had troubles. But they had happy times, too, and some good luck, and the help of friendly neighbors.

I WONDER

I wonder why the Prices decided to leave their good farm and travel west into country they had never seen.

I wonder how the Prices and their friends worked together to make their community strong.

I wonder how the pioneers at Hardenbergh's Corners chose their leaders and established a government for their community.

I wonder if it is possible to have an adventure like the Prices' today.

WORDS WE NEED TO KNOW

auger	colter	hopper	sampler
beeswax	crocks	land grant	sawmill
blacksmith	crotches	loom	sugarbush
bran	flax	millstones	tallow
carded	flint	outlet	tannery
cipher	flyleaf	plowshare	tinder box
clearing	gristmill	potash	turnpike
cogwheels	hemp	root vegetables	warp and woof

1: Off to a New Home

Polly picked up her big striped cat, Miss Muffet. "Do you remember that you were Little Miss Muffet when you first came to live with me?" she asked. "And now I have to go away and leave you forever and ever and ever."

Miss Muffet looked as if she didn't care. She tried to jump out of Polly's arms. "All right for you," said Polly, putting her down. "You'll be sorry when I'm gone."

Miss Muffet scooted for the house. She disappeared through a hole in the outer wall, beside the front door. It was as big around as a rather fat cat. In the wall inside the house was another hole the same size. This had a shutter over it, to keep the cold from coming into the room. Miss Muffet had learned how to push this shutter open while she was still

Little Miss Muffet. She could go into the house whenever she wanted to. She could not go out, however, without asking someone to open the door for her. The shutter over the cat hole opened in, but not out.

Polly went into the house, too. She looked at Miss Muffet sadly. "I'd have carried you in if you hadn't been in such a hurry," she said.

Miss Muffet arched her back against the big *loom* where Polly's mother, Mrs. Price, was working. She was taking a big piece of heavy linen cloth off the loom. She had just finished weaving this cloth, which was to be the cover for a wagon. Now she said, "Polly, you see to the dinner, will you? I'm so busy now."

Polly put the wooden plates and the pewter spoons on the table. She got

Here is the land Captain Hardenbergh tells of in his letter to the Prices. This is the Genesee country, with its deep, rich soil and beautiful lakes.

bread and butter. As she stirred the beef stew in the kettle, she said, "Mother, why must we leave our nice house and go way out to the Genesee country?"

"Your father owns six hundred acres of land out there," said Mrs. Price. "It was a *land grant* given to him by the government because he fought for our country from 1776 to the end of the Revolution. We'll have a harder life than we have in this part of the state. But after a while, we'll have a fine, big farm. It will be big enough so that each of you children can have part of it for your own when you grow up. And there will be plenty left for Father and me."

"I don't want a farm of my own. I like our little farm here."

"So do I, dear," said Mother. "I hate to leave our friends. We shall all miss our church. But many people are going west. We shall make new friends. Your father already has a good friend who lives near our land. You've heard him speak of Captain John Hardenbergh, who was the leader of his company in the Revolution. They were out there with General Sullivan. They thought even then that the Genesee country would be a fine place to live in. The soil is much deeper and richer than it is here in the northeastern part of our state."

149

Just then Mr. Price came in. He said, "I had another letter from the Captain today. He sent it by a peddler, who left it with the storekeeper at Clover Hill. Mr. Briggs drove over to the store today, so they gave him this letter to bring to me."

"What did the Captain say, Enos?" asked Mother.

"He said he was glad we were coming out. Maybe he is lonely. He said his wife had died, leaving him a beautiful little girl, Cornelia," said Father.

Polly's sad looks changed to smiles. "Oh, I'll love to help him take care of little Cornelia," she said.

"He told me how to find his house," Father went on. "It's near where the Genesee *Turnpike* meets another road.

"Now, Faith, I was wondering. Do you suppose we could get started on Monday? I want to get out there in June, if I can, so we can plant some kind of

Father reads the letter from Captain Hardenbergh.

garden. I want to get a good house built before cold weather comes."

"Well, we can try," said Mother.

Just then Polly's big brother David came in from the barn. He was not happy about moving to the Genesee country. He wanted to be a doctor, and he had begun studying with Dr. Otis in Clover Hill, the nearest village. He was afraid that he would forget all he had learned.

"Cheer up, Son," said Mr. Price. "We'll try to help you get back here, since you've got your heart set on it. But there's a good deal of hard work to do in a new settlement. You can do as much work as I can, and we'll need two men at first."

Polly put her arm around her big brother's neck. "I know how you feel, David," she said. "I don't want to go, either. I hate to leave Miss Muffet behind."

"Why can't you take her?" asked her younger brother, Timothy.

"She might get hurt by wild animals out in the Genesee country," said Mother. "We might lose her on the way. It will be a long trip in our covered wagon."

"But we could keep her safe in the wagon, couldn't we?" asked Tim.

"She's a country cat," said Mother. "She loves to play around and hunt outdoors. We couldn't watch her all the time, and a fox or a wolf might get her."

"Never mind, Polly," said Mr. Price. "We'll get you a new pet out there. Maybe you could tame a bear cub." He gave Polly's ear a playful pinch, but she didn't smile. She was sad, and she wasn't going to change just for Father's jokes. "Bears scare me," was all she said.

Tim said, "If any bears come after you, I will shoot them." He was only ten years old, but he knew that boys who went to new settlements had to be brave.

"Don't worry, Polly," said Mother. "You won't have to have a bear cub. What would we do with it when it got big? You shall have a nice tame animal as soon as it's safe to keep one."

Now Polly smiled. Mother always understood.

Just as Mother was dishing up the beef stew, a voice at the door called, "May I come in?" It was Nancy Briggs, who would soon live in the Prices' old home.

"Father sent me with the first payment on the farm," she said. She put some gold coins into Mr. Price's hand. "He will send you the other nine payments."

"Nancy," asked Polly in a worried voice, "would you like to have Miss Muffet? She's a very nice cat. She comes in through that hole near the door."

Nancy reached down and picked up the cat. For once, Miss Muffet lay still and let herself be cuddled. "I'd love to have your cat, Polly," said Nancy. "I promise I'll take good care of her."

Early Monday morning, the family was ready to start the long trip. Mr. Price and David had fitted the wagon cover over hoops of young hickory. Pots and pans were stacked in the wagon. There were straw mattresses and featherbeds rolled up and tied. The *crocks* were filled with the kind of food that would keep well—dried apples and pumpkin, pickles and salt pork. There were two smoked hams and a big cheese shaped

"How good that food looks!" thinks Tim hungrily.

like a drum. Mother had brought a crock of butter. "But," said she, "if we get hot days, that butter may not be very good." She had baked a fresh batch of bread, too. "We'll eat the wheat bread first," she said. "This Boston brown bread will keep longer. The cookies and the doughnuts should keep well in those crocks, if somebody doesn't get too hungry." She was looking at Tim, but he made believe he was looking somewhere else.

Now David brought the oxen, Buck and Bright, and hitched them to the wagon. Tim led out Sukie, the cow. He had a stick, because it was going to be his job to drive her behind the wagon. He knew, however, that he could never hit old Sukie.

David was going to lead the oxen for a while. Mr. and Mrs. Price sat on the front seat. Polly perched on her mother's small trunk. In this trunk were packed the family treasures and everybody's best clothes.

In the wagon goes Mother's trunk, filled with the family's treasures. What else did the Prices take?

"Why don't we wear our good clothes now that we're going traveling?" Polly had asked, thinking longingly of her pink checked dress with the ribbon sash.

"This is going to be a long trip," said Mother. "We might get our good clothes dirty and torn." She had packed Mr. Price's old blue Army coat, which was still the best one he had. He was wearing a deerskin jacket and his oldest wool knee breeches. Tim wore breeches of rough linen, called tow. He had outgrown his one woolen pair. All the men wore linen shirts made from cloth that Mrs. Price had woven.

Polly was wearing linen too. Her dress was just the color of her blond hair. This is the color of *flax*, from which the linen had been woven.

Mother was wearing a dress of dark brown with a short gown of calico over it

belted in at the waist. She had her old cloak, for the May nights might be cool.

As the wagon started, Nancy came to wish her friends a good trip. Polly waved good-by to Nancy and Miss Muffet.

DO YOU KNOW—

1. How Mrs. Price made the cover for the covered wagon? Why western New York State was a good place for families to move to?

2. How letters were carried in the days after the Revolution?

3. Who Mr. Price's friend in the Genessee Country was? Why he was glad the family was coming to live near him?

4. Why David did not want to move? Who was going to buy the Price's farm?

5. What kind of food the family was taking?

THINGS TO DO

1. Make a model of a small covered wagon.

2. Talk about the ways our ex-soldiers are rewarded for their services today, and decide whether these ways are better than the way Mr. Price was rewarded.

2: On into the Wilderness

Two weeks passed before the Price family reached Fort Stanwix. This was as far as they could go along the Mohawk Trail. The trail was rough, but it was wide enough for the wagon to get through. The farms were not too far apart, and the family could often buy fresh eggs or a crock of milk. There were inns or homes where they could find beds.

But Fort Stanwix was what Mr. Price called "the jumping-off place." Beyond Fort Stanwix lay the wilderness. There were hundreds of miles of almost unbroken forest. A few families from New England went through every month. Some Indians lived in the woods. But the trail would be lonely from here on.

The inn at Fort Stanwix was called the Red Lion. Its sign swung from an iron rod near the wagon road. It showed a fierce-looking lion with big white teeth and a shaggy red coat. The family enjoyed the good squirrel stew that was served to all the travelers. After dinner, Mr. Price said, "I'm going to read the newspapers. There is one from Albany that is only five days old. And I saw a New York paper that was printed a week ago Saturday. I want to find out the news now, because we may not see another newspaper for a long time."

In the morning, the family went to the store next to the inn. Father said, "Our innkeeper, Mr. Best, thought it would be a good idea to have a store. You see,

After the Revolutionary War, many families moved to the rich farm lands of western New York. The heavy lines on the map show the main roads west. The dotted lines show the less important roads and trails. Did your community grow up along an early road?

Routes West in Early New York

many people stay at his inn just before they start for the Genesee country. It's their last stop, so they're glad to buy the things they'll need on their trip.

"You'd better think of everything. This is the last store you'll see in a long time, I'm afraid."

The store was in a small log building. The front windows were not used for showing goods. They let in all the light that the store got. The little store was bursting with goods. The shelves were loaded with boxes of candles, bullets, and dyes. There were rolls of woolen cloth and stacks of shoe leather. Harness hung from the ceiling. Iron pots and pans were piled high in one corner. In another were guns. There were barrels of molasses, salt meat and fish, and whale oil for lamps. Nobody but Mr. Best could find anything in his crowded store.

"Let's buy some writing paper," said Polly. "I must write to Nancy to ask about Miss Muffet."

"We'll get some paper," said Mother, "but not very much. It costs a good deal. Besides, we shan't have many chances to send letters back to our old friends. There are no regular mails where we're going, you know."

"We'd better take some medicines, in case we get sick," said David. "I don't suppose there will be a doctor for miles around."

"Except you," said Father. "I'm sure you've learned a good deal about taking care of people."

"I hope I can help," said David quietly.

"We'll need a barrel of salt," said Mother, "to preserve meat and fish next fall."

"I'll need plenty of gunpowder," said Father, "and just fill up this pouch with bullets."

"How about sugar?" asked Tim.

"Well, we'd better take some sugar," said Father. "Next spring we can probably get some maple sugar. And we'll surely find wild honey out there. But we shall need sugar for the winter."

Why is Mr. Best's store an important place? Do you know what the Prices bought there?

When the roads were very muddy, Mother took off her shoes and hitched up her skirt.

"Shall we take wheat flour?" asked Mother.

"Yes, we'd better take some. We're going into wonderful wheat country. But we can't harvest our own wheat until next year."

"I'd better take some woolen cloth," said Mother. "I don't believe I have enough wool to keep us in warm clothes all this year and the next."

"Another thing we'll need," Father said, "is enough shoe leather for a pair of shoes apiece."

"Why?" asked Mother. "We'll be raising our own cows. We can use the hide for shoes next time we butcher a cow."

"I wouldn't be too sure of that," said Father. "The hides have to be tanned before they can be made into shoes. I don't think there is a *tannery* in all western New York State.

"I think I'd better buy a pair of glasses. I don't see as well as I did when I was young."

"I have some good glasses," said Mr. Best. "Here they are in this tray. Try some on until you find a pair that helps you."

"I have some money that I earned back home," said David. "I'd like to buy a little box of tea for you, Mother."

"You keep your money, David," said Mother, lovingly. "Tea can wait until we get rich. I know how to make a good drink out of sassafras root. Boil it up and put sugar and milk into it, and it's almost as good as tea."

Mr. Best helped Father and David load the wagon with the barrels and boxes of goods they had bought. Then Father said, "I think we'd better push on now. It's a good clear day. The trails have dried off from that last rain."

The trip from now on was quite different. The trail was narrow. Often it led through dark forests. The trees had their new summer leaves, so thick that they sometimes hid the sky. In the woods the roads were wet, because the sun could not get through to dry them. Sometimes the wagon would sink into a hole a foot or two deep. For this reason, all the fam-

155

Not a cabin in sight! Tim brings firewood as the family gets ready to spend a night in the forest.

ily walked a good deal of the way. Even Mother wanted to walk.

"The only trouble is, you'll wear out your shoes," said Father. "Better take them off. There's nobody here to see."

"Wel-l-l, if you think I should," said Mother.

"Be careful to walk in the trail," Father said. "The mud is easy on your feet. But watch out for stones or you might get a bad cut."

Mother hitched up her long skirt to keep it out of the mud. Polly hitched up her skirt, too.

Day after day the family plodded on. Sometimes Mr. Price and David had to chop down trees to let the wagon pass. Often they had to drag big branches out of the way. There were huge stumps in the middle of the trail. The wagon rocked from side to side, but somebody always steadied it so that it didn't quite tip over.

Sometimes night would fall while the family was far from any house. Then Father and David would chop branches to make a dry, springy heap. With the straw mattresses laid on it, and perhaps a featherbed, it made a fine place to sleep. But if the weather was wet, it was a different story. One rainy night everybody had to crawl into the wagon. The strong cover that Mother had woven kept off the rain, but there was no room for anybody to lie down.

The next morning, before starting off, Father and David took everything out of the wagon. They re-packed the boxes and barrels so that the mattresses could be spread over them. This kind of bed was quite bumpy, but it was better than no bed at all.

If luck was with them at nightfall, the family would see a little thread of smoke above the trees. It would tell them that some human being was near. Usually they found a *clearing* where a settler's family was living in a one-room cabin.

The travelers were always made welcome. If there was room, they were asked to sleep in the cabin. Often the settlers wanted to give up their beds, but Mother always said, "No, we'll spread our mattresses on the floor."

In some cabins, there was room for only Polly and her mother. Then the men had to shift for themselves. On clear nights, they would roll up in blankets and sleep under the stars. On rainy nights, they crawled under the wagon cover.

One family of settlers had no food except what they could shoot in the woods. Mr. Price gave them flour and cornmeal. The settlers would not take money for giving the travelers shelter. "You'd do the same for us," they would say.

Some of the homes were the poorest the Prices had ever seen. There was only packed earth for a floor. Some had a Dutch back instead of a fireplace and chimney. A Dutch back was a wall plastered with mud to keep it from catching fire. Against this wall the cooking fire was built. The smoke found its way out through a hole in the roof. At least, some of it did. The rest stayed inside.

DO YOU KNOW—

1. Whether the journey to Fort Stanwix was hard for the family? Why Father wanted to read the newspapers at the Red Lion Inn?

2. Why Mr. Best had a store near his inn? What the family bought at Mr. Best's store?

3. How the trip was harder after the family left Fort Stanwix? What some of the hardships were?

4. How the settlers proved that they were good friends to the travelers? How the family repaid the kindness they received?

THINGS TO DO

1. Draw or paint a picture of something that happened that is not already illustrated.

2. Act out a scene from the story.

Kind settlers welcome the weary travelers. Tonight they will sleep under a roof.

3: Hardenbergh's Corners

The long, tiresome journey went on for days. Everybody was tired, but everybody was excited, too. "Soon we'll be there," said Father.

Now the road went up hill and down. In the hollows there was deep mud. At one place, David and Mr. Price had to cut down logs to make a solid way across the mud.

"I hope we won't have to live in a damp, swampy place like this," said David. "It wouldn't be good for our health."

"I hope not," said Father, looking worried. He knew that they were almost at the end of their journey. Then the road leveled out, and a log house came into view. "I think this must be Captain Hardenbergh's place," said Father.

No sooner had he rapped on the door of the house than it was opened by a Negro. "Captain Hardenbergh is at his mill," said the man, "but do come in. He makes all travelers welcome."

"Captain Hardenbergh was my leader in the Army," said Father. "I have brought my family to live nearby on my land grant."

"He will be glad to see you," said the Negro. "We need more people here. Bring your family into the house and my wife will get them some hot food. We work for the Captain. I will go to the mill and tell him you are here. What name shall I say?"

"My name is Enos Price," said Father.

"Mine is Harry Freeman," said the Negro, "and my wife's name is Kate."

Harry Freeman showed the men where the oxen could graze, and then took Polly and her mother into the log house. A small, dark-haired girl toddled up to meet

Harry Freeman welcomes the Prices. "Captain Hardenbergh is at the mill," he says.

How good the deer meat and greens Kate Freeman fixed taste to the hungry Prices!

them. "You must be Cornelia," Polly said. The child was too young to say anything, but she made happy sounds as Polly picked her up.

Kate Freeman made the newcomers welcome. She poured water into the wash basin for them and got them clean towels.

Tim looked shyly in at the door, then ran back to meet his father, who had just unhitched the oxen. "Father," he whispered, "wouldn't you think he'd have a better house—a Captain in the Army and all? This isn't any better than those poor cabins we stayed at in the clearings. Will we have to live in a house like this?"

"Tim," said Father, "in the wilderness a big house isn't important. There are many other things to think about. You'll find that out when we get to our land grant."

Just then Captain John Hardenbergh came striding into the yard. "So you got here!" he cried, as he grabbed Father's hand. "And here are your boys. Let's go inside and see the rest of your family."

The Captain led the way into his house. He spoke very politely to Mrs. Price and Polly. Cornelia wriggled out of Polly's arms and ran to her father. Polly didn't blame her. She liked this tall, strong-looking, loud-voiced, kindly man.

That was why she dared to speak up and ask him the question that was first in her mind. "Is our land grant on a lake?" she asked.

"It's on a fine lake, only three miles from here," boomed the Captain. "It's called the Lake-near-the-Crossing-Place. It's fish-rich, as my Dutch grandfather used to say."

"Is it pretty, like that lake we passed this morning?"

"Yes, it's very pretty," said the Captain. "Your land is pretty, too. It's hilly, like all the land around here. But there's level land where corn and wheat will grow. This is fine wheat country."

Kate Freeman was cooking at the fire built against the Dutch back. Soon she called everybody to the plain board table. How good the deer meat and greens

159

Water pushes the wheel. It turns the millstones that grind flour. Settlers bring grain to the gristmill.

tasted! After the meal, Polly said, "It's wonderful to sit here and rest, after walking or riding over those horrid roads."

"All the same, we'd better go for a walk," said Captain Hardenbergh. "You must see our big city."

"What is the name of your big city?" asked Polly, still sitting on the bench beside the table.

"Folks call it Hardenbergh's Corners," said the Captain. "That's because my house is near the place where two trails meet."

"That's not the real reason, Captain," said Harry Freeman. "They named the settlement after you because you started it and you're helping it to grow."

"Well, never mind that," said the Cap-

tain. "Now we've got to get this pretty young lady to take a walk." He playfully pulled Polly to her feet. "If you get fat, sitting around after a full meal, you won't be pretty any more," he said, smiling at her. Then he took her arm as they started out of the house. She liked the Captain. He made her feel grown up.

"How do you happen to have Negroes working for you?" she asked. She had seen very few Negroes in her life.

"Well," said the Captain, "they belonged to my family back in Ulster County, so I brought them west with me."

"You mean they're slaves!" cried Polly, so surprised that she stopped stone still.

"I'm afraid so. Do you think that's so bad, Polly?"

"Yes, I do," she answered. Then she blushed to find herself talking this way to a grownup.

But the Captain did not seem angry. "Maybe it is bad," he said. "Anyhow, Kate and Harry are earning their freedom. Harry cuts trees and works at the mill. Kate keeps house for me and takes care of my baby. I keep an account of what their work is worth. When they have earned $300 each, I shall sign a paper saying that they are free."

"Oh, that's good," said Polly. "I knew you were a good man when I first saw you."

"Now let's walk with the rest of your family," said the Captain. "I want to tell you all about our city."

His big city was only a few log cabins. Quite near the Captain's house there was a stream of water. The only way to cross it was on steppingstones. "This is the crossing place that gave the lake its name," said Captain Hardenbergh. "Two important Indian trails cross the *outlet* here."

"What's the outlet?" asked Tim.

"It's a stream that flows from the lake. If you look upstream, to your left, you will see my mill. It's that small log building standing by the edge of the stream. We built a log dam across the outlet. The water gives me power for my *gristmill*.

"The settlers who were already here were very glad when I started this mill. They had been carrying their grain twenty miles to get it ground into flour. And they had to go right through the deep woods, too, on narrow trails.

"But they hadn't much choice. If they didn't want to take the trip, they had to grind the grain themselves. That meant hollowing out a tree stump and making it smooth. Then they had to pour the grain into the hollow and pound it by hand with a heavy wooden pestle. And that really is hard work."

"I'd like to start a little business like yours," said Father. "It will be a long time before I can grow enough crops to sell. It would be good to earn some cash money."

"I've been thinking about that," said the Captain. "There's a waterfall on your grant. You could put a mill wheel in there and get enough power for a *sawmill*. The people here need one just as badly as they needed my gristmill."

"Where would I get the saw and the other iron parts?" asked Mr. Price.

"We can send to Sterling for them. There will be somebody going through before long that we can trust. Of course, you can make the *cogwheels* of wood. That will be good whittling for you and your boys this winter."

"You are forgetting to show us your city," said Polly.

"So I am," said Captain Hardenbergh. "Look downstream a bit. Do you see all

Before the gristmill, grain was ground by hand.

those bark huts? They belong to Indians. The Indians hereabouts are good, peaceful people. The state bought most of their land, but let them stay here if they wished. A few live by themselves in the wilderness. There is an Indian, old Beaver Tail, who lives on your land. You could make him move, but I think he'll be a good neighbor."

"Where are the stores in your city?" asked Polly, teasingly.

"We haven't a single store, so far," said the Captain. "I hope we shall have one soon. But you'll be glad to know that a preacher now lives nearby. He comes here to hold church services about every four weeks."

"Have you a doctor?" asked David.

"No, we haven't," said Captain Hardenbergh. "Of course, everybody that comes here brings some medicines. There are some women who know how to nurse the sick. The Indians are a help, too. They know what plants are good for sickness. There's one good thing about a new settlement. Everybody helps everybody else."

"The next thing we should look for," said Mother, "is an inn. We want to get to bed early."

The Captain held up his hand. "Don't say any more," he cried. "There is no inn. You will be guests of Hardenbergh until you can raise your own home. And don't thank me, please," he added, as Mother started to speak.

"Will you have room for us all?"

The Captain made believe he was angry. "Mistress Price," he said, "isn't my castle grand enough for you?" Then he roared with laughter.

DO YOU KNOW—

1. How the covered wagon got across muddy parts of the road?

2. Why Tim was disappointed about the Captain's house? Why Polly was worried about the Captain's Negro helpers? Why there were Indians at Hardenbergh's Corners?

3. What the Captain's business was? What idea he gave Mr. Price about a business?

THINGS TO DO

Talk about Captain Hardenbergh. Why was he a good settler? Why did Polly like him so well? Do you know anybody who you think is like the Captain?

"The Indians here are good, peaceful people," Captain Hardenbergh tells Enos Price.

It is a beautiful day! "I'll help row!" Tim says, as he hops into the boat beside Captain Hardenbergh. Mother needs help across the wet sand. But soon the whole family is settled and on its way to see their farm land across the lake.

4: The Beginning of Polly's Falls

The next morning, Captain Hardenbergh said, "We'd better get an early start to visit your land grant."

"I'll hitch up the oxen," said Timothy. He wanted the big, kindly Captain to know how much he could help. "Will you come with us?"

"Yes, indeed," said his new friend.

"But how can you leave your mill for so long?" asked Mother.

"Harry can take care of the mill," said the Captain. "It's only a small one. Some days we don't get any grain at all to grind. Some days we get more than my mill will take care of.

"Now we'll drive out to the Lake-near-the-Crossing-Place. I have a friend, Jacob Van Doren, who has a big flat-bot-tomed boat that he'll lend to us. That's the easiest way to go to see your land grant."

The wagon jolted along the muddy, stony road. "These roads are a disgrace," said the Captain. "We'll have to pull the stumps out of them when we can find time and money."

"I'm glad we don't have to go all the way in this wagon," said Mother.

"Oh, we couldn't," said the Captain. "We'd have to follow a narrow trail right through the forest. If it weren't for the lake, we'd have to go there on foot or on horseback, if we could get enough horses."

A little farther on, he said, "Here is my friend Van Doren's place. He came from

Pioneer Settlements in Early New York

Pennsylvania. Quite a few people have come here from Pennsylvania, but more from New England."

Everybody was listening but Polly. She could do nothing but look. Right before her was the blue water of the lake, the beautiful lake that was going to be her own.

Mr. Van Doren was glad to lend the Captain and his guests the big flat-bottomed boat. "I'll put your oxen to graze while you're gone," he said. "I've got some land cleared, but no animals yet."

Polly was the first one into the boat. "You're light," said the Captain. "You can sit in that little seat in front."

"Let me help row," said Tim. Polly said nothing. She wished the boat ride would last all day. She dabbled her hand in the water as it rippled softly against the boat. At last she said, "Captain Hardenbergh, why do you live so far from the lake? I should think you'd rather live here than anywhere else."

"I picked my place because I think it's a good place for a city to grow," said the Captain. "I had my eye on that outlet. Years ago when I was here with Sullivan's army, I noticed the rapids and falls in the outlet. That gave me the idea of the mill. There are two things a settlement must have if people are to stay and be happy —a gristmill and a sawmill."

The bright sunlight on the shimmering lake made Polly blink her eyes. "We'll have to see that you get a big straw hat to keep the sun out of your eyes," said the Captain. "Some of the women around here have learned to weave good hats out of oat straw or grass."

The lake was surrounded by forests. They made a dark green dress for the gentle hills. Here and there this dark dress was mended with a patch of lighter green or of yellow. "There must be quite a few settlers around the lake," said Mother.

"Yes," said the Captain, "and they'll be glad enough to row over to see you. They'll bring their logs to be sawed as soon as your mill is ready. That's why it is good to have a mill near the lake. It's easier to travel to it by water than through the forest trails."

"Have we any near neighbors?" asked Mother.

164

"Yes. The Skinners live quite near the edge of your grant. They have a girl named Abbie, a little older than your girl here. There's their house now. We'd better head in here. That's your land ahead."

"Oh," breathed Polly. She looked at the dark pines back from the shore. Nearer there was some grassy land. A little point of bright green grass reached out into the lake as if to welcome its new owners. At one side of it, a noisy brook tumbled over the stones into the lake. Where did the brook come from? Polly followed it with her eyes back to the hillside. There she saw a beautiful little waterfall.

The flat bottom of the boat grated on the pebbles. Polly was the first ashore. She was running up the hillside toward the falls before the others had left the boat. David pulled the boat up on the pebbly shore. Then everybody began talking at once.

"Couldn't we go swimming off this point?" asked Tim.

"The lake air smells fine. Do you think it will be good for us?" asked David.

"Wouldn't that level space near the falls be a good place for our house?" asked Mother.

To all these questions, the Captain could only nod his head. Then he said, "There's one thing you ought to think about. In winter you'll be cut off from most of the other settlers. The lake freezes, at least around the edges. The trails through the woods will be choked with snow. Wouldn't you rather live at the Corners? You could sell your land and buy a lot there. People will buy farms now that they know how rich the soil is."

Polly was looking straight into Father's face, with fear and hope. She gave a big sigh of happiness when he said, "No, I don't want to change. We're used to living in the country. I don't believe we'll get lonesome. We'll have lots to do in winter, making shoes, building furniture, and so on. How do the rest of you feel?"

Polly races ahead to see the beautiful waterfall.

The rest of the family agreed with Mr. Price. "And now we'd better begin chopping," said Timothy.

"We can't begin chopping today, my boy," said the Captain, "but we might go fishing. Would you like that?"

Tim was the first into the boat. David went to cut some branches to use as fish poles. Captain Hardenbergh had brought fishlines and fishhooks. Soon the men rowed happily off, leaving Polly and her mother to enjoy the lovely view across the lake.

The men had hardly disappeared when an unknown voice spoke. A tall old Indian came toward them from the edge of the forest. He was wearing deerskin breeches, and not much else, as the day was warm.

Mother was startled for a moment, but when the Indian said, "My name Beaver Tail," she smiled at once.

"The Captain brought you," said Beaver Tail. "You must be people going to live here."

"Yes," said Mother.

"I have secret for you. Come with me."

The women were a little scared, but it must be all right, they thought. The Captain had spoken well of Beaver Tail. So they followed him up the first hill and through the woods until they reached a little orchard. There were ten or twelve twisted old apple trees. Their branches were weighted down with little hard green apples.

"I never told Captain about my orchard," said Beaver Tail, with a grin. "He here with Sullivan's men. They never found it. Captain didn't find it when he here looking over land after War. Now I am telling you. Will be many apples in fall. Use all you want. Too many for my wife and me.

"You know how to make apple pie?" he asked Polly, slyly. She nodded. "You make one for me some day?"

"Oh, yes," promised Polly. Without another word, Beaver Tail led them back down the trail to the shore. Then he disappeared.

Beaver Tail shows Polly and Mother his secret, the apple orchard.

The first supper on their new land! The Captain shows Enos and David how to cook the fish they've caught. He holds them on a branch over the open fire.

When the men returned, Tim proudly held up a string of fish. "We all caught some," he said. Then Captain Hardenbergh showed the newcomers how to cook the fish on a green stick held over a campfire.

"Were you ladies lonesome while we were gone?" he asked with a twinkle.

"Oh, not at all," said Polly, giving Mother a special look. They were not going to tell Beaver Tail's secret yet. It would be time enough when the men got their first taste of fresh apple pie.

After eating, the picnickers put out the campfire, then rested awhile on the grassy bank beyond the beach. They listened to the gentle lapping of the lake and the splash of the waterfall. A soft breeze blew from the water. Everyone was very

happy, but Polly was happiest of all. Mother, noticing her little girl's shining eyes, said, "Let's name our new home Polly's Falls."

DO YOU KNOW—

1. How the family went to their land grant?
2. How many things made Polly happy on her first visit to the land grant?
3. What the men did before the picnic? What adventure Polly and her mother had?
4. How the new home got its name?

THINGS TO DO

1. Make a table model of the place where the Price family was going to live. How can you show the lake? The falls? The beach?
2. Act out the scene of Beaver Tail's visit to the beach and what happened afterwards.
3. Talk about the way that Mother and Polly acted toward Beaver Tail. Were they scared? Did they act in a way that would build friendship? What can we learn from them?

167

"Is that an adz?" Polly asks Captain Hardenbergh, as he holds it out for her to see.

5: Work and Play at Polly's Falls

The next visit to Polly's Falls was not for a picnic. Mrs. Price and Polly didn't go this time. Captain Hardenbergh said, "This is men's work for a while now. We'll need axes and adzes."

"What's an adz?" asked Polly. The Captain showed her two that he was putting into the wagon.

"This first one is used for taking the bark off trees," he explained. "The other will make boards smooth. We can't build a boat without boards."

"I've been thinking," said Mr. Price, "that David and Tim and I had better camp up there for a few weeks. We'll have to clear some land at once if we're to get a corn crop in. Then we'll have to chop enough logs for our house.

"Now, Captain, you have been good enough to offer to help us today. We'll be pleased with your help. Then at nightfall I hope you'll row the boat back to Van Doren's and drive the wagon back here. And next time you folks at the Corners see us, it'll mean we have our own boat built."

"What will you eat, all by yourselves?" asked Mrs. Price. "You can't live on fish."

"We could if we had to," said Father. "Many new settlers have done worse. But we'll have squirrels, too."

"Oh, dear," said Polly, "must you shoot squirrels? They're so sweet."

"These black squirrels are very hard on the crops," said the Captain. "They can go right through a new cornfield and

168

leave it as clean as before it was planted. Sometimes all the neighbors get together and go on a squirrel shoot. I've known ten men to get over a thousand squirrels. It will be better to shoot them now and eat them than to wait until they've taken *your* food."

"I think Mrs. Beaver Tail will help the men out with corncakes and the like," said Kate Freeman. "She's a good soul."

"One thing you must do, Enos, before you go," said Mother. "I can't be idle while you're gone. Please set up my big spinning wheel."

"Now don't you bother to do that, Mr. Price," said Kate. "Mistress Price can use ours. I've no wool to spin. The wolves got the only flock of sheep that was ever brought to the Corners."

After the men had gone, Mother got out her big sack of wool. Some of it had been *carded*—enough for her to start the spinning. Polly and Kate Freeman went to work carding the rest. It was hard work, but they were both good at it. They liked to see the little rolls come out white and curly. Sometimes Mother took her turn at carding while Kate or Polly walked back and forth, back and forth, at the wheel.

When the wool had all been carded and spun, Kate helped Mother dye it. They boiled butternut bark. The dye bath was scalding hot when the gray yarn went into it. When the yarn had been taken out, cooled, and dried, it had a fine brown color.

After that, Kate took Mother and Polly to call on Mrs. Stebbins, who lived beyond the mill. Mrs. Stebbins had a loom. By good luck, there was no work in it now. "You go right ahead and weave

Mother spins at the big wheel, while Kate and Polly card more wool for her to spin.

your wool," she said to Mother. "I'll be glad to have company."

"I thought I would use the brown for the *warp*," said Mother. "I brought some red yarn from our old home. Do you think that would do for the *woof*?"

"I think that mixture would make a nice, warm reddish brown," said Mrs. Stebbins. "And it won't show dirt very much."

It took Mother about four hours to set up the loom with the brown wool. Then she and Polly took turns at the weaving. Mother's turn was always longer, because weaving was hard work for a young girl of twelve.

"I shall have only about six yards of wool to use this year," said Mrs. Price. "I must make your father a warm coat. He will be outdoors in bitter cold. You'll have to have a coat, too. You outgrew your old one. When are you going to stop growing, dear?"

"I'll stop right now, if you want me to," said Polly, with a grin.

"I don't believe you can. You take after your father. You children are all tall, like him. I don't know what I'll do about clothes for Timothy. He needs breeches and a jacket. I can make the jacket out of my old cloak, but what shall I use for breeches?"

"What will you use for a cloak?" asked Polly.

"I can wear your father's old Army coat. I don't have to go outdoors much, you know."

When the men came back to Captain Hardenbergh's house, Tim wanted to talk about nothing but their boat. "You should see it!" he cried. "We made it bigger than Mr. Van Doren's, even. We'll have to carry our wagon on it, you know."

"Have you got enough logs to build your house?" asked the Captain.

"I think we have," said Mr. Price.

"Then we'll have a house-raising for you on Sunday."

Mother weaves the brown wool on Mrs. Stebbins' big loom. Polly watches and waits for her turn to help.

Tim knew that this was a really big boat they were building! It would even carry the covered wagon!

"Should people work on Sunday?" asked Polly, in a shocked voice.

"Well, Polly, I'll tell you how it is," said Captain Hardenbergh. He was speaking to her in the way she liked, just as if she were grown-up. "We all have to work so hard out here on the frontier that we save Sundays for work that isn't so hard. That's almost like resting.

"At a house-raising, the neighbors get together. It's a Christian thing, working to help one another. Even preachers help at house-raisings. If you go to church first, it's all right. And if there isn't any church to go to, it's still all right."

"I think I understand," said Polly.

She understood even better on the day when the house was raised. Neighbors the Prices had never even met before came to help. But before the others came, Polly and Mother had their first look at the place where their home would be. The new boat had carried the Price family, the Captain, and some other friends from Hardenbergh's Corners to the little point of land below Polly's Falls.

Mother and Polly were surprised at the looks of their land. The little grassy point, the pebbly beach, and the water-fall were the same. But so many of the trees were gone! The piece of level land where the house would stand was bare except for three trees, left for shade. Logs were lying everywhere.

Soon friendly neighbors began to arrive. Mr. Van Doren brought some settlers from the foot of the lake. Mr. Bitner, from the east side of the lake, brought his own family and one other. "I have a keg of cider here," said Mr. Bitner. "We men can't work if we get too thirsty."

People from the west side of the lake came on foot or on horseback. Mr. Van Horn, the *blacksmith* from the hill far back of Polly's Falls, brought his wife and three children. They had had a long walk through the woods. Peter Van Horn was about Tim's age, and he said, "I'll take you to look for chestnuts later this fall. I hope the squirrels don't get them all before we do."

There was a new friend for Polly, too. The Skinners walked over from the next farm and, for the first time, Polly met Abbie Skinner. "I'm so glad you're here," said Abbie. "I have been lonesome for

171

my friends back home in New England. You and I can have good talks while we're making candles or soap. There isn't much time for anything but work in a new settlement."

The men went to work with a will. For the foundation of the house they dug a hole two feet deep. They made it fifteen feet wide and twenty feet long.

Around the edge of the hole they made a wall of logs fourteen feet high. The logs had been sharpened at the ends and driven into the ground. They filled in earth around these logs to make them stand straight and strong. An opening was left for a door on the side toward the lake. There was a smaller hole for a window high at one end.

The roof was made of pieces of chestnut bark. They overlapped one another, so as to shed water. They were held in place by poles running from front to back. There was not enough bark to cover the whole house. Father said, "Don't mind that. I'll make the rest of the roof before cold weather. There's enough now to keep us from the rain."

While the men were raising the house, the women were preparing a feast. They went to Mrs. Skinner's house, to roast a wild turkey in her Dutch oven. She had a real fireplace, which made cooking easier than it was in the Hardenbergh house and most of the others.

Each woman had brought vegetables from her garden. Many had brought cookies or a pie or a tin of gingerbread.

Polly and Abbie talked together as they helped with the cooking. "Have you any pets?" asked Polly.

The women prepare a feast, while the men help build the Price's house. Cooking in Mrs. Skinner's kitchen is easy, because she has a fireplace that holds many kettles.

The house-raising is over, and the feast begins!

"No," said Abbie. "I never had a pet. Did you?"

"Oh, yes," said Polly. Then she told Abbie all about Miss Muffet. "It was hard to leave her," she said. "I guess I never will feel at home again until I have a pet."

"I don't care so much about pets," said Abbie, "but I do wish there were some boys my age near here. Don't you ever worry about getting married?"

"No," said Polly. "I know just the kind of man I want to marry. I don't worry about boys. I think I can find the man I want." She was thinking about Captain Hardenbergh, who treated her like a lady. She was thinking how she would like to take care of little Cornelia. But she didn't tell Abbie what she was thinking.

The men sat around on stumps or fallen tree trunks while the women brought the food. They washed it down with Mr. Bitner's cider. They drank toasts to all the things they cared for most. "Here's to our country, the United States of America," said Mr. Price.

"To our president, George Washington," cried the Captain, lifting his mug of cider, "first in peace as he was first in war."

"To freedom!"

"To the heroes of the Revolution who won freedom for us."

"To the Governor of New York State, George Clinton," said Mr. Skinner. "Long may he live!"

They drank to the new settlers. They drank to Captain Hardenbergh and his gristmill. They drank to the sawmill they hoped Mr. Price would build. They drank to Hardenbergh's Corners, which would soon be a big town, they said. They drank to the Lake-near-the-Crossing-Place. They drank to Polly's Falls.

Then everybody sang "Yankee Doodle," "Bunker Hill," and "The Liberty Song."

When the men had rested long enough after dinner, the games of strength began. First came wrestling. This started with the smaller boys. As soon as one boy had out-wrestled another, he took on a new boy. Little by little, the older boys

173

The men and boys play at many games of strength. Can you name some of them?

came in, and then the men. Finally only David and Captain Hardenbergh were left wrestling. The Captain was more than fifty years old, but he was so strong that he was a match for the younger man. Neither could get the other down. At last everybody shouted, "A tie! A tie!"

Next there were running races along the shore. There was broad-jumping and there was high-jumping. Some of the men pitched horseshoes, which Mr. Skinner brought from his horse-shed.

It was dark when the party broke up. "Oh, let's not go away!" said Timothy. "Let's sleep in our new home."

"We haven't any of our furniture here," said Mother.

"We could sleep outdoors," said Tim. "It's warm enough."

"Listen! What was that sound?" asked Mother.

"That was a wolf howling, Ma'am," said Mr. Bitner. "Wait till later at night. You'll hear them howling like ghosts. Some of them may *be* ghosts."

"I was just joking about staying here tonight," said Tim.

DO YOU KNOW—

1. What were the men's first tasks at Polly's Falls? What they built before they returned to Hardenbergh's Corners?

2. What was Mrs. Price's big job while the men were gone? How Polly helped?

3. Why all the neighbors came to Polly's Falls on a Sunday? How everybody helped? What friends Polly and Tim made? What kinds of fun the men and boys had after the big job was done?

THINGS TO DO

1. Try making a model of the house that was built at Polly's Falls.

2. Ask your librarian or your music teacher for books that give the words and music of songs that people sang after the Revolutionary War. Learn to sing those that you like best.

3. Visit a museum or a library where you can learn about a loom. Learn to weave.

6: First Days at the New Home

It was two weeks after the house-raising. Polly and her mother were still living in the Captain's house at the Corners. "When can we move to our home?" Polly teased.

"Just as soon as your father gets the house ready for us," said Mother. "He will have to make a place for me to cook. I'm afraid it will be a Dutch back. It takes so long to build a good stone fireplace and chimney."

Mother was right. A Dutch back wasn't a very safe way of cooking and of heating a house, but everybody would be careful.

At last the day came when Father and David brought the boat down the lake and into the outlet. They tied it up at the landing above Hardenbergh's dam and began loading it with the furniture from their wagon. The largest pieces were the two benches from the old farmhouse in eastern New York. Between them stood Mother's little rocking chair, a barrel of pewter and crockery for serving food, the trunk of clothing, and some food bought from farmers near the Corners.

At last everything was aboard the boat, except the wagon and the oxen. The men would have to come back later for them. Captain Hardenbergh with little Cornelia in his arms came to bid the family good-by. "Keep pretty and don't get fat, Miss Polly," he called, as the boat moved up the outlet. Harry and Kate Freeman waved from the landing.

Mother was very quiet as Father and David rowed slowly toward Polly's Falls. She was planning ways to make the new house seem homelike. She knew she would have a hard job.

And so she did. There were no beds, no cupboards, no tables. Most of the household things had to be kept in barrels or baskets when not in use. Mrs. Beaver Tail gave Mother a finely woven basket of

The Price family loads the boat with furniture for their new home.

rye straw in which she set her bread dough to rise.

Nobody minded sleeping on mattresses spread on the floor. The family was used to it by now. Polly wanted to sleep outdoors. She loved to look up at the stars shining like hundreds and hundreds of candles. She loved to see the same stars shining up at her from the still, dark lake.

But Tim spoke to her of the wolves. "Maybe," he said, "they are ghosts that sound like wolves." She decided that it might be better to sleep indoors.

The men were busy outdoors from dawn to nightfall. They were clearing the land as fast as they could. They needed a big field for winter wheat. They hoped to have a pasture for the cattle by another year.

Now the cattle had to be driven to the woods every day. There they nibbled the leaves they could reach. If food was scarce, David cut some of the higher branches from the trees. Sometimes the deer found these branches before the cattle did. Then Father or David found the deer, and the family had deer meat for dinner.

The cattle had to be brought home late in the afternoon. Wild animals prowled the woods at night, looking for a good meal. A cow or an ox would have suited them very well. Sukie wore a bell to help the men find her, and the oxen were always nearby. Polly, Tim, and Mother had been told not to go to the woods after dark.

The men cleared one piece of land at a time. First of all, the small trees and underbrush were cut. Timothy helped with this job. Then he helped drag away the cut brush and the fallen branches.

Next the big trees could be cut. It was easy to get at them with no brush in the way. Father and David did this job very carefully. They planned to make the trees all fall in the same direction. On the hills, the trees were cut so that they could be rolled downhill. "This is hard work," David would say when he came home very tired, "but I like it. Every day I can see the clearing get bigger."

The trunks and big branches, cut into logs, were left lying on the field for about two months. By this time, they were usually quite dry. Then they were set afire. The fire burned all the small trees and weeds. It destroyed some of the logs and blackened the others.

Tim drives the cattle into the woods, where they will nibble on leaves. Sukie leads the way, her bell ringing merrily. If food is scarce, David will have to cut some of the higher branches for the cattle.

The oxen were used to pull the remaining logs off the fields. The logs were piled into huge heaps, then set afire.

"How I hate to see that fine wood burn," said Mother. "It would make furniture and all sorts of good things."

"It isn't all wasted," said Father. "We shall collect the ashes. You'll use some in making soap, and we'll send the rest to the ashery. We'll get a few dollars from them. They will be made into *potash* to use in making glass or other things."

One Saturday afternoon, the men finished burning a log heap. Mr. Skinner had been helping them, just as they sometimes helped him log his fields. They had collected the ashes in barrels. This was hard, dirty work. The men were covered with smoke and ashes. Their feet were smarting from walking over stones and briers. The pioneer men almost never wore shoes in the summer. Shoes were hard to make and were saved to be worn in cold weather.

The three men and Tim went down to the lake to wash. "How lucky we are to live near a lake!" cried Tim. "We can get clean and have fun at the same time." Then he dived from the boat into the deep water.

The men swam for a time, until Mr. Price said, "Let's go over to the south field and pick some blackberries. My wife was saying she'd like to make some blackberry pies. Your folks must come over and have supper and some pie with us, Joel," he added to Mr. Skinner.

When everybody's basket was full, Father said, "I'll take these berries to my wife. Suppose you fetch your family for supper now, Joel."

Mrs. Skinner shows Mother and Polly how to shoot.

When Mrs. Skinner came, she was carrying a gun. When Mrs. Price saw her friend with the gun, she said, "I wouldn't dare touch one of those things."

"You'd better learn," said Mrs. Skinner. "You and Polly both. Women who live in the wilderness have to know how to shoot, and to shoot straight. After supper Abbie and I will show you how. They say a woman can teach a woman to shoot better than a man can."

DO YOU KNOW—

1. What the house at Polly's Falls was like when Mother and Polly went there to live? How the family lived?

2. How the cattle were fed and cared for?

3. How the men logged a field or a hillside? Why it was hard, dirty work?

THINGS TO DO

1. Ask your librarian for a book that tells what ashes were used for, and how pioneers made soap.

2. Draw or paint a picture of some happening in this chapter that is not shown.

Captain Hardenbergh's mill is the place to hear the latest news!

7: A Visit to Hardenbergh's Corners

On Monday, Father said, "I'm going to row down to the foot of the lake today. I want to take those ashes down to the Corners. The Captain will get a chance to send them to the ashery at Log City some day soon, I'm sure. Polly, would you like to go with me?"

"Oh, may I, Mother?" cried Polly.

"I think so," said Mother. "You got a lot of flax spun last week. You may have a day off."

"May I wear my shoes?"

"Children don't wear shoes in the summer, except to church," said Mother. "I don't know when Father will get time to make more shoes. You'd better save yours for the winter."

"All right," said Polly, but she sounded a little sad. "I wish I had something new to wear."

"I'll let you wear my white collar over your yellow dress," said Mother. "Fasten it with your silver pin."

"Oh, thank you, Mother!" cried Polly, and soon she was scampering down to the shore where Father was waiting for her.

They rowed down the lake and into the outlet. At Hardenbergh's Landing they tied up their boat.

"We'll go to the mill first," said Father.

There were several men at the mill, waiting for their grain to be ground. Everybody was telling the news because this was the only place where people from far away got together.

Harry Freeman came upstairs with a linen sack full of flour that had just come through the mill. He spoke to Mr. Bump, who had brought the wheat. "Do you want the *bran* sifted out?" he asked.

178

"Yes, please," said Mr. Bump. "My wife uses the bran in dyeing wool."

Harry Freeman sifted the flour. Into a big basket, finely woven, went the flour. The bran stayed in the sieve.

Polly whispered to Father, "Didn't Mr. Bump have to pay for getting his wheat ground?"

"Oh, yes," said Mr. Price. "Captain Hardenbergh takes a small part of all the wheat he grinds. That's his pay. He sells the extra wheat he gets, or he trades it for something else he needs."

The Captain poured more wheat into the *hopper*, and the big *millstones* began grinding. Polly went over to talk to the Captain while he was watching the millstones. "There are lots of people here today," she said.

"Yes," said Captain Hardenbergh, "and I hope there won't be any more. My mill can't grind more than twelve bushels a day. I'm planning to get another set of millstones before next summer."

The Captain worked at the hopper a minute, and then he said, "What brings you and your father here today? I know you haven't any wheat planted, and your corn isn't ready yet."

"Father brought some ashes," Polly said. "We burned a lot of logs. He thought maybe we could find a way to send the ashes to the ashery at Log City."

"Your father is in luck," said the Captain. "Mr. Higgins from Log City is here today. He has his oxcart, so I know he'll be able to take the ashes. Next time he comes to the mill, he'll bring your father the money."

Mr. Higgins had another idea. "Could you use a sheepskin?" he asked. "A wolf killed my only sheep last night. I shot

Polly watches Captain Hardenbergh as he puts wheat into the hopper where it will be ground. Harry Freeman sifts the flour as it shoots into the bin below.

the wolf before he tore the sheep to pieces, so the skin is in good condition. But I don't know how to tan it, and we haven't a tannery in Log City yet, or for twenty miles around. I'll trade it for your ashes if you can use it."

"I don't know how to tan sheepskin or anything else," said Mr. Price.

Polly said, "Beaver Tail knows how to tan deerskin. Maybe he could help us with this. I heard Mother say that she needs something to make Tim some winter breeches."

"Mr. Higgins," said Father, "I'll make the trade with you. It doesn't give me cash money, which is what I need. But you'll oblige me by taking my ashes to Log City."

Just then there was a commotion around the door. A tall, lanky fellow with two small trunks slung over his shoulder on a strap came into the mill.

"The Yankee peddler!" cried Captain Hardenbergh.

"Will he be coming to our place?" asked Polly.

"No," said the Captain. "He couldn't get through that Indian trail, with his horse and his two trunks. He stops only at mills and houses on the Genesee Turnpike and the other main roads."

"Well, then," said Polly, "I'd better remind Father of the things Mother needs. She has had trouble with the last pins she bought. The heads kept coming off. I'll ask the peddler if he has the new kind made all in one piece. The heads can't come off those."

"Yes, I have the new pins, young lady," said the peddler. He was swiftly unpacking his trunks. He spread his goods out on the benches and, when the benches were full, on the floor. In one place were spices. In another were

The Yankee peddler shows his goods to the settlers. Can you name some of the things he has to sell?

combs made from horn. And next he put down buttons of bone, brass, pewter, and even silver.

"Let's get Mother some silver buttons," said Polly.

"No," said Father. "They cost too much. But we'll buy her a piece of lace for a new collar. You can hide it until her birthday."

"Can't we buy some of these little books for Tim?" asked Polly. "I don't want him to forget how to read, now that there's no school for him to go to. These books will help him."

"Yes, we'll get him as many of the little books as we can buy for a copper coin," said Father.

The peddler grinned at Father. "I'll trade you ten books for the silver pin the little lady is wearing," he said.

"Oh, no," said Father. "That pin has been in our family for a hundred years. I'll pay money for the books."

"Three, then," said the peddler, "three for a copper."

Polly started to say, "I'll give up my silver pin," when the Captain took her gently by the arm.

"Come over here a minute," he said, leading her away. When they were in the far corner, he whispered, "Your silver pin is worth many times as much as a copper. The peddler knows this. So does your father, but many people do not know the worth of jewelry. They will trade lockets and golden pins for a few goods. The peddler sells jewelry at a high price when he gets back to Albany or Boston or wherever he came from."

"But that isn't fair," said Polly.

"No, it isn't," the Captain agreed, "but some peddlers have tricks like that. However, we put up with them. We couldn't get along without peddlers here in the wilderness."

While the Captain and Polly were talking, Mr. Price was buying a present for Polly. It was pink ribbon for a pretty sash. This would be her birthday present from him and Mother.

When Polly returned, Father bought some whole cloves and a small box of ginger. "Let's take a little pepper, too," said Polly. "It will be fine on the rabbit and raccoon meat Mother cooks."

"All right," said Father, "and I'll get a little tea for your mother. She hasn't had a cup of tea since we left our old home. Then I mustn't spend any more."

The peddler was doing a good business. The men who lived near the Corners had gone to fetch their wives. "I hate to think of the money she'll spend," said one of the men, "but she'll never forgive me if I don't tell her the Yankee peddler is here."

At last everybody was through buying. Polly could not believe her eyes as she watched the peddler pack his trunks. The whole mill was full of his goods. There seemed to be enough for ten trunks. But in almost no time he had stowed them all neatly away. He lifted the trunks on their leather strap and slung them over his shoulder as easily as Polly could have lifted Miss Muffet. In a second he was outside and on his horse. "I'll see you next year, folks," he shouted.

"By the way," said the Captain, "we have new neighbors, the O'Brien family. Mr. O'Brien is going to start a little store in his house. Then we won't have to wait for the peddler."

DO YOU KNOW—

1. Why Mr. Price was going to Hardenbergh's Corners?

2. Why Hardenbergh's mill was a place for meeting and telling the news? What other ways did people in pioneer days have for finding out the news? How the Captain's mill worked?

3. Why peddlers were welcomed by people in the new settlements? What kinds of things they sold? Why Mr. O'Brien was going to start a little store in his house?

THINGS TO DO

Act out some of the scenes in the mill. Perhaps groups of children might act out different scenes and put them together to tell the whole story of Polly's visit to the Corners.

Off he goes with his wares! Soon Hardenbergh's Corners may have its own store.

The door is finished, and now the deed box is on its new shelf.

8: Getting Ready for Winter

When Polly got home, she rushed into the cabin to tell Mother about the peddler. "We got good pins for you, Mother, all made in one piece."

"I got something else," said Father. "I got us a deed box."

Polly looked at the box he handed to Mother. It was a tin box about the size of a small loaf of bread, but not so high. It was painted black with red roses and green leaves on the cover. There was a clasp, but no lock. "What's it for?" asked Polly.

"This box is for our important papers," said Father.

Polly did not know what he meant. She knew that all paper cost a good deal of money. But she did not know why some papers should be more important than others. Seeing her puzzled face,

Father laughed. "It's like this," he said. "We have a paper that proves this land belongs to us. If anybody ever tries to take our home away, this paper will protect us. It's called a deed."

"What other important papers have we?" asked Polly.

"We have the paper that Mr. Briggs signed when he bought our old home," said Father. "He wrote on this paper that he would send us money every year until the farm was all paid for."

"Another important paper," said Mother, "is the one that tells when your father and I were married. Others tell when you children were baptized."

"Why do we need a box for these papers?" asked Polly.

"This tin box will keep them safe and clean," said Father. "We shall tell our neighbors where we keep it. If our cabin should catch fire when we are away, they will save this box first of all. When we build a fireplace, we shall keep our deed box on the mantel. Until then, I suppose we'd best make a little shelf for it right inside the door."

"That will be good," said Mother. "I wonder when we are going to get our house finished inside."

"We'll get at it just as soon as we build a pen for our cattle, Faith. When cold weather comes, wild animals may get after them. We must protect them."

"You're right, Enos," said Mother. "Make the animals safe first. What would we do without them?"

The next day Father and David went to work on the cattle pen. They built a strong fence of solid logs, high enough so that a wolf could not jump over it. "Maybe I can build a little shed for the cattle before snow flies," said Father.

"The next thing for us to do," he went on, "is to put up a door for the house. We can't have panthers and wolves coming to visit us."

He and David smoothed some boards with an adz. "What will we use for hinges?" asked David.

"Old Beaver Tail said he would help us with hinges," said Father. "He has some deerskin straps that will do very well. Tim, will you go to Beaver Tail's hut and get the deerskin straps?"

"Oh, yes," cried Tim, and he was off. He chatted awhile with his Indian friends. Then Beaver Tail gave him the deerskin straps for the door. "How is the sheepskin coming along?" asked Tim, as he was leaving.

"It all right, I think. I never tan anything but deerskin before. I hope same way work with sheepskin."

Tim got back just as the men were fitting the door into place. They hung it on its deerskin hinges. It would have no lock, but the men made a latch fastened with a string. When the latch string was out, people could come in from the out-

The cattle pen is built by notching logs with a hatchet and fitting them together.

David seals the walls of their new home with mud,
while father makes furniture.

side. When it was in, the door could be
opened only from the inside.

Next the men finished covering the
house with a bark roof. They left a hole
above the Dutch back, and daubed it
with mud.

The beds were built next. Mr. Price
had saved some good stout *crotches* from
the trees that had been cut down. There
were four for each bed, one at each corner. He sharpened the ends and drove
the sharpened ends into the ground.
Then he put a long pole along each side of
the bed, held up by the crotches at the
foot and the head. Across the poles he
put boards. These would support the
straw mattress.

Mother was very happy about the
beds. She unpacked her pretty quilts.
"These were too good to use while we

slept on the ground," she said, "but they'll
make our house look like a real home.
Now that we have only one room, we
must do our best to make it pleasant to
live in.

"I'm worried about the window," said
Mother. "It will let in the cold winds."

"I'm going to use oiled paper to cover
the window," said Father. "Some light
will come through, but not much cold.

"Another thing I must do is to close up
the cracks in the house walls and the
door. I'll fill in the cracks with mud
which will dry hard and solid. I'm going
to dig a hole inside our house to get earth
to use in making the mud. I'll leave a
hole just big enough for storing *root vegetables*. We'll cover them with earth and
some boards. If we're lucky, they'll last
all winter."

A surprise! Mother serves the two steaming apple pies to her family and the Beavertails.

A few days later the house was as cozy as it could be made. "A good thing, too," said Father. "It's time to plant our winter wheat. Maybe we will not have much, but there will be enough for us and maybe a few bushels for the Utica wheat market. Wheat from the Genesee country is the best. Everybody wants it."

"But tonight," said Mother, "we're going to celebrate. I want you to invite Mr. and Mrs. Beaver Tail for supper. I have planned a surprise for everybody."

"I'll go and ask them," said Tim, darting out of the house.

Mother winked at Polly. The men did not yet know Beaver Tail's secret. Polly had gathered all the apples she could find under the twisted apple trees of the old orchard. Mother had hidden them in the floor hole.

When the men had gone outside, Mother began making pie crust dough of the wheat flour and bear fat that Kate Freeman had given her. Polly cut up enough apples for two big pies. Mother put the dough for the bottom crusts into two pie tins. She heaped the pie tins with apples and put on the top crust. She pinched the edges of the top and bottom crusts together, and made a pretty design of tiny holes in the top of each pie. Then she set each pie tin in a bakepot that hung over the fire.

By the time the men came in, the pies were done and had been hidden under a huge kettle. Soon Mr. and Mrs. Beaver Tail came, and everybody sat down to a meal of stewed rabbit and hot corn bread.

"Don't get too full," said Mother.

"Why?" asked Tim. "We'll just get some of that old stewed pumpkin."

"Guess again," said Mother, smiling.

At this, she brought out the apple pies. Beaver Tail grinned. "I knew you'd do what you said, Miss Polly," he said. Then he told his secret, and everybody laughed and had another piece of pie.

DO YOU KNOW—

1. What a deed box was? What papers the Price family had to protect? Whether your parents have important papers and, if so, what?

2. How Father and David put up a door? How they made the house a more pleasant place?

3. How Mother and Polly baked pies? Where they got the apples for the pies?

4. How the Price family and the Beaver Tail family showed that they were good neighbors?

9: *Tim's Adventure*

David was having trouble plowing the field for wheat. The plow didn't turn up the soil as it should. "Let me look at the plow," said Father.

He felt of the *plowshare* and the *colter*. "They're both dull," he said. "We need a blacksmith to sharpen them. Mr. Skinner takes his horse to Mr. Van Horn's to be shod. But how can we take our plowshare and colter there? They are too heavy to carry. Our wagon is too wide to go through that narrow trail to the blacksmith's."

"I have an idea," said Tim. "I could ride Mr. Skinner's horse, old Sally. We could put the plowshare in one end of our big *hemp* bag and the colter in the other end. You could put the bag over the horse's back."

"The plow parts wouldn't balance," said Father.

"I'll sit on the middle of the bag and anchor it. That will keep it from slipping off," said Tim.

"Maybe Mr. Skinner needs his horse for plowing," said David.

"He's chopping trees today," said Tim. "I was over there this morning. He said that Sally needs new shoes, but he hasn't any time to take her to the blacksmith. I could get her shod while I was there."

"Do you think you could find your way?" asked Mother. "It's three miles up the hill from here."

"The trees are marked all the way," said Tim. "Mr. Skinner showed me the kind of marks to look for. Besides, old Sally knows the way. Ever since the house-raising, I've wanted to go up there to see Peter. I never had time before."

Tim was happy, and everybody else was pleased with his plan. Mr. Skinner was glad to have Sally shod. Father was glad that his plowshare and colter would be repaired. He put them into the big hemp bag, which he placed over Sally's back.

As Tim was climbing onto the horse, his mother said, "You can't wear those torn breeches. What would Mistress Van Horn think of your mother? You must wear your new sheepskin breeches."

"The plowshare and colter are dull," says Father. "They must be sharpened."

"Won't they be too warm?" asked Tim.

"I'm afraid they will," said Mother, "but at least you'll look as if you had a mother who cares how you are dressed."

Tim struggled into the new breeches. They were rather tight and short. He was growing long-legged, and one sheepskin was hardly enough to make a pair of breeches for him. "They'll have to do," said Mother. "I haven't enough wool to make you another pair this year. Next spring we'll take some sheep to double, and I'll have enough wool for us all."

"What does that mean, Mother, taking sheep to double?" asked Tim.

"We'll borrow two or three female sheep from another settler. The sheep will have lambs. That's what we mean when we say they double. There will be two sheep for each one. We shall feed and take care of them all. A year later, we'll give back a sheep or a lamb for each one we borrowed. Everyone gains by this plan. The settler we borrowed from gets a year's free care and food for the sheep we give back. We get the extra sheep or lambs to keep for our own."

"That's a good plan," said Tim, as he rode away on old Sally.

It was a warm autumn day. White clouds rode high in the sky. They came together, made a darker mass, then parted again. Sometimes they covered the sun, but not for long.

Tim could see the blue sky and the clouds through the leafy branches overhead. The woods were cool. He could follow the marked trees without trouble. The way led uphill, so he did not try to hurry old Sally. He munched some corn

Tim and old Sally make their way to the blacksmith's through brightly colored woods.

"This must be the top of the world!" Tim thinks,
as he looks at the beautiful countryside below.

bread as he rode along. It was hard to balance the plowshare and the colter. Aside from this, he enjoyed everything.

It was early afternoon when he reached Mr. Van Horn's house and forge. Peter came running out. "Oh, at last you've come to play with me!" he cried.

"Maybe I can play later," Tim answered, "but first I have to do some business with your father."

"He's out in the far field," said Peter. "If you ride up this path, you'll find him."

Up the path rode Tim. When he reached the hilltop, he looked around him on all sides. "This must be the top of the world," he thought. Behind him lay *his* lake, the Lake-near-the-Crossing-Place. Ahead of him was a much larger lake,

which the Indians called the Lake-of-the-Boat-Landing. "This is a fine place," he thought. "Some day I'd like to have a house on a hill where I could see two lakes."

At the end of the field he saw Mr. Van Horn coming slowly toward him. Mr. Van Horn was a very short, very fat man. He did not like to hurry. When at last he and Tim met, he agreed to go down to his forge. "Too bad Peter isn't big enough to help at the smithy," he said. "Farming and blacksmithing together are too much for one man."

Slowly he went down the hill. Slowly he blew up the fire in his forge. Slowly he put new shoes on Sally's hoofs. Then he went to work on the plowshare.

189

"Now don't get excited, Sonny," the blacksmith tells Tim. "I'll be finished before it rains."

While Tim waited, he went with Peter to look for chestnuts. The ground was littered with the shiny brown nuts. The boys ate all they could hold and brought a big basketful to Mrs. Van Horn and the younger children.

Back at the house, Peter's little brother asked Tim, "Where did you get those breeches?"

"Mother made them for me," said Tim. "Beaver Tail tanned the sheepskin."

Mrs. Van Horn looked at the sheepskin and felt of it. "I'm afraid it isn't very well tanned," she said. "I hope we'll have a real tannery here at the Corners before long."

Tim went back to the forge. How slow Mr. Van Horn was! He was sharpening the colter, but stopped ever so often to rest and to talk to anybody who would listen.

"Blowing up to rain, I think," he said. "Those clouds look like it."

"If it's going to rain, couldn't you please hurry?" asked Tim politely. He knew he shouldn't say it. Children were supposed to keep quiet even when they were right.

"Now don't get excited, sonny," said Mr. Van Horn. "I'll have your job done before it rains."

"But I've got to get home, too," said Tim. He was a little afraid he was going to cry, and he knew that a man of ten should never cry. Quickly he said, "Mr. Skinner sent you this bag of corn for shoeing Sally. Is it enough?"

"I guess so," said Mr. Van Horn. "What did your father send for sharpening the plowshare and the colter?"

"He sent money," said Tim. "He hasn't anything else because we haven't been here long enough to grow crops."

"Money will be fine," said Mr. Van Horn. "I almost never see any cash money. There's going to be a store down near the big lake, I hear, so I'll be needing money."

190

At last the work was done. Tim paid the blacksmith, who put the big bag on the horse's back.

The sky was dark and threatening as Tim started toward home. "You'd better stay here overnight," called Mrs. Van Horn, but Tim shook his head. He felt that he had a job to do and that he must do it.

The clouds were piling up overhead. A cold wind was blowing the leaves from the trees. Tim shivered in his linen shirt. He was glad he was wearing the sheepskin breeches.

Sally knew the way home. She went steadily on, though the thunder was rumbling. All around, Tim heard the crack and crash of big branches in the wind. Sometimes a branch fell across the path. Sally found her way around it and back to the trail.

It was now as dark as night in the woods. Looking up, Tim could see only

a little light in the sky. The massed clouds were moving forward, always right over him, it seemed.

Suddenly, with a great crash of thunder, the rain began falling. It came in a flood. It didn't seem that it could be falling in drops. Rather, it seemed as if it were pouring from a million buckets.

Sally stopped and shook herself. It was hard going. Tim said, "Go on, Sally. Nice oats at home, remember?" He patted her neck and she started on again.

She plunged through a brook swollen with the flood. The water came up to Tim's feet. But the horse scrambled up the bank on the other side. She kept going, back toward the trail that had been blocked by the brook.

Tim shivered. Everything he had on was wringing wet, even the new sheepskin breeches. He pulled them down to cover his cold knees. But what was this? A piece of the sheepskin came off in his hand. "I'd better not do that again," he thought. "These breeches have to last me all winter." Then he noticed that Sally had stopped again.

The wind blows and great dark clouds gather in the sky, as Tim leaves the Van Horn's house.

Old Sally stops before a fallen tree! The storm whips around them as Tim tries to urge her on.

She did not go on when he spoke to her. A flash of lightning showed him why. A huge tree lay right across the trail. It was so big that there seemed no way to get around it. Now Sally was shivering too. Perhaps the wind and the rain and the lightning had scared her. Perhaps she was only cold. Whichever way it was, she seemed ready to spend the night in this place.

Tim thought of all the wild animals of the woods. He thought of the ghost stories he had heard. What should he do? He couldn't find his way home in the dark. He couldn't find his way back to the Van Horn farm, either.

"Well, then, I'll just have to spend the night on horseback," he thought. As soon as he had made up his mind, he was not so scared any more. "I'd better not go to sleep, though," he went on. "These plow parts will slip and carry me off with them."

Back at the house, Mother and Polly were worried. All their men were gone. Mr. Price and David had rowed down the lake to get some wood for their mill wheels. They knew that a settler had cut down a huge tree. It was so large around that a slice of the trunk would be big enough for the largest wheel.

Late in the afternoon, the men were not yet back. Their flat-bottomed boat was nowhere to be seen. The wind was blowing. The lake no longer had that beautiful blue brightness that Polly loved so. It was gray-green and sad-looking.

192

Across the lake a sheet of grayness came toward them. "That's rain," said Mother. "It will hit our men out in the middle of the lake. This wind . . ." then she stopped, because she didn't want to scare Polly.

"You mean the wind might tip their boat over?" Polly asked. "I don't think so, Mother. This lake and all the lakes hereabout are well known for their sudden squalls. That's why people build flat-bottomed boats, so the Captain said. It's hard to tip them over."

"Polly dear," said Mother, "you are a comfort to me."

"I think I see a boat now," said Polly. The sky was dark, but in the clearings and on the lake there was still some daylight.

Polly was right. The boat came to the shore, and David pulled it up onto the pebbles. Then he and Father hurried up toward the cottage.

"Where's Tim?" asked David.

"He hasn't come yet," said Mother. "He should be here any minute now."

"He should have been here long before this," said Father.

"It's still early," said Mother, but she looked worried.

"It's early, but it must be as dark as night in the woods," said Father. "We'll have to go and look for Tim at once. He must have lost his way. Who knows what has happened to him?"

Mother and Polly were both white with fear. "What can we do?" asked Polly in a choking voice.

"Get a pine torch lighted in the fire," said Father. "Get some other pine knots for us to carry. We'll light them from

this one. It may be a long search. Better give me my *tinder box*. The rain might put out our lights."

It did not take Father and David long to find Tim. He was not far from home. He was sitting straight upright on Sally, clutching her mane. He looked a little pale. When he saw David clearly, he let out a shout of joy. "I was afraid you were ghosts," he said.

The men led the horse down the hill to their house. Then David took her back to Mr. Skinner.

As Tim went into the cabin, Mother and Polly grabbed him and hugged him. "Oh, what a terrible time you've had!" cried Polly.

"It wasn't so bad," said Tim, grinning.

He had no bad effects from his adventure, but his sheepskin breeches were never again the same. After they dried, they were very tight. Whenever he was out in the rain after that, he tried to stretch them. This worked well until they dried. Then they shrank and were smaller than ever.

DO YOU KNOW—

1. What a plow was? Why its parts had to be sharp? How Tim took the plow parts to the blacksmith?

2. How Tim got into a dangerous adventure? Whether he did the best he could?

3. What happened to Tim's sheepskin breeches? Why he had this trouble with them?

THINGS TO DO

1. Ask the librarian to help you find books and pictures that tell you about a blacksmith's work. Read Longfellow's poem "The Village Blacksmith." Talk about whether this blacksmith was like Mr. Van Horn.

2. If you know a farmer, ask him how he plows his fields. Find out how his way is different from the way the settlers plowed.

10: Winter at Polly's Falls

Winter came fast. There was just time for David to make a shed for the cattle before the first snowstorm blanketed the countryside.

With little outside work to do, Mr. Price went to work making boots for the men and shoes for the women. Another job that Mr. Price and David did was to shape the cogwheels for the sawmill they were going to build. They had big slices of the trunks of trees. These they shaped into wheels. They whittled cogs for the wheels. Timothy liked to help with the whittling.

Mother and Polly spun flax and knitted stockings. They also had to make candles. Mother melted *tallow* and *beeswax* in a big kettle. She and Polly fastened wicks to a rack. When the melted mixture was just warm enough, they dipped the wicks into it. As soon as the tallow had hardened on the wicks, they dipped them again into the warm mixture. They kept up the dipping until the candles were thick enough.

When Father and David were out hunting for deer or rabbits, Mother and Polly had many a long talk. Polly liked best to talk about Captain Hardenbergh. "He's such a fine gentleman," she said. "Do you think I'm too young to marry him? He talks to me just as if I were a grown-up young lady. I know I could take good care of little Cornelia. She loves me already. And soon his slaves will have their freedom. Then I could keep house for him. There's only one thing I would try to get him to change. He ought to have a real fireplace for me to cook on, instead of a Dutch back."

"Polly dear," said Mother, "I wouldn't think too much about marrying the Captain. He is a very fine man, but he is too old for you. I have heard that there is a young lady, ten or fifteen years older than you, that he likes very much."

In the winter Father makes shoes for the family, while David makes a shed for cattle.

Polly looked sad. "I had to give up Miss Muffet and now I'll have to give up the Captain," she complained. "I ought to have a new pet, at least."

Mother gave Polly a loving look. "That sounds more like my own little girl," she said. "I'm sure you'll get a pet before you get a husband."

The winter seemed long to everybody. At last March came, with one warm, spring-like day. Mother was glad. She said, "Now we'll get some fresh meat. We've been running short on food. There's only a little flour left, and a little corn meal."

Mr. Price went hunting and got a fine deer. David went along the shore until he was in front of the Skinners' house. "Have you some corn meal we could buy?" he asked. "Father will make you each a pair of shoes if you can help us with corn meal and flour. He has some leather left from what he bought at Fort Stanwix."

The plan was welcome to the Skinners, because their shoes were almost worn out. On the day they came over to have Mr. Price measure their feet, Mr. Skinner said, "I have to start on a trip to Sterling this afternoon. Just before the big snow, I heard about a man there who may buy my farm in New England. He's tired of trying to get along in the wilderness. He sent word for me to see him when I could. I guess now's the time. With this thaw, Sally can get through the trails."

"If you're going to Sterling," said Father, "maybe you can bring a straight saw and some metal parts for my sawmill. You know I want to get it built by summer."

DO YOU KNOW—

1. How the men spent their time in the winter? Why winter was a good time for such work? What was the winter work that Mother and Polly did? What the family had to eat in the wintertime? Did they have enough?

2. Why Mr. Skinner wanted to go to Sterling? What Father wanted him to bring back?

THINGS TO DO

Collect pictures of bears and other wild animals that lived in western New York in the time of the settlers. Read about them.

Father and Tim work on the cogwheels for the sawmill. Mother is dipping candles.

11: Tim's Cash Crop

Tim's father had given him a piece of land up in the northwest corner of his lot. The place was wooded, mostly with maple. Mr. Price said to Tim, "You can work it as a *sugarbush*, if you want to, Tim. Your mother would be glad to have sugar and sirup. If you make more than she can use, maybe you could sell it for cash money.

"I don't know much about sugar making," he continued, "but you could ask around and maybe find out. I'd be glad to help when I have time. You will probably need Buck and Bright, too. Let me know when you find out what you need to get started."

Tim was pleased and excited. He would have a cash crop of his own! The only problem was how to go about it. He asked at the Corners, and no one knew. Finally David brought Tim a printed leaflet that had been sent to Mr. Hardenbergh. The leaflet urged people to take up land in western New York. It

Tim learns how to make sap buckets of birchbark.

told some ways of making a living there. One of these was a cheap and easy plan for making maple sirup and sugar.

Tim read the plan carefully. It said that by tapping eight hundred trees, you could make forty hundredweight of sugar. But when Tim read about the things he would need for doing the job, he got discouraged. He knew he would never be able to get them all together.

A few days later Tim was out squirrel-hunting. He had just put the third squirrel into his hunting pouch when a shadow fell across his face. Even before he turned to look, Tim knew it was old Beaver Tail. No one else could walk so silently.

The two friends were always glad to see each other. Beaver Tail admired the squirrels Tim had in his pouch, then said, "You got nice stand of maple here, Tim. Why you don't work it?"

"I'd like to," answered Tim, "but it's too big a job for me alone, I guess. David and Father are too busy to help much."

"Maybe old Beaver Tail can help," said the Indian.

Tim grinned. "You mean it, Beaver Tail? You'd help me work the sugarbush?"

Beaver Tail nodded. "This good time to start, Tim."

"Yes," answered Tim. "I was reading a leaflet about sugar-making. It said this was the right time of year for it. The sap is just beginning to rise. The only trouble is you have to have a lot of things."

Tim puts spouts into the maple tree, while Beaver-tail pours maple sap into a large wooden trough.

"What things?" asked Beaver Tail.

"Oh, spouts, and buckets, and troughs. Things like that," answered Tim.

"Beaver Tail has jackknife. Tim has jackknife. We make those things," said Beaver Tail.

"Father said he would lend me the team of oxen for the heavy hauling," said Tim. "But we're not ready to start."

"We have time to make tools," said Beaver Tail. "These trees not quite ready for tapping. Maybe you start with fifty trees, Tim," said Beaver Tail. He went on to tell Tim how they could make sap buckets of birchbark.

The spouts could be made of alder sticks. One twelve-inch length split in half would make two spouts.

It took the two friends several days to get everything ready. They both worked with their jackknives, peeling birchbark. Then they folded it into square-sided buckets. Each bucket was made of one piece of bark. It was folded in such a way that there were no seams or holes. It had no handle, either.

When they had finished the buckets, Beaver Tail tested a couple of the maple trees to see if they were ready. He did this by making gashes through the outer bark. The sap began to drip immediately, so he knew that they were ready.

Mr. Price loaned Tim an *auger* to drill the trees. With the bark buckets piled into one another, the alder spouts in a sack, and the auger hanging from Tim's belt, the two friends went off to the sugarbush.

Beaver Tail showed Tim how to bore the trees and insert the spouts. Under each spout, on the ground, they placed a bark bucket. Each day Tim had to go around to look at all the buckets. If they were full, he poured the sap into a big wooden trough that Beaver Tail had hollowed out of a tree trunk.

DO YOU KNOW—

1. What a sugarbush is?
2. What animals were generally used for hauling things on a farm in Tim's day?
3. When sap begins to rise in the trees?
4. What material Beaver Tail planned to use for the sap buckets? What a trough is?

THINGS TO DO

New York State produces much maple sugar. Find out where the maple groves are and visit one if you can. If you can't, visit a museum where there is a display of modern methods of maple sugar production.

197

12: Making Maple Sugar

In the meantime there was other work to be done. Wood had to be gathered for the sap-boiling fire. This is where the oxen, Buck and Bright, came in handy. Tim yoked them and hitched them to a flat sled. Then he drove them into the woods and gathered as much fallen timber as he could find. Many of the blown-down trees were too big to handle. From these Tim cut branches until he had a large enough pile for the fire.

There were only patches of snow left on the ground, but a sled was still easier to manage than a cart. Sometimes, when the wind was right, Mrs. Price and Polly could hear Tim calling "Gee" and "Haw" to the oxen. This was how he made them turn to the right or the left.

In a few days, the big trough was almost full of sap. Tim borrowed his mother's biggest iron kettle. He got another from Mrs. Skinner. These were the kettles that were used in melting tallow for candles. He borrowed iron dippers and skimmers, too. They were all

loaded onto the sled and dragged to the maple grove by Buck and Bright.

That morning Tim's father asked, "Who is going to set up the lug poles and hang those heavy kettles on them? I have a little time today, and I'd like to do that much for you, Tim."

So it was Mr. Price who drove upright poles into the ground and set the lug poles across them. Before the lug poles were put into place, one of the two iron kettles was hung over each. Tim had brought *flint* and tinder to start the fire under each kettle. Beaver Tail began ladling the sap from the trough into the kettles.

It seemed a long time before the sap began to boil. But when it did, it made a lovely smell mixed with the woodsmoke in the cold air. As the sap boiled up and formed a scum on top, Tim skimmed this off and threw it away. When both kettles had boiled down to about half the liquid they had started with, Tim and Beaver Tail together emptied one into

Everyone comes out for the last boiling of the maple sirup. Do you know what things are being done?

the other. Into the emptied one they poured fresh sap from the trough, and continued to boil both kettles.

Finally the sap in the first kettle began to thicken. Beaver Tail raised a little of the sirup on a stick to see whether it was ready to strain. He said that before it got too thick, it should be strained through a woolen cloth. Then it should be allowed to stand in a wooden tub overnight. The next day it should be boiled up again for the last time.

Tim went home that night to tell Polly and Mother that the sugaring-off would be the next day. They would surely want to come to that. Even David was planning to come. Mrs. Price gathered up all the cookie molds, butter tubs, and milk pails she could find. The sirup would be poured into them to harden into sugar.

The last boiling was the most fun. This time when Tim skimmed off the top,

he was careful to throw it onto patches of clean snow. It made a kind of maple candy in the snow. Everyone picked up handfuls of it to eat. The taste was delicious.

Beaver Tail kept testing the sirup with a stick to see how thick it was getting. Finally he told Tim it was ready for the last test. He held the dripping stick out to Tim and said, "Take pinch of sirup between thumb and forefinger. Pull fingers apart and see if sirup forms thread."

At the first try Tim said, "Ouch!" and put his fingers into his mouth as fast as he could. He tried again and this time the sirup was warm and sticky. Everyone watched as he pulled his fingers apart. The sirup formed a thread. "It's ready, it's ready!" cried Tim.

Everyone got busy with dippers and ladles, filling the molds with hot sirup. Beaver Tail said it shouldn't cook any longer, or it would set too hard, or burn.

A month later, the sap had stopped running. When all the sirup was finally cooked down and poured into molds, Tim said to Beaver Tail, "There's enough for us all and some left over to sell."

Then David spoke up, "By the way, Tim, I saw Captain Hardenbergh down at the Corners and told him about your sugar. He said he'd be glad to let people know you had some to sell. You could move it down to his house if you want to. What are you going to do with the money?"

Suddenly Tim became very shy. He answered slowly, "Well, I was thinking you'd need some to go to school to study medicine, David. And next time the peddler comes through I'd like to get something for Mother, and maybe for Polly, too. She's been so lonesome without Miss Muffet. And I need a new jackknife. I dropped mine the other day and

Buck stepped on it. Snapped the blade right in two."

David laughed and put his hand on his younger brother's shoulder. "First get your new jackknife, Tim. Then get something for Polly and Mother, if you want to. But don't worry about me."

DO YOU KNOW—

1. What kind of cart Tim used to haul wood?
2. How Tim made the oxen turn?
3. What Tim boiled the sap in? Why the sugaring-off was fun for everybody?
4. How Beaver Tail had Tim test the sirup?
5. What Tim was going to do with the extra sugar? What Tim planned to do with his cash?

THINGS TO DO

1. Make a sap bucket like the ones Tim and Beaver Tail used. It can be made of heavy paper, or birchbark, if you can get it. You may have to soften the bark in warm water before it will fold easily without breaking.
2. Make maple sugar out of maple sirup. Make maple sugar candy as the children in the story did. (You may use ice cubes instead of snow, if necessary.)

"I can buy something for everyone!" Tim thought, pouring sirup into the buckets.

In their new sawmill Father and David cut logs for many settlers around the lake.

13: *David's Good Luck*

Now that spring had come, David was busy helping his father build their little sawmill. They built a water wheel below the falls. This wheel would make all the other wheels move. These were the cogwheels that the men had whittled out during the long winter. The saw that Mr. Skinner had brought from Sterling was set into place. The cogwheels would make it move up and down to cut the logs into boards. A shed was built to cover the machinery.

Soon men from all the nearby farms around the lake were loading their logs into boats and bringing them to the new sawmill. Mr. Bitner was one of the first to come.

While he was waiting for Father to saw his logs, he said, "I was down at the Corners yesterday. Captain Hardenbergh said that there's going to be preaching at his house Sunday morning. I suppose you'll be going?"

"Yes, indeed," said Mr. Price. "We'll take the Skinners, too."

"By the way," said Mr. Bitner, "I understand your son David wants to be a doctor. He may be in for some good luck. A new man has come to the Corners, a doctor. Crossett, his name is. He might teach David how to be a doctor.

"Now don't say anything to the boy about it. I'm going to the Corners early Sunday. I'll put a bee in Crossett's bonnet. Then he can talk to David himself."

On Sunday the family got ready bright and early for the trip to Hardenbergh's Corners. The ride to the foot of the lake in the bright sunshine was lovely. All the world looked happy.

Captain Hardenbergh's house was crowded with people glad to be at church again. The preaching was good. Everybody said "Amen" loudly after each prayer. They sang the dear old hymns at the top of their voices. At the end, Mr.

Price said, "Preacher Irish, will you come to Polly's Falls some Sunday? We could find a lot of folks round about who'd like to have some praying and preaching."

"I will plan on it," said the preacher.

Captain Hardenbergh asked Preacher Irish, Dr. Crossett, and the Price family to stay for dinner. While Kate Freeman was stirring the big kettle of bear meat, Dr. Crossett and David had a quiet talk in the far corner of the cabin.

The doctor said, "I'm thinking of settling here at the Corners. These people need a doctor. The only worry I have is that they live so far apart. That means a good deal of traveling, and I'm getting on in years. I need a young helper. If I could get a young fellow to help me, I'd be willing to teach him all I know about doctoring. Would you know of any young man who would like this kind of job?"

"Oh, Doctor Crossett!" David cried. "I want the job more than anything else in the world."

"A doctor's life isn't easy," Dr. Crossett says, but he can see how eager David is to begin work.

Dr. Crossett said, "You needn't decide in a hurry. A doctor's life isn't easy, especially in a new settlement. You'll have to take long rides when you're dead tired. You may have to be awake all night long, watching a patient. Your time will belong to whoever needs you. Are you up to that kind of life?"

"Sir," said David, "if my parents can spare me, I will accept your offer."

"When you decide, let me know," said Dr. Crossett. "I shall want you to come and live with me as soon as I get my house raised. I am planning to have a drug shop in my house. You will tend the shop while I am out visiting patients. You'll learn about drugs, and you can study when there isn't any business at the shop."

"I thank you for your offer," said David. He and the doctor shook hands just as Kate Freeman called the guests to the dinner table.

On the way home, David told the family about Dr. Crossett's offer.

Father said, "We'll miss you, David. But you may never get another chance as good as this."

Tim spoke up. "Don't worry, David, I'm big enough now to do your work and mine too."

DO YOU KNOW—

1. How Father and David built the sawmill?
2. How Mr. Bitner showed that he was a good friend of David's?
3. How David was to help Dr. Crossett? Why David thought he should wait awhile before accepting the doctor's offer?

THINGS TO DO

Read about what it was like to be a doctor when David was a young man. Discuss this with the rest of the class.

14: A Town Meeting

The little settlement was growing. New people were coming in. Some farmed and others began to work at trades. Many, like Mr. Van Horn, the blacksmith, did both. The settlers didn't see very much of one another, because everyone was so busy. When they did get a chance to get together, they sometimes talked about things that were problems to all of them. There were public roads, education, stray animals, and other matters that each family could not take care of for itself.

Captain Hardenbergh heard more talk than anyone else because he lived right at the crossroads. At last he decided that the men must all get together to talk over their problems. He set a day for a town meeting and sent Harry Freeman out to tell everyone. All males sixteen years old or over were supposed to come in to the

meeting at Hardenbergh's house at the Corners.

Harry went first to Crossett's store. He found David Price there tending the shop. David said he would come, and he would tell anyone who came into the store, too.

"I know one thing my father would like to bring up at the meeting," he told Harry. "He's been worrying that Tim wouldn't have a chance for an education. I don't think Tim cares. He can already read and write and *cipher*. That's all right if he stays at farming. But Father doesn't want him to feel that he can never change his mind."

"There's something I'd like them to talk about, too," said Harry. "Of course, I'm not a free man yet, so I can't come to the meeting. But I'd like it if Hardenbergh's Corners was a real town. Then they would have a clerk to write the records of important things that happen. Some day I will be a free man. And when I am, I want that to be written down in a book, so that folks will know."

The day for the meeting came and all of the settlement men left their work to come into the Corners. Some of them drove ox teams, some rode horseback, and others walked. It was hard for many of them to leave their work, but they came as a duty.

When the men had gathered at Hardenbergh's house, there were not more than twenty in all. Captain Hardenbergh called the meeting to order.

"I am glad to see that you could all come to the meeting," he said. "I guess everybody is here except Sam Crossett."

David spoke up then and said that Dr. Crossett would be there as soon as he could make it. He was tending Peter Van Horn, who was down with a fever.

Captain Hardenbergh continued, "I have made up a list of the usual town officers. After I have read them to you,

I'd like anyone who has any other ideas to get up and speak. I'm not the head man here. I'm just talking to get things started."

He began to read his list. "First we need a supervisor to be the head man and town clerk. Then we need a few people to see about schools, and a constable to keep law and order."

There was a laugh when he said this, and Hardenbergh answered with, "I know we are all law-abiding citizens. But there will be newcomers. Some of them may be people who could not make an honest living back home. We've got to see that they do, here."

He went on with his list, saying, "We'll need an assessor to figure out how much tax each of us should pay. We'll also need a tax collector."

Mr. Skinner stood up and said, "The state is anxious to have this land settled. They've offered to help with the highways. But we will have to take care of our own public paths. One of us ought to look after the boundaries and fences."

The early settlers elected their own town officers just as we do today.

"All right," said Captain Hardenbergh. "Then we will need path-masters and fence-viewers. Any other ideas?"

Mr. Stebbins said, "We ought to have a pound-keeper to look after stray animals. Someone will have to take charge of them until the owners show up. We'll all have our cattle's earmarks recorded by the town clerk, too. That will help."

"There's one other thing," said Dr. Crossett, who had just come in. "Who is going to look after those who have bad luck and can't take care of themselves? We may have some widows and orphans before this year is out. We should have an overseer of the poor to look after them."

When the list of officers was complete, the men began nominating and voting Someone nominated Captain Hardenbergh as supervisor and town clerk, and everyone stood up and said, "Aye." When they got around to the committee on schools, Captain Hardenbergh asked for volunteers. Mr. Price said he would be willing to take charge.

Dr. Crossett said he knew a young man back east who would be willing to come out as schoolmaster. His name was Noah Parish and he was a friend of the doctor. He wanted to settle out west and had asked the doctor to let him know what chances there were for a young man. The settlers would not be able to pay him much. He would have to board around at the houses of his pupils.

It wasn't long before every man at the meeting had been named to some office. There was one job left and no one to take it. It was the job of pound-keeper. Finally Captain Hardenbergh agreed to

Pioneers earmarked their cattle so they would know who owned them, just as cattle are branded today.

take it. "I guess it won't be much of a hardship for a while," he said, laughing.

"I wouldn't worry about it too much, Captain," said Mr. Price. "I've got a daughter who is mighty fond of animals. Just bring your strays over to her and she'll take care of them."

DO YOU KNOW—

1. How people made a living in the little settlement of Hardenbergh's Corners?

2. Some of the problems that worried all of the settlers? What Mr. Price's problem was?

3. Why Harry Freeman wanted to live in a town that had a town clerk?

4. How people in those days could tell their cattle apart? How we do this today?

THINGS TO DO

Look up the history of your community. Find out when it was settled and how big it was after the Revolutionary War. How did people make a living in your town?

15: *Morning at School*

It was a beautiful day. The sun was bright, the sky was soft blue, and the air was just warm enough. As Tim started off toward school, he wasn't so sure he wanted an education that day. The outdoors looked mighty fine.

Tim's feet were bare, but on his head he wore a battered straw hat. This shaded his eyes and allowed the sun to bring out a few freckles across the bridge of his nose.

From his hand swung a strap in which three slim books were tied. One of them was the New York Primer, another was the Testament. The third was a plain copy book.

On the first pages of the Primer were printed the letters of the alphabet. Beneath each letter there was a two-line rhyme. Tim knew these rhymes by heart. His favorite was the one which went with the letter T:

Young Timothy
Learnt sin to fly.

He liked that one because you had to say Timothy a little different to make it rhyme with *fly*.

When Tim reached the schoolhouse, it was still early. Some of the older boys were already there. It was Tim's week to open the schoolhouse for the master. He hurried into the log building to see that everything was in order.

At the back of the room were the high benches for the older boys. Toward the front were the low benches for the smaller children. One of these was overturned. Timothy righted the bench and picked up a torn copy book and some goose quills that were scattered on the dirt floor. These he placed on a narrow shelf which ran along the back wall.

Just above the narrow shelf there was another deeper, sloping shelf which the scholars used to write on. The only desk in the schoolroom was the one used by the master. Beside the master's desk, in the front wall of the room, was a fireplace.

There were only two windows in the room, one on either side. Instead of glass, the windowpanes were made of brown paper which had been greased with lard. These didn't let in much light, so in the summertime the door was always left open.

As Tim tidied up the room, he could hear other boys arriving. They played outside until someone shouted, "There he is. Master Parish is coming!" There was a rush and a scramble, and all the boys ran pell-mell into the room. It was surprising how much noise twenty barefoot boys could make on an earthen floor.

They were still shifting and shoving each other on the oak benches when Schoolmaster Noah Parish came in.

"Good morning, gentlemen," said the master, as he seated himself at his tall desk.

"Good morning, Master," answered the boys.

"We will begin the day as usual," said the master.

The older boys knew what he meant. They already had their books open at the right page. Standing at their places, they read aloud a passage from the Testament. While they were reading, the smaller boys tried to keep still. This wasn't so easy. Some of them were no more than six years old. Their legs were too short to reach the floor. As they became restless and bored listening to the older boys, they began to swing their legs against the bench and against each other. Soon they were giggling and laughing. Then, suddenly, "Silence!" roared the master, and his ruler came down with a clap on his desk. A shiver went through the little ones, and they stopped giggling. There was a moment of complete stillness. Then the older boys went on reading aloud.

When the reading was finished, it was time for a writing lesson. Even the smallest boys had copy books with blank pages in them. The master sharpened their quill pens for them. One of the older boys mixed the ink powder with water. The master went around the room writing something at the top of a blank page in each boy's copy book.

Pioneer families used these books. At the top are a primer like Tim's and a horn book. At the right are two story books. What are the other two?

In some of the older boys' books he wrote: *Procrastination is the thief of time*. They had to copy this out all down the page. In the books of the smallest boys the master wrote no words, only straight lines and curves. These the boys had to copy as exactly as they could.

Tim was in the middle group. He could read and write well, but not such long words as the older boys. In Tim's book the master wrote: *Patience is a virtue*. Tim ruled his paper and copied the sentence in neat, round letters as many times as he could on the page. He finished his lesson before anyone else, and then didn't know what to do. To pass the time, he picked up his copy book and began scribbling on the *flyleaf*. First he drew a picture of Sukie. Then he began to write: Ten weeks will never go away, never, never, never, never, never, never never neverneverneverneverev—

"But there are only nine of them left this summer, Tim." It was the schoolmaster speaking. "Even that is hardly time enough for you boys to get an education. We can't keep school in the winter, because you can't get here through the snow. In the spring and fall your fathers say they need you to help with planting and harvesting. And now you are here in body, but your minds are somewhere else."

The master was scolding, but not very hard. Tim was a good scholar, not usually an idle boy. But the master knew that even a good scholar, if he had time on his hands, might get into mischief.

DO YOU KNOW—

1. What Tim wore on his feet on his way to school? What books he carried?
2. How many rooms the schoolhouse had?
3. How the schoolroom was furnished?
4. How the boys addressed the teacher? How writing was taught?
5. Why school was held in the summertime?

THINGS TO DO

Make some quill pens and try writing with them. Goose quills are good to use because they are big enough. Cut the quill end at a slant like a pen point.

"Young man, what have you there in your hands?" the schoolmaster asks sternly.

Whoosh! Bang! Crash! The schoolroom shakes as the boys scramble and play.

16: Afternoon Session

The morning session droned on until noon. Tim's group read from their Testament. Then the youngest boys were given syllables to repeat aloud. At the top of their shrill little voices they sang out:

Ba Be Bi Bo Bu
Fa Fe Fi Fo Fu
Ma Me Mi Mo Mu—and so on. From this they were supposed to learn that the sounds were the same as the printed syllables in their Primers.

Finally the master said it was time for lunch. Most of the children had brought lunches with them. The schoolmaster was boarding out that week with the Huggins family, who lived close by. He went home with the two Huggins boys for his lunch.

Before he left he spoke to Tim. "Remember, Timothy Price, that this week it is your duty to tend the schoolhouse while I am gone. See that the smaller boys don't get hurt, and mind there's no trash on the floor when I get back."

Tim said he would do his best and the master left. For a while the only sounds were the eating of lunches and the friendly chatter of the boys. When the older boys finished their lunches, they decided it would be fun to give Tim some trouble. One of them began throwing scraps of his lunch on the floor, calling out to Tim, "Mind there's no trash on the floor when I get back!"

Another one wadded a piece of paper, dipped it in an inkwell, and tossed it at Tim, chanting,

Timothy Price
Is much too nice.

Tim dodged the ink ball. In a minute, everyone was throwing ink balls, Primers,

209

"Shh!" Tim tells the boys when he sees the master. What fun to bar him out! But what if he tells their parents. The little boys begin to cry.

copy books, and anything else they could pick up.

When the scramble was over, Tim began collecting the trash and putting it into the fireplace. The day was warm, so he made only a small fire with a handful of twigs just big enough to burn the ink-soaked papers. The twigs were green and the fire was still smoldering when someone shouted that the master was coming back. One of the big boys said, "Let's bar him out. Let's bar the master out!"

The smaller boys picked up the shout, "Let's bar the master out!" Some of them had heard of the custom. Some had not, but thought it might be fun. Tim knew

that once or twice in a term schoolboys would get the master out of the building, then bar the door and windows so that he couldn't get back in. They'd spend the rest of the day romping and playing. When the master finally gave up trying to get in, they'd all run out and go home.

So now the older boys dragged one of the heavier benches to the front of the room and stood it firmly against the door. The windows didn't need guarding, because they were small and placed high in the wall.

Tim had decided he'd never get through the day without punishment, so he might as well join the fun. He pushed a bench against the wall under the window and put a stool on top of it. By climbing on top of the stool, he could peek through a hole in the greased paper and see the master.

As Schoolmaster Parish neared the door, he stopped. Something was wrong. It was all so quiet. And why was the door closed? He lifted the latch and pushed. Nothing happened. From his perch on top of the stool, Tim signaled the others to be quiet.

By now the master knew very well what was going on. He stepped back from the door and called to the boys, "Boys, I am not going to force my way in. But you will all answer for this tomorrow. You may even answer for it tonight, if I tell your parents."

Tim saw the master turn away. He dropped down from his perch, and whispered, "What will we do? He's going to tell our parents!"

"Oh, I don't want to be whipped!" cried one of the small boys.

By now they were all feeling a little scared and didn't even want to play. Some picked up their Primers and began studying. About five minutes passed quietly when one of the boys spoke up, "Tim Price, what did you build that fire out of? It's smoking something awful."

"I guess it's just because the door is closed and there's no draft," answered Tim. He walked over to the fireplace and looked up the chimney. "I can't see daylight up there," said Tim. "Something must have fallen on top of the chimney."

One of the little boys said to Tim, "Couldn't you climb up onto the roof and see what's the matter, Tim?"

"Anyone could," said one of the older boys. "There's a tree with a branch that reaches right out over the roof on that side. I'd have to stand on somebody's shoulders to get up the trunk. Then it would be easy."

This seemed like a good idea to all of them. The door was unbarred and the

boys rushed outside, glad to be breathing fresh air again. When they got around to the chimney side of the building, they decided it would be easier for Tim to stand on a tall boy's shoulders, than the other way around.

With much grunting and scraping of shins, Tim reached the lowest branch. From there on it was easy. He climbed from one branch to another, and then eased out onto the one which hung over the roof of the schoolhouse. The boys below shouted directions to him. He couldn't see very well because the leaves were so thick.

A boy called from below, "I can just see you. You are right over the roof. Let yourself drop down. Your toes are almost touching the roof now."

Tim dangled for a moment. He was trying to peer through the leaves and see just where he would land. Then he dropped with a thump to the roof. As he recovered himself and sat up, he couldn't believe his eyes. There was the schoolmaster sitting on a board placed squarely

Covering their faces and tripping over benches, the boys race out of the schoolroom.

Tim is amazed! There sits the master, right smack on top of the chimney, laughing at him.

over the chimney flue! His arms were folded and he was laughing at Tim.

From below the boys were calling, "What's wrong up there? Did you find anything?"

"There's nothing wrong—exactly," answered Tim. "Only Master is sitting on the chimney!"

The boys below thought he was joking. But in a moment they saw the master and Tim looking down at them. They were glad to find that the master was laughing. He was so pleased with the joke he had played on the boys that he couldn't be stern. He called down, "First you barred me out, and now I have smoked you out. Shall we call it even and go back to our studies?"

With great relief all the boys said, "Yes!" One of the little ones called up tearfully to the master, "You won't tell my papa on me, will you?"

"No, I won't tell your parents," said the schoolmaster. "But I expect all of you to study twice as hard this afternoon."

DO YOU KNOW—

1. What Tim was supposed to do while the master was away? How the older boys teased Tim?

2. What "barring the master out" meant?

3. Why the boys quieted down after Tim saw the master turn away?

4. Why the master didn't punish the boys?

THINGS TO DO

Act out a morning session in an early American school. Pretend that you are the scholars and your teacher is the master or mistress. Divide the class into three groups according to height. The small ones can be the young boys, the medium-height children can be the middle group (Tim's), and the tallest children the older boys. The teacher can give you lessons to learn. While one group is reciting, the others should study and be very quiet.

17: Polly Makes a Sampler

Polly was recovering from a fever. No one knew just what it was. They thought that she had probably breathed too much of the wind from the marshes. Genesee Fever they called the sickness. Some of the workmen on the turnpike had been taken to bed with it. Dr. Crossett said that the only way to treat it was to keep the patients in bed. They should be kept warm when they had the chills, and cooled off when they burned with fever.

Polly was over the worst of it. She shook with chills only once in a while. Her knees were still weak but her spirit was improving. Today she asked her mother if she could sit up in bed and do something.

"I feel so useless," she said. "I think I'd feel better if I could help you."

"Why, you are still weak as water, young lady," said Mrs. Price. "I want to make sure you are over that fever. No one puts a harness on a sick horse, you know."

"I could sit at the flax wheel," said Polly.

"No, you couldn't," said her mother. "I don't have enough flax ready for spinning."

"We will all need some woolen stockings for winter," said Polly. "Why don't I knit some? That isn't hard or tiring."

"Oh, there is still plenty of time for that," said Mrs. Price. "If you must do something, why don't you work on your *sampler* for a while? Since we left our old home, you haven't had much time for pretty things like that."

"I'd almost forgotten about it," said Polly. "Do you think you could find it in the trunk?"

"Well, I'll rummage around until I do," answered Mrs. Price. She opened the trunk and looked all through the clothes waiting to be mended and other odds and ends. At the bottom of the trunk, still flat in its wooden frame, was the sampler Polly had begun two years earlier.

"I found it, child," said Mrs. Price, bringing Polly the sampler, the needles, and a handful of colored silks from the trunk.

Polly's sampler was a square of hand-woven linen cloth stretched in a wooden frame. At the top of the square Polly had already stitched the letters of the alphabet, both large and small. Following the letters were the numbers from one to nine. Then Polly had added a row of birds, one of animals, and still another of flowers. Most of the work was done in cross-stitch, but in a few figures she had shown off some of the fancy stitches her mother had taught her. These were feather-stitch, mouse-stitch, back-stitch, whip-stitch, and fern-stitch.

Only about one third of the linen square was left to work on. Polly wanted to embroider it with a short poem, then add her name and the date and she would be through with it.

"What verse shall I use?" asked Polly.

"Why, I'm sure you could find something nice in the Bible," said Mrs. Price. "When I was a girl there were little printed books with verses for samplers.

Most of them were long and hard. I remember I chose an easy one. It was:

> Here is my sampler,
> Here you see
> What care my mother
> Took of me."

"Oh, I like that one," said Polly. "I'd like to use it for mine, too. It would show that you took care to educate me, just as your mother did with you."

"I think my old sampler is still around, if you would like to see it," said Mrs. Price. "I remember that I rolled it up and tucked it into a corner of the trunk before we came here."

Mrs. Price went over to the trunk again and soon came back with a rolled piece of linen in her hand. When she unrolled it Polly saw that it was longer and narrower than her own sampler. The stitches were extremely fine. Polly wondered how anyone could take so much pains with

Mother shows Polly the sampler she once made.

needlework. Her mother's work was much finer than her own.

"Remember, dear," said Mrs. Price, "that I didn't grow up on a frontier farm. We were always busy, to be sure, but we had much more time for sewing fine seams than you have now. Why, I never had to milk a cow or make soap. You have already learned those things. One day, Polly, you'll make some man a fine wife."

Polly looked sad for a moment. She had heard that Captain Hardenbergh was going to be married. "Oh, why couldn't he have waited for me?" she thought. Then with a toss of her head she answered her mother. "I like milking cows and making soap, Mother. And by the time I am grown up I'll know how to do many more things."

Mrs. Price sighed. "When I was young, Polly, it was not thought proper for a young lady to know too much. I learned to read but not to write."

"How times have changed," said Polly, as she bent over her sampler.

"Yes," said Mrs. Price, *"and it's always for the best.* Remember that, Polly."

DO YOU KNOW—

1. What Mrs. Price meant when she said, "No one puts a harness on a sick horse"?
2. Why Polly felt useless? What her mother suggested?
3. Why Polly was sad when she thought of Captain Hardenbergh?

THINGS TO DO

Talk about samplers and look at examples of them. You can see them in museums, in books, or possibly right at home. Do you know the names of the different stitches? Why was skill in sewing important in Polly's time?

The circus girl seemed to float over the horse's back! How the settlers loved it, but the show's star couldn't perform. She and her puppies watched it from their basket.

18: *Polly Gets a New Pet*

One day a troupe of players came through the Corners. There were two men, a woman, a horse, and a dog. One man was a magician. The other could bend his joints all sorts of ways. The woman could stand on the horse's back while he galloped. What's more, she could stand either on her feet or upside down on her hands.

But it was the little dog that was the star of the show. They said she could jump through hoops and waltz on her hind feet. She could hold her tail in her mouth and spin in circles so fast it made you dizzy to watch. She could also count from one to ten by barking. Uncle Billy, the magician, who was the leader of the troupe, said that she was a real wonder dog. The only trouble was that just now she was too busy to perform. She was nursing a brand new litter of six puppies!

When the troupe stopped at the Corners, Uncle Billy spoke to Captain Hardenbergh. "We'd like to pass the night here, friend," he said. "We have no money to pay for lodging, but we would be glad to perform for our bed and board."

"You're welcome to stop," said Captain Hardenbergh. "Maybe I can get some of the townspeople to come in and see the show."

"The more the better," said Uncle Billy. "We charge no admission, of course, but you won't mind if we pass the hat, will you?"

"You may pass the hat, if you like," said Captain Hardenbergh, "but you won't find much hard money in this settlement."

"Every little bit helps," said Uncle Billy, "and we don't care if it's American or British. We'll take farthings, half-pennies, dimes, or pistareens."

Word was sent out that there was going to be a show at the Corners. All those who could spare time came in to see it. David was not too busy that afternoon, and Dr. Crossett told him the change would be good for him. Mr. Price and Tim came in from the farm. Mrs. Price stayed home with Polly, who was still not well enough to get out of bed.

Polly cuddles the puppy Captain Hardenbergh has brought for her. Now Polly's Falls is really home.

Before he left, Tim said, "I'll tell you all about it, Polly. They say the dog isn't working because she has a litter of pups. I'll take a peek and tell you what they look like."

Everyone enjoyed the show, and when Uncle Billy counted the money in the hat, he found about two dollars. Some of the coins were brand-new copper cent pieces made in New York State that year.

After the show, Tim asked to see the wonder dog. Uncle Billy pointed to a basket standing by the fire. When Tim looked into the basket, he saw a lovely brown-and-white spaniel nursing six tiny puppies. Their eyes were not yet open.

Tim asked Uncle Billy if he could buy one of the pups for his sister. "She's sick," said Tim, "and I think she'd get well faster if she had a pet of her own."

"Why, one of those wonder pups would cost you a mint of money, son," answered Uncle Billy. "Besides, they're too young to take from their mother."

Tim was disappointed. He had thought he might be able to buy one with some of the money he had made selling his maple sugar. "How do those dogs keep up with you when you're traveling?" he wanted to know.

"Why, bless you," said Uncle Billy, "those dogs don't walk. They stay right in the basket with their mama, and they all ride on the back of the horse. The rest of us walk."

"Don't they ever fall out?" asked Tim. "Our roads are pretty rough."

"They haven't fallen out yet," said Uncle Billy. "Didn't I tell you they were wonder dogs?"

The day after the show, Captain Hardenbergh came hurrying over to the Price farm. Mrs. Price opened the door and said, "Land sakes, Captain, you seem to be in a great hurry."

"I've got to see Miss Polly," said Captain Hardenbergh. "I hope she's feeling better, ma'am."

"Oh, I'm feeling much better," called Polly from the bed in the corner. "What are you carrying under your coat, Captain Hardenbergh?"

"That's what I came to see you about," he answered. "After that troupe left this morning, I heard something whimpering down the road a piece. When I went to look, it was one of those spaniel puppies. The horse must have stumbled and pitched one of them out, right into the mud.

216

"I'm the town pound-keeper, you know. So I guess it's my job to take care of him. But he needs to be fed pretty often. He isn't weaned yet."

Polly held out her hands and Captain Hardenbergh put the puppy into them. "Your father said that if I ever had any trouble with my job I should come to you, Polly."

Polly cuddled the soft little puppy up to her cheek. She was so pleased and happy that for a moment she couldn't speak. When she lifted her head, her eyes were shining. "Mother and I will take care of him, Captain Hardenbergh," she said. "We'll spoon warm milk into him until he's as fat as a butterball.

"Now it really feels like home again, doesn't it, Mother?" she continued with a happy sigh. "David is studying medicine, Tim is going to school, and I have a new pet."

"Frontier life is hardest of all on you women, I guess," said Captain Hardenbergh. "But with everybody's help this will be a town we'll all be proud of."

DO YOU KNOW—

1. Why the star of the troupe wasn't performing when they came through the Corners?
2. What "lodging" means?
3. Why Polly couldn't go to the show?
4. How the players collected money?
5. Where Tim got the money with which he was going to buy a puppy?
6. How it happened that Polly got a new pet after all?

THINGS TO DO

1. Talk about frontier life as the Price family knew it. How was it different from the life of the Dutch settlers? In what ways was it the same?
2. Act out a performance of the troupe that visited the Corners.
3. Find out how stray animals are taken care of in your town. Perhaps your teacher can arrange a visit to a shelter for homeless animals.

A New Look at Polly's Falls

THINGS TO TALK ABOUT

1. Suppose that you and your family were to take a trip from eastern to western New York State today. How would you travel? What route would you follow? How would you dress for the trip? How long would it take? How would you plan to get food on your trip? What would you need to take with you besides clothing? In what ways would your trip be different from that of the Price family?

2. Think about the largest store in your community. What things are sold there that Mr. Best sold? What things are sold there that were not found in Mr. Best's store? What things are sold there that the Price family had never heard of? What things are sold there that the Yankee peddler carried? What things that the peddler could not carry can be bought in a modern store? Compare modern stores with pioneer stores.

3. In what ways was Beaver Tail a good neighbor? Captain Hardenbergh? How did the Price family and the Skinner family help each other? How many ways can you think of in which neighbors helped the new settlers in pioneer days? How can we help new neighbors in our own communities today? How are our ways different from the old ways? How are they the same?

4. What things did men do to earn a living in pioneer days? How many of these things are still done? What new ways do men have of making a living today? How did women and children help in making money in pioneer days? Do women have more or fewer kinds of jobs today? Do children help make a living for their families nowadays?

HOW TO FIND OUT MORE ABOUT THE PIONEERS

1. Try to find out how your ancestors first came to your community and why they came. Trace the route they followed on a map or a globe. Find out when they came, and whether they had hardships like those that the Price family went through.

2. If your town has a Historical Society, ask somebody who belongs to tell you what the oldest houses and buildings are and who built them. Visit some of these houses or buildings and see if you can see how they are different from newer buildings.

3. Visit the nearest museum that shows things used in pioneer times. If there is no such museum near you, write to the New York State Historical Association at Cooperstown to ask what booklets they have about pioneer matters in which you are interested.

4. Each child in the class may take this job: To find an older person in the community who can remember stories his or her grandparents told about the old days. Perhaps some of these persons would be willing to visit your class and tell what they have heard about early days in the community.

5. Read stories or history books telling about pioneers in other parts of our country. See whether their troubles and good times were like those of the people you have read about in the story of the Price family.

RECORDS TO ENJOY

Adventures in Folk Song: We start a New Country, Album FSP 1, G. Chandler. Songs sung in colonial days.

Ballads of the Revolution, 1767–1775, FP48–1 (10″ LP), Folkways. Sung by Wallace House with guitar accompaniment.

By Wagon and Flatboat, 10 and 12, Series 3, G. Chandler. Sung by Johnny Tremain.

Folk Songs of Our Land, Mercury Childcraft 9. Sung by Jack Russell.

Hudson Valley Songs, Album 611, Disc Co. of America. Frank Warner and balladeers.

School Days—Songs to Grow On, Album 604, Disc Co. of America. Sung for children by Pete Seeger, Lead Belly, et al.

Who Built America, FP2 (LP), Folkways. American history through folksongs.

BOOKS THE TEACHER MAY READ TO YOU

Berry, Erick, *Hearthstone in the Wilderness*, Macmillan, 1944.

Berry, Erick, *Sybil Ludington's Ride*, Viking, 1952. A story of our Revolution.

Carmer, Carl, *Too Many Cherries*, Viking, 1949. A story of New York State today.

Emerson, Caroline D., *Pioneer Children of America*, Heath, 1950.

Fenner, P. R., *Yankee Doodle: Stories of the Brave and Free*, Knopf, 1951.

Steele, William O., *The Golden Root*, Aladdin, 1951. A pioneer family living in North Carolina have a visit from a mysterious stranger who changes their lives.

Weber, Alma B., and others, *Coonskin for a General: Stories of Great American Cities*, Aladdin, 1951.

BOOKS TO READ AND LOOK AT

Berry, Erick, *Hay-foot, Straw-foot*, Viking, 1954. A Yankee Doodle story.

Coatsworth, Elizabeth, *Away Goes Sally*, Macmillan, 1951. An exciting trip taken about the time of the Price family's trip.

Coatsworth, Elizabeth, *Five Bushel Farm*, Macmillan, 1939.

DeAngeli, M. L., *Shippack School*, Doubleday (Junior Books), 1939. The story of a boy in school long ago in Pennsylvania.

Fretwell, J. H., *Down the Hudson*, Nelson, 1935.

Gilchrist, M. E., *The Story of the Great Lakes*, Harper, 1942.

Johnson, S. J., *Debby*, Longmans, 1940.

Mason, M. E., *Susannah, the Pioneer Cow*, Macmillan, 1941.

Meadowcroft, E. L., *Along the Erie Towpath*, Crowell, 1940.

Orton, H. F., *The Treasure of the Little Trunk*, Stokes, 1932. A story about the travels of a family into the Genesee country.

Perkins, L. F., *Pioneer Twins*, Houghton, 1928.

Sickels, E. R., *The School Bell Rings*, Scribner, 1942. A history of schools.

Wilkins, Eva, *Weaver's Children*, American Book, 1914.

Woodward, Hildegard, *Jared's Blessing*, Scribner, 1942.

Another Look at Indians, Settlers, and Pioneers

Now you have read three stories of people who lived in your state before you were born. First you read about Cokoe and the Indians. Next you read about Teunis and Lisbet and the first Dutch settlers in New Netherland. And finally you read a story about Timothy and Polly and David and their life as pioneer children in western New York.

Although they were different people living at different times, you saw that their lives were much alike in many ways. People have the same problems everywhere. It is the way they solve the problems that makes the difference.

All Communities Must Have Food

The first big problem people have is getting food. They must have food to live. They may simply gather wild food, if they live in a place where it grows. The Indians gathered wild seeds and berries, nuts and roots. They had to keep track of where they grew and what time of year they ripened. They also planted gardens so that there would be food close to home. Their garden food, corn and beans and squash, could be eaten fresh, or dried and stored to use in winter, when there were no wild foods to gather. They fished and hunted wild animals for meat.

The first Dutch settlers brought dried and salted food from Holland. But remember how happy they were to have the first fresh corn and strawberries, the deer meat and turkeys! However, they

didn't depend on these wild foods so much as the Indians did. They planted garden crops as soon as they could. To their own familiar crops they added the ones they learned about from the Indians. None of the wild animals in this part of the world had been tamed by the Indians except the dog. It was not long before the Dutch brought cattle over, and soon began raising herds to furnish meat and milk and butter and cheese.

Pioneer families, moving from eastern to western New York, had the same problem all over again. They had to have food. To get their food they farmed the land. They shot wild animals. They raised cattle and sheep, and chickens and pigs.

How does your community solve the problem of getting food for everybody? Could you live like the Indians by hunting and gathering wild foods? How far would you have to go every day to gather enough food for your family? Do many families in your community raise their own food? How much of it do they raise?

All Communities Need Shelter

Another problem everybody has is shelter. In some climates this is not so very important, but in our climate it is. Our houses give us shelter from the rain and snow and the cold. The Indians built wigwams and longhouses for the same purpose. We may think their houses were much simpler and easier to build than ours. But did you ever try to strip the bark from a tree in one big piece? Did you ever think how hard it would be to cut down a tree with a stone axe?

When the Dutch settlers left the shelter of their ship, they had to build homes on land. They had not brought bricks and tile and lumber with them on shipboard, so they had to use the materials that they found here. These were trees and bark, and cornhusk mats made by the Indians. Some of them even adopted the Indians' style of house.

The pioneers in their turn had to build houses for shelter. They built houses of logs and stone, and some built sod houses. It was hard work, but they had some things to make it easier that neither the Indians nor the first Dutch settlers had. They had horses and oxen to help them haul heavy loads.

Other Community Problems

There were many other problems in all of these communities, just as there are problems in your community today. There were problems of getting from one place to another, of taking care of the sick, of keeping in touch with other communities. And then there was always the problem of raising and educating the children. Whether it was at home or in school, there was always some plan for teaching children the things they would need to know when they grew up. Cokoe learned from his parents and his uncle, and by watching other grownups. Lisbet and Teunis learned by helping their mother and father. Later the Krankenbezoeker was going to give them lessons.

In pioneer days some people still thought only boys needed to be educated in schools. Most girls learned whatever they needed to know at home.

One thing which helped all of these communities solve their problems was co-operation. People helped each other with jobs that were too hard to do alone. Do you remember how the whole Indian village went shad fishing? And do you remember the house-raising for the Price family?

Does Your Community Have Problems?

Are there any problems in your community which people solve by working together? Do you co-operate at home, at school, and with your playmates? Remember to do this and you will find that your life will be much happier.

Glossary

This glossary contains the words in this book that have meanings or pronunciations that may be new to you. Most of the words have been printed in *italics* in the book. You can use the glossary just as you would a dictionary. It gives only the meaning that a word has in this book. In your dictionary you may find other meanings for many of the words. Each word is respelled to show you how to pronounce it. You can learn the sounds the marked letters stand for by seeing how they are used in the easy words below.

Key to Pronunciation

ā	āte	ĕ	bĕd	ô	fôr	ū	ūnit
â	bâre	ē	bakēr	ŏ	hŏt	û	hûrry
ă	ăt	ī	bīte	o͝o	go͝od	ŭ	ŭp
ä	fär	ĭ	ĭt	o͞o	so͞on	u̇	circu̇s
å	åbout	kw	qu in quick	oi	oil	z	s in ribs
ē	bē	ō	gō	ou	found		

A heavy accent mark (′) means that the preceding syllable should be stressed more than any other syllable. A light mark (′) indicates a somewhat lighter stress.

Adriaen Tienpont (ä·drē·än′tēn′pont). Governor of Beavertown in Skipper May's absence.

adz (ădz). Tool with a curved cutting edge.

Algonquin (ăl·gŏn′kwĭn). Group of Indians.

auger (ô′gēr). Tool, like a drill, used for boring holes in wood.

Bastiaen Krol (bäs·tē·än′krōl). Beavertown's Man of God and Comforter of the Sick.

Boterberg (bō′tēr·bĕrg). Dutch for Butter Mountain.

boundary (boun′då·rĭ). A line, real or imaginary, that limits an area of land.

bran (brăn). Grain coverings which are broken and separated from the flour.

breechcloth (brēch′klôth′). A small garment worn by Indian men and boys.

card (kärd). To clean wool by combing it with a toothed tool or wire brush.

ceremony (sĕr′ĕ·mō·nĭ). A set of actions to be carried out on special occasions.

char (chär). To burn an object slightly.

clan (klăn). Group of people related by blood, or people grouped together.

clearing (klēr′ĭng). An area of cleared land surrounded by forest.

cogwheels (kŏg′hwēlz′). Toothed wheels that lock so that one wheel turns the other.

Cokoe (kō′kō′). A young Lenni-Lenape boy.

colter (kōl′tēr). Cutting part of a plow that cuts the upper layer of soil.

crotch (krŏch). Forked part of an object.

cruller (krŭl′ēr). Sweet, twisted doughnut.

Daniel Van Krieckebeeck (vän krē′k′·bāk). An important soldier at Beavertown.

Donderberg (dōn′dēr·bĕrg). Dutch word for Thunder Mountain.

featherbed (fĕth′ēr·bĕd′). A cloth case filled with feathers to make a mattress.

felt (fĕlt). Cloth made of wool fibers or hair pressed into a firm material.

flax (flăks). Fibers from the stems of flax plants; prepared for spinning.

flint (flĭnt). Hard stone that makes sparks when struck against steel; used as a match.

Genesee (gĕ·nĕ·sē′). Land in northwestern New York to which the Price family moved.

gourd (gōrd). The dried and cleaned fruit shell of a gourd plant; used as bowls.

gristmill (grĭst′mĭl′). Place where grain is ground into flour.

hemp (hĕmp). Long plant with tough fibers, used in making rope and coarse cloth.

hopper (hŏp′ẽr). Part of a mill that receives grain for grinding.

Iroquois (ĭr′ŏ·kwoi). Group of Indians.

Jan (yän). Maritje's little brother.

Johanna (yō·hän′nǎ). Kip Teunissen's wife.

Joost (yōst). A friend of Teunis.

Kip Teunissen (kĭp tū′nĭs·s'n). The Dutchman who took his family to the New World.

Krankenbezoeker (krän′k'n·b'·zōō′k'r). Man of God and Comforter of the Sick.

Lammetje (läm′mĕ·chù). Teunis' baby sister.

leek (lēk). Vegetable like an onion.

Lenni-Lenape (lĕn′ĭ lĕn′å·pē). Tribe of Indians; members of the Algonquin group.

Lisbet (lĭs′bĕt). A young Dutch girl.

loom (lōōm). Machine to weave cloth.

lugpole (lŭg′pōl′). A pole on which kettles are hung over a fire.

Mahican (må·hē′kǎn). Tribe of Indians; members of the Algonquin group.

manito (măn′ĭ·tō). Indian spirit or god.

Maritje (mär·ē′chù). A friend of Lisbet.

millstones (mĭl′stōnz′). Two flat round stones for grinding corn, wheat, or other grain.

Mohawk (mō′hôk). Tribe of Indians; members of the Iroquois group.

Mohican (mō·hē′kǎn). Tribe of Indians; members of the Algonquin group.

Mollie Grietje (mōl′lē grē′chù). St. Nicholas' wife.

Mokween (mō′kwēn). Mahican Indian boy.

mortar (môr′tẽr). Lime, sand, and water mixed, to hold bricks or stones together.

mortar and pestle (pĕs′'l). Hard bowl and tool for grinding and pounding matter.

New Netherland (nū nĕth′ẽr·lănd). Dutch colony in southeastern New York.

nominate (nŏm′ĭ·nāt). To name a person as a candidate for office.

pewter (pū′tẽr). A mixture of tin and lead.

plowshare (plou′shâr′). Part of a plow that cuts furrows into the soil.

porthole (pōrt′hōl′). Round opening in the side of a ship to let in light and air.

Primer (prĭm′ẽr). Book used to teach children to read and spell.

quest (kwĕst). A search for something.

quiver (kwĭv′ẽr). Case for carrying arrows.

sagamore (săg′å·mōr). Less important chief among North American Indians.

sawmill (sô′mĭl′). Place where logs are sawed into boards.

Seneca River (sĕn′ē·cå). River in west central New York.

skimmer (skĭm′ẽr). Long-handled, shallow spoon used to skim liquids.

Soningo (sō·nĭng′gō). Cokoe's uncle.

storage (stōr′ĭj). Storing place.

sugarbush (shŏŏg′ẽr·bŏŏsh′). Woods of maple trees; used for getting sugar and sirup.

suppawn (sū·pôn′). Indian food of corn meal.

tallow (tăl′ō). Hard sheep and cow fat; used for making soap and candles.

Tamquid (tăm′kwĭd). Cokoe's father.

tannery (tăn′ẽr·ĭ). Place where animal skins are made into leather.

Teunis (tū′nĭs). A young Dutch boy.

tinder box (tĭn′dẽr bŏks). Box for carrying flint, steel, and material to make fires.

tomahawk (tŏm′å·hôk). Lightweight ax; weapon and tool used by North American Indians.

trencher (trĕn′chẽr). Shallow wooden dish for carving meat and serving food.

tribute (trĭb′ût). Payment of money from one nation to another for peace.

trough (trôf). Long, narrow container.

turnpike (tûrn′pīk′). Road that has or did have a gate where travellers must pay.

Walloons (wäl·lōōnz′). French-speaking people from Flanders who moved to the Netherlands.

wampum (wŏm′pŭm). Shell beads.

warp (wôrp). Threads that run the long way.

wigwam (wĭg′wŏm). American Indian hut.

wilden (wĭl′d'n). Dutch name for Indians.

Woodland Indians (wŏŏd′lănd′ ĭn′dĭ·ănz). Indians of the eastern forests.

woof (wŏŏf). Threads that run cross-wise.

Index

The following index of places and things is arranged in alphabetical order. It will help you find the text information, pictures, and maps you need in your work. Italic letters before certain page references tell you what you will find: *m.* stands for *map*, *p.* stands for *picture*. The index will also help you when you are planning a report on a large topic such as **communication** or **being a good citizen**.

Acknowledgments

DRAWINGS AND MAPS ARE THE WORK OF THE FOLLOWING ARTISTS:
Cohen, Ben, 17
Frankenberg, Robert, 145, 148–152, 154–163, 165–206, 208–216

Magnus, Al, 8–9 (map), 31, 58, 80, 83, 87, 153, 164
Mars, W. T., 13, 16, 18–30, 32–57, 59–65, 68
Robison, Robert, 1, 4–12
Royt, Kevin, 207

Sumley, Al, 14–15, 70–71, 146–147
Van Dyke, Joyce, 220
Zalusky, Bernard, *cover illustration*, 69, 72–79, 81–82, 84–86, 88–142